Evaluating Performance
in
Physical Education

EVALUATING PERFORMANCE IN PHYSICAL EDUCATION

B. DON FRANKS
Temple University

HELGA DEUTSCH
University of Illinois

ACADEMIC PRESS   New York and London

A Subsidiary of Harcourt Brace Jovanovich, Publishers

ACADEMIC PRESS, INC.
111 Fifth Avenue, New York, New York 10003

United Kingdom Edition published by
ACADEMIC PRESS, INC. (LONDON) LTD.
24/28 Oval Road, London NW1

LIBRARY OF CONGRESS CATALOG CARD NUMBER: 72-88369

PRINTED IN THE UNITED STATES OF AMERICA

Contents

Chapter 1. Functions of Testing

Chapter 2. Test Evaluation

Chapter 3. Administration of Tests

v

Chapter 4. Subjective Evaluation

Chapter 5. Interpretation of Test Scores

Chapter 6. Optional Supplement to Interpretation of Test Scores

Preface

Evaluation is an important and necessary function of all teachers. The teacher is charged with the responsibility of evaluating students, the curriculum, and teaching methods. Tests play a vital role in this process. The teacher of physical education is faced with many problems common to any teacher, as well as with some problems which are unique to this field.

This book includes much of the conventional material, such as the place of testing in physical education, selection, construction, and administration of written, performance, and fitness tests, as well as some elementary statistics which are important in the evaluation and interpretation of students' scores. The unique features of the book include its flexibility, the introduction of nonparametric statistics, a section on subjective evaluation, and a theoretical model for physical performance and fitness.

Nonparametric statistics are included because we believe they are more practical for application by the public school teacher. This is true mainly because they do not demand as strict adherence to the theoretical assumptions underlying parametric statistical techniques. They are also easier to use (without the necessity of computer or calculator) and are easier to teach to students who may lack a good background in mathematics.

The inclusion of a section on subjective evaluation should be of value to all teachers in the field since much of our evaluation is subjective in nature. It is an attempt at resolving such problems as how to evaluate movements which take short periods of time. The physical educator must be able to make subjective judgments systematically according to a predetermined objective scheme.

A third feature of the book is the presentation of a model for physical performance and fitness. The content of the model is not as important as the hierarchical concept that will allow students to place different components of performance and fitness into perspective.

Although this book was written primarily for students just beginning their study of evaluating performance, there is a flexibility which allows it to be adapted for more advanced students. The potential flexibility can be seen in Chapters 5 and 6 (Interpretation of Test Scores and Optional Supplement to Interpretation of Test Scores) in which both the simpler (nonparametric) and more complex (parametric) statistical procedures are included. The statistical procedures that would be most appropriate for the background and interests of a particular class can be chosen. The major source of flexibility for the other portions of the book will be in the use made of the problems at the end of each chapter.

Many have assisted us directly and indirectly in this endeavor. Although they did not collaborate with us directly, we were certainly influenced by the teaching and ideas of such men as T. K. Cureton, A. W. Hubbard, and G. C. Moore. More directly, we appreciate the initial involvement and continual encouragement of our good friend Earle Zeigler. The typing of Mrs. Doreen Knight and Mrs. Lillian Simkins was indispensable. The general support from department heads, such as Rollin Wright and Joe Oxendine, helped in numerous ways. Finally, reading and commenting on the manuscript by various students, such as Mrs. Janet (Vanourek) Taylor, helped us get a feel for student reaction to the material presented in this form. We extend our sincere thanks to all involved.

Don Franks
Helga Deutsch

To the Instructor

There is no one "correct" way to use this book or teach a course in evaluating performance through testing in physical education. The interests, background, and your judgment concerning the needs of the students and the resultant objectives (and their relative importance) will, of course, determine the usefulness of particular portions of this book. We did think, however, that it would be beneficial to share some of our thoughts on how this book might best be used in such a course. These suggestions are obviously that—suggestions to be used, adapted, or disregarded as you attempt to provide the best possible experiences for your class.

Class Project(s)

We have included a few problems at the end of each chapter. In order for the material to have relevance, it should be adapted to the present and future needs (situation) of the student. These problems can be used for "laboratory" sessions, separate independent projects, as a part of a larger term project, or as a basis for further class discussion. Below are some further suggestions concerning the scope and evaluation of these problems.

ASSISTANCE WITH PROBLEMS

Chapter 1

PROBLEM: To differentiate between test and measurement and then to suggest ways in which evaluation might be used in terms of student performance, curriculum planning, guiding students, public relations, motivation, and research. We suggested that the student do this with a test taken in a physical education class. You may want to assign a particular test to be analyzed in this way, or, if practice teaching, the student might want to use a test that is being used in this situation. The first part of the problem is simply to determine if the difference between the tool (test) and the act of getting scores using the test (measurement) is understood. The second part of the problem is aimed at developing an approach to evaluation which will permeate the entire course. Emphasis on the "why" of evaluation (how it can be used) rather than the "how to do" can aid in making this course relevant.

Chapter 2

PROBLEM: To select a test to measure a specific objective in a particular physical education class and to justify the selection. The problem should be evaluated in terms of the procedure used to make the selection rather than an agreement with the actual selection. If the purpose of the problem is simply to select a test, then the teacher might want to arbitrarily assign a specific class and objective to be tested. If the students are practice teaching at the same time, the teacher may ask them to use one of the units in one of the classes in which they are involved. A third alternative is to have this problem as a part of a larger term project in which students select a class, determine objectives, tests, and develop a grading plan.

In any case, the students should cover the following points in their justification of selection of a test:

1. Validity: through expert opinion and use and strong relationship to criterion measure; also, are the responses characteristic of what is expected.

2. Reliability: through high correlation between test and retest and little systematic shift as a result of retest.

3. Objectivity: through close agreement with different scorers.

4. Applicability: through evidence that it can be used with the particular sex and age group involved.

5. Standardization: through instructions for pre-test, administration, and scoring of test.

6. Practicality: must meet limitations of cost and time.

Chapter 3

PROBLEM: To make detailed plans for administration of a test to a particular class. Our suggestion would be to have the students use the same test they selected in Chapter 2. One option available for discussion of this problem would be to have one student test the entire class and then have the class discuss ways the test administration could have been improved. Another possibility would be to divide the class into several small groups and have a student in each group administer a test. The small groups would then discuss it and report back to the group as a whole. A reporter for each small group would be chosen in advance.

Chapter 4

PROBLEM 1: Evaluate a performance of a simple skill. Select a "simple" skill such as a forward roll. Analyze the factors which are most important in the proper execution of the skill. It would be advantageous to record the performance on tape or loop film of 4 or 5 subjects of varying skill which can be reviewed as often as desired by your students. Hand out a rating sheet to each student and carefully discuss how it is to be used. Have some students present a justification for their evaluation.

PROBLEM 2: Rate a team during game play. Have the students rate a team during game play using a rating form developed by you and a rating form which they themselves have developed. Again, it would be advantageous if the game could be taped so that grades could be reviewed and justified by the students. Also discuss the student-developed rating forms in terms of simplicity, logicality, clarity, ease of recording, and pertinent points to be evaluated.

PROBLEM 3: Develop a rating scale for a skill or routine. Have the class discuss the rating form itself as well as any difficulties encountered in the evaluation period.

Chapters 5 and 6

PROBLEM 1: Weigh each class member. Check pre-test instructions (food, water, etc.); wearing apparel; posture on scales; number of trials; etc.

PROBLEM 2: Select a sample from the class representative of different weights. Divide the class into three or four groups and select a random sample from each group (if groups are unequal, proportional numbers from each group should be chosen for sample).

PROBLEM 3: Determine the median and percentile scores for the entire class and for the sample. How well does the sample represent the class? Point out that the sample is an estimate and that differences for different samples will exist.

PROBLEM 4: Determine reliability of the sample. Check both for relative position (correlation) and systematic change (Wilcoxon test for paired groups). Discuss possible causes of inconsistency.

PROBLEM 5: Measure the height of the sample. What is the relationship between height and weight? Point out that correlation differs for different groups.

PROBLEM 6: Divide the class in half according to height. Take a random sample from each half. On the basis of these samples, what is the difference in body weight for persons of different height? Use the Mann-Whitney U test; discuss significance level, what it means, etc.

Chapter 7

PROBLEM: Establish a specific grading plan for a physical education class. This plan should be evaluated in terms of completeness and consistency. The students should be encouraged to develop plans consistent with their own grading principles (e.g., a student may believe that grading should be based on improvement and thus should be evaluated on the basis of his ability to set up a grading plan to do that). Some of the items necessary for developing a grading plan are (1) selection of a particular class; (2) specific objectives for the class and their relative importance; (3) specific content of the class; (4) tests to be used to measure the attainment of the objectives; (5) standards to be used for the grading plan (perhaps in a point or percent breakdown).

If the sole purpose of the problem for the class is the grading plan, the teacher may want to arbitrarily assign items 1–3. The class could answer item 4 as part of their assignment for Chapter 2 and item 5 for this chapter. If the students are involved in practice teaching at the same time, the teacher may ask them to use one of the specific classes in which they are involved. A third alternative is to select this problem as a larger term project and have the student do all the items. A final suggestion would be to ask the class to do this problem in terms of a test and measurement class.

Chapter 8

PROBLEM 1: Divide one of the four major components of performance and fitness into different subdivisions. The main criteria for evaluating this chore (and problem 4) are completeness and logical groupings; there is no one "correct" answer.

PROBLEM 2: Select, or develop, a test for one level of one of the components of performance and fitness. This could be used to help a beginning class become more familiar with the literature by having them "select" a test. The development of a test might be a good project for an advanced class. In either case, they should refer back to Chapter 2.

PROBLEM 3: Analyze several "fitness tests" to determine what levels of what components are tested. The teacher might want to select some tests, articles, or books for a beginning class. It might remain open for an advanced class.

PROBLEM 4: Using a hierarchical model similiar to the one in this chapter, develop your own content for physical performance and fitness. An alternate problem would be to compare models developed by other people (such as Åstrand, Cureton, deVries, Falls, and Fleishman).

Chapter 9

PROBLEM 1: Have the students formulate one question for each form described. Student questions should be evaluated in terms of the following points:

1. What is the purpose of the question? What is being asked?
2. Is the question clear or ambiguous?
3. Is it simply stated with no superfluous wording?
4. Is textbook language avoided?
5. Are the foils plausible?

PROBLEM 2: Have the students develop, administer, analyze, and interpret the test results and analysis. When evaluating the test as a whole take the following into account:

1. Are the directions clear?
2. Do the directions include all pertinent information?
3. Is the item analysis properly interpreted?

An alternative exercise would be to have the students select one area and formulate a question of each type for that area.

Chapter 10

PROBLEM: How does one answer an important question in our field? Again there is no one correct answer. The attention given to the selection (or construction) of valid tests and the mode chosen to answer the question are the major factors to be considered in evaluation. In general, this problem is designed to initiate the students' thinking about "next steps." It should provide an opportunity for the instructor to discuss this book and course in terms of the students' present situation and future plans.

Statistical Procedures

We share the concern of many students and instructors that an adequate study of statistical procedures in test and measurement classes is almost impossible because of the limited time available for this unit, the lack of mathematical background of some of the students, and the amount of information and calculating skill necessary to solve even some of the simpler procedures (such as r and t). It has proved difficult to help students get beyond the details of the computation to see the overview and the reasons for the procedures.

We believe that the use of nonparametric statistical procedures will greatly assist you in helping the student learn more about the "why" of statistical procedures. The calculations involved in these procedures are so much easier to use and understand that it will free you to spend more time on the uses of the procedures. Thus we recommend that most classes use only Chapter 5 (nonparametric statistical procedures). In the discussion of the nonparametric procedures, it would be useful to mention the parametric counterpart (Chapter 6) since the students will encounter these procedures in much of the literature. However, it is not necessary or even desirable to use both chapters in detail. For example, when discussing the Mann-Whitney U test for determining the difference between two independent groups, it should be pointed out that this test achieves the same thing the t test does for difference between independent groups. The class should work the example only using the Mann-Whitney U test and skip the computation of the t test. Although you may not be as familiar with these nonparametric procedures and feel more comfortable with the parametric tests, we strongly encourage you to try the nonparametric procedures. If you would like an additional reference to use with this portion, we would recommend Siegel (see Chapter 5 for full reference).

The parametric procedures are included in Chapter 6 not only for comparative purposes but also for use with advanced classes (comprised of students who have had previous test and measurement class, a prior unit on statistical procedures, good math background, can use calculators, etc.) for which these may be more appropriate. In these cases, the emphasis should be placed on Chapter 6, with Chapter 5 used for review and comparative purposes.

Subjective Evaluation

The impression is sometimes given that unless something is measured in thousandths of a second or millimeter we have not really evaluated it. Few really important decisions (whether by teachers, coaches, executives, statesmen, or anyone else) are made purely on the basis of objective evidence. We certainly do not make our personal decisions on this basis. It behooves us therefore to learn how to systematically observe performances so that we can attain that "objective subjectivity" in our evaluations. Let's not apologize for subjective evaluations, but realize that they are necessary in many cases. If we do them well, our overall evaluation is strengthened by the inclusion of elements that can only be evaluated subjectively.

Physical Performance and Fitness

This chapter may well be the most exciting *and* disappointing one in the book. It is our hope that this chapter will allow students to understand (put into perspective) the maze of information about performance and fitness; that they will be able to understand that *both* the "general motor ability" and "specificity of motor skills" proponents have something to say; that there are some large general components in that human abilities are related to each other and that there are unique characteristics in the most minute portions of skills and/or the human body. In addition, we hope that students will be better able to sort out the literature and realize that findings in one component at one level apply only to that level of that component. And we hope that students will be able to make more intelligent decisions concerning the area(s) they want to emphasize in their professional lives.

This will be a disappointing chapter if one expects to find a listing of specific tests. We purposely avoided doing that because we believe the first priority is to gain an overall perspective of this area. We believe that the inclusion of specific tests prior to that understanding would hinder this goal (just as we believe the inclusion of complex statistical procedures has hindered the overview of the reasons for statistical procedures). This does not mean that the selection and (or) construction of specific tests for specific levels of particular components are not important, but we believe that this selection and construction can be done better after an understanding of Chapters 2–8, rather than as a part of them. This is obviously a good topic for projects, as has been suggested after Chapter 8. (See also Appendix D.)

Conclusion

The final chapter is an attempt to put the content of this book into a broader perspective. It is an effort to say, "this is only the beginning." Our hope is that it is the kind of beginning that will provide the interest and some of the tools for going further.

One textbook cannot completely fulfill the interests and purposes of a specific class. It is expected that you will want to supplement this book with articles and other books to enrich the experiences of the students in your class.

CHAPTER 1

Functions of Testing

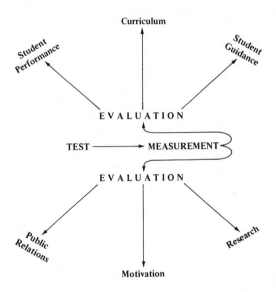

Words such as tests, measurements, and evaluation are so emotion-laden that to many of us they conjure up the same symptoms that we encounter when we visit the doctor or dentist. Students of all ages may find that they experience butterflies and general nervousness. Unfortunately, tests are viewed by many as never-ending barriers that must be surmounted before our life's work can be undertaken. These reactions are often understandable because the area of tests, measurements, and evaluation is often misunderstood and therefore misused by many teachers. An understanding of this vital area of the teaching–learning process as well as student empathy will help the teacher place testing in its proper perspective. Two questions provide an appropriate beginning for this understanding:

1. What terms are used to differentiate the tools used, the act of using the tools, and the interpretation and use of the process?
2. In what ways does evaluation assist the teacher?

Definition of Terms

Although the terms test, measurement, and evaluation are often used interchangeably, technically they have precise meanings with definitely different nuances. The 1968 edition of *The Random House Dictionary College Edition* defined these words as follows:

Test—the *means* by which the presence (or) quality···of anything is determined.
Measurement—the *act* of ascertaining the extent···of something. (*Note:* composite of definitions of measurement and to measure.)
Evaluation—to determine or *set the value* or amount of; to appraise.

The vertical jump, then, is a tool (*test*) which takes meaning as the teacher or student *measures* the jump. *Evaluation* occurs when the results are compared or used in relation to predetermined criteria. Evaluation occurs when a student's score is interpreted by comparison with class or nationwide norms or with a previously stated objective.

The Role of Evaluation

When we profess to become teachers, we also accept the responsibility for making judgments. We must assess, fortunately or unfortunately, our students, which in many instances will have implications for their future. This weighty responsibility—judging people—must be accomplished objectively and judiciously.

From the definition of terms, the first step in evaluation is to determine clearly the objective of the course and/or the program. These objectives will reflect the desires of the institution (grade level or school) as well as the teacher's own philosophy. Once these objectives have been established and are clearly understood by students, parents, and administration, the guidelines for evaluation (grades) will have been accepted.

However, the purpose of tests and measurements is much broader than grading. Besides being administered to *assess student performance and/or progress*, test scores also give the teacher insight into the *validity of his methods*. If the majority of students in a class do poorly on a certain question or topic, the teacher knows that something went awry between the presentation and reception (teacher–student) of the information. Therefore, in addition to realizing that review of the material is necessary, the teacher should reflect and correct the methods used in presenting this aspect.

Judicious use and interpretation of test scores can be an advantageous tool in *curriculum planning*. A simple example of how test scores may be used in this area follows. A community has just begun to sponsor a swimming program for all youngsters. On testing in the physical education swimming classes, instructors find a definite increase in the number of students who have acquired the basic skills. If this trend continues, the school may reduce the number of beginning classes offered and replace them with advanced or specialized swimming classes. In keeping attuned to students' needs as reflected in test results, a teacher can provide more meaningful experiences to his students.

One of the physical educator's greatest problems is class size. Although improvements have been made in this area, the ideal of individual instruction will rarely if ever be possible in public schools; therefore this problem will always exist. Tests and measurements can assist the teacher with this problem by giving him an objective measure for *guiding students*. With information obtained from tests, he can group his students homogeneously. This will enable the teacher to work with each individual (group) according to ability. In so doing, the teacher will no longer have to gear the work for one level and hope that the other children or adolescents will catch up or advance on their own but can work with each group in turn either in separate classes or within the same class.

Discovering students' strengths and weaknesses through testing and then recommending ways for enhancing and/or improving each is another phase of the guidance function of testing. Since ramifications in concrete terms are more readily understood by students, parents, and administrators, the *public relations* aspect, which is important for teachers, the program, and the school, is also positively affected through a carefully developed testing program. A valuable by-product in the determination of strengths and weaknesses might be in the development of a proficiency program which would have tremendous influence in allowing the student to progress at his own rate as well as offering him the most well-rounded, meaningful experiences possible.

Another aspect in which tests and measurements can make a valuable contribution is *motivation*. Two techniques predominate.

1. *Self-testing.* This occurs when the student competes against himself by observing the progress of his own scores on a test. Charts may be kept denoting weekly, monthly, or yearly progress. Many "formal" tests become self-testing activities with slight modifications such as a chalk line rather than having to measure each jump. Students of all ages are responsive to the immediate feedback which they receive in events such as jumping and throwing.

2. *Competition.* Posting norms, be they class or national norms,

allows the student to ascertain exactly where he stands and offers him guidelines for establishing realistic goals. This technique, although extremely valuable, must be used with caution. Although we live in a competitive world, undue stress of competition in class may frustrate students and therefore work negatively in motivating a student to improve.

Tests and measurements are also a vital tool in practically every type of *research*. It is one of the primary means for collecting data. Therefore it is imperative that all physical educators have training in this area, since it is through research that knowledge is enhanced and teaching is upgraded, resulting in improved experiences for the students.

In this instance research is used in its broadest sense. It refers not only to the work done in laboratories but also to the systematic investigations made by *all* teachers in the field. Many examples have already been cited under categories such as guidance and curriculum planning.

Summary

Tests and measurements are tools that can be used for evaluation, guidance, curriculum planning, public relations, motivation, and research. Therefore, the teacher may be prone to overuse this tool or may be so overwhelmed as to avoid it completely. Either choice is poor, since the role of the teacher is to provide meaningful experiences for pupils in order for them to learn about themselves and their environment. To use this technique to greatest advantage, 10 to 15% of the total class time could be spent in some kind of measurement.

The use of tests and measurements is limited only by the teacher's imagination. Its value, however, depends on judicious application.

Problems

Choose a test given to you in a physical education class.
1. What is the test?

2. What is the measurement?
3. How could an evaluation of that test be used in terms of
   A. Student performance
   B. Curriculum planning
   C. Student guidance
   D. Public relations for the class and/or program
   E. Motivation of the students
   F. Research associated with the class

References

Barrow, H. M., and McGee, R. *A practical approach to measurement in physical education.* Philadelphia: Lea and Febiger, 1964.

Grounlund, N. E. *Measurement and evaluation in teaching.* New York: Macmillan, 1965.

Scott, M. G., and French, E. *Measurement and evaluation in physical education.* Dubuque, Iowa: W. C. Brown Co., 1959.

Smithells, P. A. and Cameron, P. E. *Principles of evaluation in physical education.* New York: Harper, 1962.

Test Evaluation

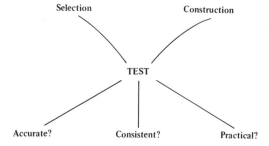

The selection of good tests is essential for all persons in physical education. Evaluation and research can be no better than the tests used. Appropriate testing tools are, therefore, a prerequisite for evaluation of the pupil, the teacher, and the program.

Criteria for Test Selection

The following questions are important ones to consider in the selection of a test.

1. How well does the test measure what it is purported to measure?
2. How consistent will the results be under the same conditions at different time intervals (for example, one minute, one week, one year later)?
3. How consistent will the test results be for different testers?
4. How appropriate is the test for your particular purpose and group?
5. What other things would change a person's score (time of day, time since last meal or physical activity, temperature, humidity, condition of floor or field, etc.)?
6. How much does it cost in terms of time, space, equipment, and staff?

RELATIVE QUESTIONS

These questions are the *degree* to which a test will satisfy a particular criterion, since they cannot be answered in an absolute sense with yes or no. The question is not, Is the test consistent, but rather, How much fluctuation can we normally expect in using the test? It is important to know whether the normal fluctuation of a test is 2%, 10%, or 50% before using the test. From among less than perfect tests, one must choose the test that more nearly meets the criteria.

Test Construction

The test constructor has an obligation to provide answers to the above questions. These questions can be answered by establishing the degree of validity (question 1), reliability (question 2), and objectivity (question 3), and by obtaining information concerning different groups (question 4), standardized instructions (question 5), and practical considerations of cost and time (question 6).

Validity

Validity is the ability to determine how well a test measures what it is supposed to measure. It is important, since invalid tests are irrelevant to the tester's intentions. Even if a test could meet the other criteria (was consistent, could be used with a particular group, was standardized, was objective, was easily administered, etc.), it would not be useful unless it measured the characteristic the tester wanted to measure. To exaggerate and make the point, one might be able to measure height consistently, objectively, with any age group or sex, in a standardized way, with little equipment, and in a short period of time; however, it would not yield much information in the evaluation of a pupil's cardiovascular fitness. It would be helpful only if one were interested in the pupil's height.

There are three types of validity: (1) Do experts believe the test to be valid? (2) Does it compare favorably with valid tests of the same thing (and/or does it differentiate among groups differing on this trait)? (3) Does the test respond as a measure of this characteristic could be predicted to respond in different situations?

EXPERTS' OPINION

This type of validity is only as good as the logic and quality of the experts making the judgment. Persons who understand the trait to be measured give their opinion concerning whether or not a particular test will measure that trait. Favorable opinions concerning a test from knowledgeable persons can be viewed as one form of validity for a test.

RELATION TO VALID TEST

The second type of validity depends on having an accepted test of the same characteristic (criterion test). If a valid criterion test is available, then the new test can be compared with it to determine the degree to which they measure the same thing. If a good criterion exists, the primary purpose for developing a new test would be for wider application, usually because of practical considerations such as time and cost.

Criterion groups can be used to validate a test in much the same manner as criterion tests. If there are groups that differ on the characteristic being measured, then the degree to which the test can differentiate among the groups supports its validity.

RELATION TO THEORY

The third type of validity can never be completely established. It is based on a sound theory about the characteristic being tested. A thorough knowledge of the characteristic being measured will enable one to know what tests should have a direct (positive), low, and inverse (negative) relationship to the trait in question. If the test has the same type of relationship to these other tests, then this supports the validity of the test. The underlying theory about the characteristic being measured will also suggest how this test should respond to different situations, and this, too, can be studied to determine the degree to which the new test responds as predicted.

EXAMPLE OF VALIDITY

To illustrate the three types of validity, let us assume that we want to find a test for cardiovascular fitness that could be given to large groups by physical educators. First, we could read the literature and talk to qualified persons in physical performance and fitness. We might find that the time for a distance run, such as the two-mile run, would be recommended as a test of cardiovascular fitness that could be used in mass testing situations. The fact that this measure has been used by persons in this area and is recommended by experts would be some evidence of the first type of validity.

Let us assume that, after a thorough search of the literature, it was found that maximal oxygen intake was the most valid test of cardiovascular fitness (criterion test). The next step would be to see if the two-mile run is highly related to maximal oxygen intake in groups similar to those we want to test. If a high relationship is found (that is, persons scoring high on maximal oxygen intake tend to have faster two-mile run times), then this is evidence of the second type of validity.

Let us assume further that a thorough knowledge of cardiovascular fitness indicates that it is highly related to high stroke volume and better heart rate adaptation to submaximal work; is inversely related to symptoms of various cardiovascular diseases; and is not related to small motor skills and academic acheviement. If the two-mile run time was highly, inversely, and not related, respectively, to these other tests, this would be additional support for its validity as a test of cardiovascular fitness.

One would suspect that cardiovascular fitness would be worse in extreme temperatures, in high altitudes, during fatigue, etc. The response of the two-mile run as predicted to these conditions would add support for its validity. In addition, one might expect cardiovascular fitness to improve as a result of a regular program of endurance training, to decrease as a result of being bedridden, and not to change as a result of regular participation in shuffleboard. Again, the validity of the two-mile run could be studied to see if it responds as predicted to these conditions.

In short, the two-mile run would be validated as a test of cardiovascular fitness by (1) opinions of cardiovascular experts, (2) demonstrated high relationship to a criterion measure of cardiovascular fitness, and (3) its response to different conditions and situations in the same way that a test of cardiovascular fitness would be predicted to respond (based on the best information available).

Reliability

Reliability of a test means the degree to which one can expect the results to be consistent. It is important, since the confidence the teacher has in being able to test the pupil's ability depends largely on the consistency of the test; that is, the higher the reliability, the less likely the test score will be due to the fluctuation of the test rather than a reflection of the pupil. Although validity involves more than reliability, reliability is a necessary element in validity. A test could measure something consistently, but it may not be the trait it is supposed to measure (thus it would be reliable but not valid); however, it could not be valid unless it was first reliable (a test could not measure what it is supposed to measure unless it measures it consistently).

Reliability can be determined by testing the same group of pupils in the same condition on the same test with a set time interval between tests. Two questions should be asked concerning the consistency of a test given twice to the same group in the same condition—(1) to what degree does the test rank the pupils in the same order both times (from best to poorest), and (2) do pupils tend to appreciably change scores on the test simply by retaking the test?

Relative Position

The consistency in the order of the pupils is usually determined by the correlation (relationship) between the two tests. The higher (positive) the relationship, the more reliable the test is with respect to the differentiation among the pupils (relative position). That is, a a high positive correlation would be indicative of a similar score on the two tests.

Systematic Changes

The difference in score due to retesting is often neglected in the determination of reliability, but it is needed to detect any systematic changes made by the entire group (which will not be detected by correlation). The two testing periods can be compared on the same group to determine whether there is a difference in the actual test scores (absolute values) between the two testing periods on the same test.

FLUCTUATIONS

Low correlations can be caused by fluctuations (errors) in the equipment, the measurement, and/or the pupil (intraindividual variability). The reliability should be reported for short time intervals (which minimize intraindividual variation) *and* for the time intervals normally elapsing between test administrations. Thus, if a test would normally be administered before and after a six-week unit, then the six-week reliability should be reported; if it is normally administered annually, then the reliability over one year should be reported, etc. Obviously, the longer the time interval, the larger will be the intraindividual variation and the lower the reliability. The reliability of tests should be established for each particular situation and group for which the test is used.

OBJECTIVITY

A related question concerns the consistency of a test with different testers. The objectivity is relatively easy to determine by a comparison of independent scorers on the same test and same pupils. Reliability and objectivity can be increased by training the testers and having them use standardized procedures and instructions in administering and scoring the test. The scorers should make *independent* determinations (that is, the test should be scored in such a way that a scorer cannot be influenced by other scorers).

Standardized Instructions

Since reliability and validity are established by using particular instructions to ensure standard conditions, it is important to include these instructions with the test. The instructions should include (1) pretest rules concerning food, physical activity, rest, and other matters that might affect the test, (2) detailed procedure for administering the test, including modifications for different ages and sex, and (3) instructions for scoring the test.

Norms

Most variables change with age, and many are different for males and females. Therefore the typical scores and range of scores should be reported for age groups, by sex. These norms will help the pupil compare himself with similar pupils on particular tests. Careful attention to the group used for establishing the norms will provide more meaningful use of norms (for example, if the norms were based on Olympic champions, they would hardly be useful for postcoronary patients).

Practical Matters

The practical considerations will not validate tests or establish their reliability, but many good tests cannot be used because of cost and time. Although we would hardly be expected to minimize the importance of testing, it clearly has a secondary role to teaching. Therefore it should not take a disproportionate amount of class time. The cost of testing is a limiting factor in almost all cases—how much space, how much equipment, how many persons are needed to administer and score the test? Test constructors should give a realistic estimate of these factors. Ideally, one should search for the perfect test and not have to be concerned with such mundane items. In practice, however, one must often ask, What is the most valid and reliable test that can be given to 50 pupils in 30 minutes?

Summary

Selection (and construction) of a test is based on the degree to which the following criteria are established. The test

1. Measures what it is supposed to, as determined by experts' opinions, relation to valid tests, and theory

2. Is consistent, as determined by reliability and objectivity
3. Is appropriate for the particular group to be tested
4. Includes standardized instructions and is feasible in terms of time, space, equipment, and staff

Problem

Select a test to measure a specific objective in a particular physical education class. Justify your selection.

References

Barry, A. J., Webster, G. W., and Daly, J. W. Validity and reliability of a multi-stage exercise test for older men and women. *Journal of Gerontology*, 1969, **24**, 284–291.

Cowell, C. C. Validating an index of social adjustment for high school use. *Research Quarterly*, 1958, **29**, 7–18.

Cronbach, L. J. *Essentials of psychological testing*. (2nd ed.) New York: Harper, 1960.

Feldt, L. S., and McKee, M. E. Estimation of the reliability of skill tests. *Research Quarterly*, 1958, **29**, 279–293.

Franks, B. D., Wiley, J. F., and Cureton, T. K., Jr. Orthogonal factors and norms for time components of the left ventricle. *Medicine and Science in Sports*, 1969, **1**, 171–176.

Henry, F. M., and Farmer, D. Functional tests: II. The reliability of the progressive pulse ratio. *Research Quarterly*, 1939, **9**, 81.

Hoyt, D. P., and Magoon, T. M. A validation study of the Taylor manifest anxiety scale. *Journal of Clinical Psychology*, 1954, **10**, 357–361.

Jetté, M. Progressive physical training on anxiety in middle-aged men. Unpublished M.S. thesis, University of Illinois, 1967.

Jetté, M. The long-term effects of an exercise program on selected physiological and psychological measures in middle-aged men. Unpublished Ph.D. thesis. University of Illinois, 1969.

Kerlinger, F. N. *Foundations of behavioral research*, New York: Holt, Rinehart and Winston, 1966.

Liverman, R. D. Daily variability of a three-minute work test. In B. D. Franks (Ed.), *Exercise and Fitness—1969*. Chicago: Athletic Institute, 1969.

Marmis, C., Montoye, H. J., Cunningham, D. A., and Kozar, A. J. Reliability of the multi-trial of the AAHPER youth fitness test. *Research Quarterly*, 1969, **40**, 240–245.

McArdle, W. D., Zwiren, L., and Magel, J. R. Validity of the post-exercise heart rate as a means of estimating heart rate during work of varying intensities. *Research Quarterly*, 1969, **40,** 523.

Munro, A., Joffe, A., Ward, J. S., Wyndham, C. H., and Fleming, P. W. An analysis of the errors in certain anthropometric measurements. *Internationale Zeitschrift Angewandte Physiologie*, 1966, **23,** 93–106.

Orlee, H., *et al.* Evaluation of the AAHPER youth fitness test. *Journal of Sport Medicine and Physical Fitness* 1965, **5,** 67–71.

Strong, C. H. Motivation related to performance of physical fitness tests. *Research Quarterly*, 1963, **34,** 497–507.

Wilmore, J. H., Girandole, R. N., and Moody, D. L. Validity of skinfold and girth assessment for predicting alterations in body composition. *Journal of Applied Psychology*, 1970, **29,** 313–317.

CHAPTER 3

Administration of Tests

Score Card					
					Date
Number		Name			Birthday
Tests	Trials			$\bar{X}$	Rating
	1	2	3		
A					
B					
C					
D					
E					

What Do I Do
After
the Test?

Efficiency, which results from thorough planning, is a prerequisite of testing. Since time is at a premium, every word and action must be predetermined in order to accomplish the most in the least amount of time. The same may be said for good teaching. Actually, testing requires the same and at times more precise planning than does good teaching. Testing as well as teaching may be divided into three steps: preplanning (preparation), testing (instruction), and follow-up (feedback) periods. This chapter deals with the following question.

> What should be done prior to, during, and after the administration of a test?

Preplanning

Appropriate tests must be selected. The criteria for selection have been delineated in Chapter 2. Among others, they include consideration of age, sex, group size, time available, test purpose, scientific value (validity, reliability, objectivity), and availability of leadership, facilities, and equipment.

FLOOR PLAN

After the tests have been selected, the facility should be organized for most efficient use. Factors such as group structure, traffic pattern, and student fatigue must be considered so that tests may be administered safely and accurately to the greatest number of students in the shortest time. In developing a plan for rotation, tests should alternate in regard to muscle groups involved as well as degree of activity (most and least strenuous). The traffic pattern should avoid student meandering and confusion concerning test locations. Each area should be clearly marked and a floor plan prominently displayed.

The above organization assumes that sufficient leadership is available and that a number of different tests requiring a similar amount of time will be administered simultaneously. If one test proves to be more time-consuming than others, two or more stations should be provided for that activity. This reduces the possibility of a delay in one area which may cause confusion and unnecessary loss of time. Also, when students are forced to wait for an undue amount of time, there is an increased tendency toward discipline problems.

The need for additional leadership may be met by using other teachers, leaders' groups, senior students, or parents. When additional personnel are involved, the teacher in charge must assume the responsibility for training the individuals *prior* to the day the tests will be administered. A time-consuming but recommended procedure is to have these leaders actually experience the tests. This increases their familiarity with the test and also offers an opportunity to check on potential delays due to traffic pattern or timing of the tests.

GROUP ORGANIZATION

A number of means are available for organizing the students. The above system assumes individual or group rotation. That is, each individual is responsible for completing a set number of tests. On completion of one test a student is free to go to any area for the next test. This procedure is useful when one is working with older pupils (upper elementary school), since it also teaches self-direction. An alternative form, that of squad rotation, is recommended for young students and is equally effective with older students. This technique allows the squad to rotate as a group from test to test. With younger students it would be essential to assign a group captain, usually an older child, to direct the group from one test area to another.

The most economical procedure in testing is to administer the same test to half the group while the rest of the class acts as scorers. Then partners change places, and the test is repeated (mass testing). This procedure is recommended when facilities, equipment, and the type of test permit.

Score Cards

The purpose of the test and the rotation procedure selected will determine the type of score card used. If an individual or partner system is selected, an individual score card will be needed. This points to one of the disadvantages of individual rotation. Students may lose or mutilate their score cards, making them useless as permanent records. Mutilation is a less serious problem, since the scores can be recorded on another card. Although loss of a card does not occur often, it can be avoided by carefully controlling the collection of the score cards before the students leave the testing area.

When squad rotation is used, the leader may be charged with the responsibility for carrying the group's score card. A card for a squad is a shortened form of the class roll, listing only members of the squad. No matter which form is used, all score cards should include names, tests, date of testing, room for scores including all trials, a place for calculation or score conversions (norms, etc.), and grades.

When testing occurs over a two-day period, the teacher must be certain to collect the cards after the first day and redistribute them on the next. These procedures must also be preplanned. If individual cards are used, they should be returned to a designated place or collected as the students leave the gymnasium. If squad cards or class rolls are used, they should be returned directly to the teacher.

Cards should be alphabetized or ordered systematically to be redistributed as students enter the gymnasium. If squad cards are used, organization will be facilitated if squads are previously informed as to where they should meet.

Score cards should be developed before the day of testing. When squad or class rolls are used, the teacher can have names already entered. This procedure becomes cumbersome when individual cards are used. Therefore, an alternative would be to have a model drawn on the board which the students can copy. Ideally, forms should be preprinted to which students need only add their names. This procedure is also helpful when squads are used.

WRITTEN INSTRUCTIONS

All standardized tests should include written instructions. These guides for the teacher should define the purpose of the test, dimensions, markings, equipment needed, directions, scoring procedure, and data for reliability, validity, and objectivity. The teacher must be thoroughly familiar with the test layout, directions, and equipment involved prior to administering the test. Before the day of testing the teacher should prepare a second form giving the key points of the test to be presented to the students or underline those points on the original form.

Having become thoroughly familiar with the test(s) to be presented and having carefully planned the organization and rotation, the teacher has one task remaining before testing day. He must prepare the students by informing them of the purpose for testing and of any special equipment which they must supply, as well as giving them procedural cues such as special formations, if any, to be used on entering the gymnasium for the next class meeting.

Testing Day

The teacher should arrive early to post norms and the diagram of the testing stations. Equipment should be carefully checked and placed in position before the class arrives. Extra pencils, stopwatches, and score cards should be easily accessible.

PRELIMINARY INSTRUCTIONS

As the class arrives, score cards should be distributed and the students should be seated in a position where they can see the teacher as he explains the tests. The teacher should stand in a position where he can see and be seen by everyone. Instructions are given to the entire group before they divide into squads for testing. Even if trained leaders are used who are to handle the entire administration of a test, the teacher should review the purpose of the testing situation and the overall procedure (squad rotation, traffic pattern, collection of score cards at the end of testing) and set a positive, efficient tone for the day.

TEST INSTRUCTIONS

In administering a test, the teacher should present the following information to all students. The purpose of the test must be clearly delineated so that all students understand what the test is designed to measure. A careful explanation of the test should be given. Key points should be emphasized. The instructions are more easily understood if the explanation is given in units and follows the order in which they occur in the test. A demonstration should be given, since students are often more receptive to pictures than words. The factors to be watched by scorers should be reemphasized, and then students should be asked if there are any questions. If starting and stopping signals are used, they should be distinctive and should be described before testing begins. Although the teacher has memorized the test, he should always have a written form available. Instructions should be standardized and should be concisely presented in language appropriate to the age group.

Not only should test instructions be standardized, but procedures and environment should also be the same for all students. This necessitates the establishment of a policy on the permissibility of pretest practice. If one student is allowed to practice, all students must be given the same privilege. In a test requiring a throw for distance, practice allows warm-up which may play a vital role in the prevention of injuries. Care should be taken, however, that students do *not* warm up to the point of fatigue. Consideration should also be given to the absurdity of having students warm up and then sit around waiting their turn. All factors, then, including space dimensions, equipment, warm-up, instructions, number of trials, and time between trials should be kept constant to assure equivalent conditions for each student.

PERSONNEL

All personnel involved in testing must be carefully trained. When a mass testing procedure is followed, the teacher should emphasize the scoring technique to be used.

When testing stations are used, one person should be designated as being in charge of each station. This leader should be thoroughly versed in the test and should be responsible for the rotation and scoring at his area. Each area should have sufficient personnel assigned to it so that time will not be wasted in retrieving balls or recording scores.

DISCIPLINE AND SAFETY

Students should be kept involved with meaningful duties and experiences if discipline is to be maintained. For this reason testing should be carefully planned, positively conducted, and efficiently managed. A discipline problem not only leads to poor use of time but may also present a safety hazard to the individual and others. Therefore safety should be stressed for each event and in developing the traffic pattern. Whenever possible, students should be occupied with such things as scoring, equipment retrieval, and assisting in every possible way. Extra equipment should be available in case of damage or repairs. If students understand the purpose of the tests and are kept involved with meaningful experiences, few discipline problems will arise.

Follow-up

After all scores have been accurately recorded, the score sheets should be returned to the teacher who now must interpret the scores. Room is available on each card for conversion into norms and/or grades. Profiles are recorded on a permanent record or directly on the score sheet. Before the score sheet is returned to the student, a permanent copy is recorded. The results should be made available as soon as possible, with an explanation of how they will affect the work to follow—that is, whether groups will be formed on the basis of the test results or whether his program will be accelerated. Each student, individually when possible, must be assisted in properly interpreting his results and in developing concrete steps toward formulation of a meaningful program.

Hints

When giving directions to a group, present the information before sending the groups to their testing stations. In dividing students into groups, use color-coded or numbered sheets to efficiently assign students to their testing stations.

Students will take as much time as is given to them. Therefore, be certain to use distinctive signals for starting and stopping. Inform the students that following the signal for stopping you will say, "Next, ready, go," and will expect them to be prepared. In this way time will be saved.

When timing a test that involves more than one testing station, know the number in each group and make appropriate adjustments if the groups are uneven.

Areas should be premarked for more efficient reading of scores. This is true for any tests that involve throwing or jumping for distance. Another time-saving technique is to read only the best of three trials when that is the score used. If only one stopwatch is available to test a class in a run, read off the time at each tenth of a second and have partners watch when their partner crosses the preestablished line.

When testing the high jump, test all subjects at the same height before progressively raising the cross bar.

Summary

Accurate results depend on "good tests" properly administered. This requires careful planning with clear, concise directions that are readily understood by the students. Properly trained assistants are a necessity. The one factor not yet considered is the student himself. It is assumed that each student is trying his best on each test. To assure this, the teacher must properly motivate the student. This is done by being sure that the student understands why the tests are given and how the scores will be used. Positive encouragement during the test itself is permitted if each student is so motivated. The problem is that students react differently and therefore varied methods are appropriate. Since this is not always possible, it might be advisable to use only mass techniques such as establishing a positive, efficient environment when one is working with older students. When elementary-age youngsters are being tested, individual techniques may be useful provided that care is taken not to "overmotivate," which would cause students to try "too hard" and thereby lower their scores.

Problem

Select a test. Make detailed plans for administering this test to a particular class.

References

Barrow, H. M., and McGee, R. *A practical approach to measurement in physical education.* Philadelphia, Pennsylvania: Lea and Febiger, 1964.

Hanson, D. L. Influence of the Hawthorne effect upon physical education research. *Research Quarterly,* December 1967, **38,** 4.

Scott, M. G., and French, E. *Measurement and evaluation in physical education.* Dubuque, Iowa: W. C. Brown Co., 1959.

Starr, H. M. How to fit in fitness testing. *Journal of Health, Physical Education and Recreation,* March 1959, **30,** 18.

CHAPTER 4

Subjective Evaluation

What Are the Important Elements in the Performance?

How Do I Set up Subjective Rating Scales?

Rating Scale		
		Date
Number	Name	Rater
Performance	Rating	
1		
2		
3		
4		

Scale (see definitions):
5 Excellent
4 Above average
3 Average
2 Below average
1 Poor

How Do I Use This
Rating Scale?

Subjective evaluation takes many forms and is used by *all* teachers. It necessitates a reliance on training and experience. If a teacher does not shy away from correcting errors in his pupils, why is he hesitant to evaluate a student's performance? Difficulty arises because this technique involves qualitative rather than quantitative judgments. Correction of errors and subjective evaluation require similar kinds of analysis and comparison with *predetermined criteria*. An appropriate description of this technique would be "objective subjectivity."

The questions to be answered prior to subjective evaluation are as follows.

1. What are the components to be evaluated?
2. Which ones should be evaluated subjectively?
3. What rating scale will be used?
4. How will each point on the scale be defined?
5. How many students will be rated at one time?
6. In what situation will the rating be done?
7. What type of rating form will be used?
8. How many raters will be used?

Development of Categories to Be Rated

The first crucial question to be resolved when preparing to evaluate students is to determine the components to be judged. This is decided before the semester begins and is done in conjunction with the development of a unit plan. The teacher carefully considers those skills required for the game. Once this decision has been made, he must determine which skills are to be evaluated objectively (skill tests) and which subjectively. Subjective evaluation complements and supplements objective measures and should not be used redundantly. That is, if a skill test is administered to determine the number of baskets made in 30 seconds (or field goal average for a game), this criterion should not be used to subjectively evaluate shooting skill. However, it would be appropriate to subjectively evaluate the "type" of shot used in game play and the manner of execution, as opposed to whether the basket is made.

The following analysis illustrates how the teacher may determine which elements to evaluate subjectively as well as develop an overall scheme for doing so. The student should recognize it as only an example of the procedure that might be followed.

The game of basketball taught to beginners includes many essentials such as running, jumping, passing, shooting, rebounding, and offensive and defensive patterning. All these aspects should be evaluated. Shooting, passing, running, and jumping can be readily evaluated objectively by timing for speed, by counting baskets made, or by measuring height jumped. If all aspects are deemed equally important and if time permits, a skill test is selected (according to the criteria established in Chapter 2) to measure each phase. If there is not sufficient time to measure all these components, those least important are eliminated. In this way only one shot or pass may be tested and the running test may be deleted, since rarely does a basketball player run for a long distance without suddenly having to change direction.

The teacher may feel that it is important not only to evaluate the student's ability to handle the ball in a structured situation, such as how many baskets he can make in 30 seconds or how many passes, but also to have an indication of how the student uses these skills in a game situation. Again, the elements to be evaluated must be determined. Therefore, the teacher would like to evaluate shooting, passing, guarding, rebounding, and teamwork not for the number of baskets made (which is accomplished through objective tests) but for how all these skills are adapted during game play. Each phase then is further analyzed so that shooting is now thought about in terms of positioning, using the appropriate shot for the situation, the flight of the ball, the timing of the shot, etc. Passing, guarding, rebounding, and other aspects deemed important are similarly analyzed.

Because such a listing would be unwieldy, the teacher must condense and reorganize these factors. An example of the result of such retrenching is given in Form 1. Where play and classtime permit, it would be advantageous to rate each aspect of the specific skill executed. Because of time and the complexity of the game of basketball, a more realistic rating sheet would use only the major headings (Form 2).

FORM 1

Basketball
Subjective Grading Sheet

	Names of Players							
I. Shooting								
A. Type								
B. Execution								
II. Guarding								
A. Body position								
B. Arm position								
C. Balance								
III. Passing								
A. Type								
B. Accuracy								
C. Force								
IV. Rebounding and jump balls								
A. Position								
B. Timing								
V. Teamwork								
A. Assists teammate								
B. Uses players to greatest advantage								
C. Uses self to best advantage								

Scale: 5   Excellent
      4   Above average
      3   Average
      2   Below average
      1   Poor

FORM 2

Basketball
Subjective Grading Sheet

Names of Players

I. Shooting									
II. Guarding									
III. Passing									
IV. Rebounding and jump balls									
V. Teamwork									

Scale: 5   Excellent
      4   Above average
      3   Average
      2   Below average
      1   Poor

Form 3 is an example of a scale that requires judging each aspect of a skill in connection with a balance beam routine which students create, including all the activities outlined as well as two movements which they select. In this case, students are rated on each aspect— base of support, alignment, etc. Every level of execution must be carefully considered before testing begins. All of these scales can be adapted to as many levels of discrimination as the teacher desires. Each is but an example which should be adapted for a particular situation before being used.

The purpose of the rating scale will determine the number of categories involved. For example, if the teacher desires to divide the class into three groups, three categories will suffice. However, if the rating scale will be used for grading purposes, a minimum of five divisions is desirable. Basically, the number of categories to be used will be determined by the degree of discrimination desired. Each unit of discrimination will have to be defined so that the rater (teacher) and those to be rated (students) will have a clear picture of what excellent, above average, average, below average, and poor performance is, relative to the aspect being judged. It has been found more convenient and useful to employ numerical ratings as opposed to words or letters when

FORM 3
Basic Movement
Balance Beams—Rating Scale[a]

Name _____   Section _____

Area I:
    Creative combination _____

Area II:
    Synchronization of movement _____

Area III:
  A. *Mount*
    Body weight controlled in straight line _____
    Balance before beginning step _____
  B. *Forward Walk*
    Alignment _____
    New base of support _____
  C. *Back Walk*
    New base of support _____
    Alignment _____
    Leg moved from hip _____
  D. *Turn*
    Weight over base on balls of feet _____
    Center of gravity not lowered until turn is complete _____
  E. *Lunge to Beam*
    Adequate base of support
      immediately assumed _____
    Alignment (down and up) _____
    Weight controlled when lowering _____
    Weight controlled on recovery _____
  F. *Leg Swings*
    Weight balance over base _____
    Movement initiated from hip _____
    Alignment _____
  G. *Dismount*
    Body weight controlled _____
    Step down and back from beam _____
    Erect standing position (end) _____
  H. *Optional* 1
    Control _____
    Alignment _____
    Complexity _____
  I. *Optional* 2
    Control _____
    Alignment _____
    Complexity _____

Scale: 5   Excellent   2 Poor   Total points _____
       4   Good   1 Very poor Grade _____
       3   Fair

[a] Used in the Department of Physical Education for Women, University of Illinois, Champaign-Urbana.

subjectively rating. This not only saves time during the actual rating but also gives greater flexibility in analyzing the grades or adding them to develop a composite score.

Developing the Rating Sheet

The rating sheet should be developed before the rating process begins. The type of rating sheet to be used will be determined by (1) whether an individual or an individual within a group will be observed, (2) whether one or many skills will be rated, and (3) the degree of discrimination desired. This latter point will depend on the purpose of the rating session. It may be for classification, achievement, or grading, to name a few. In the examples above, the basketball rating sheet (Form 1) allows members of two teams to be rated simultaneously, whereas Form 3 permits a maximum observation of two people only.

A rating sheet must be simple to be used with accuracy. It should be easily read and logically written. Before using it, the teacher should be familiar with the criteria and the rating sheet to permit the most accurate rating possible in the shortest amount of time.

Observations

Subjective evaluation, when well done, is relatively time-consuming and strenuous in that it requires complete concentration on the task. Therefore, observations must be carefully preplanned and organized. Ratings must be done more than once, particularly if they are done during game situations. In these situations three observations would normally be the minimum to provide adequate information for an accurate judgment, since individuals will be observed in slightly different situations involving the same techniques.

The environment and other conditions during the rating situation should be kept constant. That is, if one team or individual is rated in a competitive environment with observers present, all teams or individuals should be rated under similar conditions. Therefore, either the level of competition should be equated, or each player or team should be observed as they compete against every other individual or team.

This last condition, although possibly ideal, raises the problem of time if classes are large. Therefore, equating competition for rating purposes may be the most practical way of organizing these sessions.

Subjective evaluation requires focusing on the individual with *predetermined criteria* in mind for the purpose of rating the degree of skill attained. Although there is a similarity in observation for the purpose of correcting errors (used in teaching), the mind set of the teacher is quite different when grading. For this reason observations made during teaching without this specific focus lead to inaccurate and often invalid grades. It is impossible to use the cumulative observations made during the regular teaching process for "objective subjectivity." One reason is the "halo effect"—the influence a student's personality or attitude has on his skill rating. The teacher must constantly guard against being influenced by a student's attitude while evaluating achievement. Arguments such as "Johnny has worked hard on this for two weeks so I'll give him a B" or "Sarah could execute this stroke more efficiently if she'd only work harder so I'll lower her grade" have no place in subjective grading.

To overcome this aspect, the teacher, when conditions are appropriate, should observe each pupil doing one skill before beginning to rate a second skill. For example, in rating students on five dives, all students should be rated on the front dive before any student is evaluated on his back dive. When students are permitted to select their own dives, the teacher should rate all who have elected dive A before beginning to evaluate dive B. Thus the rater does not have to switch from one set of criteria to another and therefore achieves increased accuracy in evaluation.

Rating each student on one element before proceeding to the next also allows the teacher to focus on each student individually and, in a manner of speaking, assures "equal time" for each student. This also safeguards against the "halo effect," since all of us have a tendency to recall pleasurable and satisfying experiences (the courteous student) more readily than others.

Types of Rating Forms

Rating forms serve different functions and therefore appear in different ways. *Check lists* and *incidence charts* are often used by students in rating each other. They may also be used to pinpoint strengths and weaknesses. They are of value in helping a student to focus his attention on the play that is occurring on the court rather than expecting the novitiate to select pertinent points from a great deal of activity. An example of a checklist appears below.

The following is an example of an incidence chart on which students check appropriate areas as they occur.

These two rating forms are useful in involving students who are not playing at the moment. Focusing the students' attention on a specific aspect or aspects of the game enhances the learning of the "spectator" who will soon become the participant. Students can also use these ratings to improve their own and a partner's skill. That is, student A watches student B and then meets with him to explain his observations. Including students in the teaching situation helps to develop better understanding and increase their motivation. This kind of individual instruction can also improve their skill. As an evaluative technique to be used for grading, we have found these systems to be too cumbersome and time-consuming, and their reliability may be questionable. Since they involve a great deal of writing (checking), the teacher may find that too much time is spent with attention diverted from the game itself, causing him to miss many grading opportunities.

	Batting[a]	Date	_____
Subject	_____	Rater	_____

      Holds bat at end of handle
      Has hands together
      Keeps elbows away from body
      Steps into ball
      Overstrides
      Uses body behind swing
      Swings too early
      Swings too late
      Has smooth swing
      Swings too hard

---

[a] Partial list. Student checks those aspects that are appropriate.

Basketball[a]

Date _____

Subject _____   Rater _____

Passes	Accurate (flight)	Straight	Arched	Fumbled
Push				
Underhand				
Hook				
Bounce				
Chest				

Shots	Accurate (flight)	Hard	Soft	Made
Lay-up				
Push				
Set				
Free throw				
Hook				
Jump				

[a] Partial list.

Achievement Chart—Swimming[a]

Name _____

Turtle float
Prone float
Back float
Flutter kick, one width
Whip kick, one width
Scissor kick, one width
Front crawl, one length
Back crawl, one length
Elementary backstroke, one length
Breastroke, one length
Surface dive
Plunge dive
Spring dive

[a] Partial list—check as completed.

A modification of the checklist type of rating sheet can be used as an achievement chart on which to record a student's progress on a pass-fail basis. The student or teacher checks off the successful completion of a specific skill, and in this way the student can keep track of his progress. An example of this type of achievement chart is a modification of the American Red Cross Swimming Progression shown here.

A valuable aid would be the addition of pictures depicting various levels of performance. Then, after the subject's form is compared with the criteria, a judgment is made. This procedure is often used in rating posture.

Different Forms for Rating

The usefulness of a rating sheet depends on the teacher's training and experience as well as on the skill to be rated. An example of vari-

---

Subjective Evaluation of the Swing

Form A

Using a 10-point scale, rate the four students on the loop films as fairly as possible.

For each grade given, explain how you arrived at this particular grade (what you used as criteria for your evaluation).

Subject A
Grade: _____

Subject B
Grade: _____

Subject C
Grade: _____

Subject D
Grade: _____

Name _____ Date _____

---

ous forms used to rate will be given for a particular skill. The task was a pendulum swing in three-quarter time involving the whole body. The following sheets were developed by Drs. Deutsch and Hoyman* for the purpose of establishing guidelines for subjective evaluation. Films were taken of four students who varied in skill. Teachers and upper-class physical education majors rated the quality of the swing, using each of the sheets. The five rating forms are presented to give the reader an idea of different forms that may be used in evaluating the same activity.

Subjective Evaluation of the Swing

Form B

Using the scale shown below, rate each of the four students on the loop films. For each grade given, explain how you arrived at this particular grade with reference to following criteria in the specified order:

1. Trunk involvement	Scale: 1– 2	Very poor
2. Knee involvement	3– 4	Poor
3. Arm involvement	5– 6	Fair
4. Range of movement	7– 8	Good
5. Rhythm	9–10	Very good
6. Coordination		

Subject: _____

Grade: _____

Subject: _____

Grade: _____

Name _____   Date _____   Trial No. _____

---

* Dr. Annelis Hoyman, Associate Professor, Department of Physical Education, University of Illinois, Champaign-Urbana.

Subjective Evaluation of the Swing

Form C

Using the scale shown below, rate each of the four students on the loop films. Evaluate the performance in terms of the following criteria in the specified order:

A. Arms

1. Use of gravity	Scale: 1– 2	Very poor
2. Amplitude of the swing	3– 4	Poor
3. Time per period (round trip)	5– 6	Fair
4. Speed at various points in the arc	7– 8	Good
	9–10	Very good

B. 1. Knee action (coordination)
2. Total body involvement

Subject: _____

Grade: _____

Subject: _____

Grade: _____

Name _____ Date _____ Trial No. _____

Form A is an open-ended sheet which was favored primarily by people who taught dance and were very experienced in analyzing and assessing movement. An analysis of the criteria used by the raters showed that each followed a consistent pattern that resulted in watching the movement in its entirety and then a careful analysis of the parts involved. The majors found that they needed more guidelines than this form provided. In general, the majority of the people who used this form agreed with the majors.

Form B was generally well received by all experienced teachers who used this sheet. It was too general when used by majors. Most raters again viewed the entire movement before concentrating on its parts and recommended inclusion of a category of this type. This type of rating sheet is also applicable to other movements. Again it must be emphasized that each rater had to define for himself what each numerical rating would be for the trunk, knee, etc. Since the ratings were relatively similar among judges, all of whom had previous experience in teaching such a movement, their own guidelines appeared to be in agreement with those established by others.

Whereas Form B was patterned after an anatomical or kinesiological format, Form C used a rhythmical concept. It met with average acceptance by experienced teachers but was not very helpful when used by majors who lacked experience. Some individuals praised the order of the outline, while others felt that this form overemphasized the use of the arms.

Experienced teachers rated Form D as only generally acceptable, feeling that it was too restricting in form and terminology and too cumbersome. The majors felt that it was very useful and appreciated the guidelines which were included. Experience resulting in increased self-confidence has positive implications for subjective evaluation.

Some experienced teachers and all the majors thought that Form E was useful in judging the total body swings of the subjects. Other experienced teachers felt that it was too restricting and cumbersome.

The experienced raters were relatively consistent regardless of the form used. Each had a systematic way of viewing the movement when they used the open-ended form. Nearly all experienced judges favored some guidelines in the form of some key areas to observe (Form B) rather than a more detailed form. Inexperienced raters favored the more rigid forms such as D or E. Although Forms B and D offered a more kinesiological analysis while Forms C and E emphasized rhythmic aspects, the experienced raters were relatively consistent in their judgments. Preference thus appeared to depend on training and experience. It is hoped that these forms give insight into a means for developing your own forms when subjectively evaluating a skill.

The purpose of the movement to be rated, reflected in the teaching method used, also has bearing on the type of rating form used. Referring back to the Balance Beam Form, one can see that the object of

Subjective Evaluation of the Swing

Form D

Using the criteria and the rating scale shown below, rate each of the four students on the loop films

Subject: _____   Grade: _____

	1–2 Very poor	3–4 Poor	6–7 Fair	7–8 Good	9–10 Very good
1. Trunk involvement	Stiff	Slight uneven	Lacks coordination	Limited range	Range, coordination
2. Knee involvement	Stiff	One pump or exaggerated	Two pumps, lacks coordination	Two pumps, jerky	Range, coordination
3. Arm involvement	Limited range, no coordination	No use of gravity	Limited range, coordinated but jerky	Limited range, but coordinated	Range, coordination, uses gravity
4. Range of movement	Narrow, stiff	Range all right, but forced	Limited but relaxed	Limited but coordinated	Sufficient range, relaxed coordination
5. Rhythm	Absent	Jerky	Not even	Lacks stress, otherwise all right	Stress even, relaxed
6. Coordination	Work in parts	Arms and legs not together, uses trunk	Arms wide and legs narrow, or vice versa	Use of entire body, but lacks smooth transition	Movement spreads smoothly throughout the body

Name _____   Date _____   Trial No. _____

Subjective Evaluation of the Swing

Form E

Using the criteria and the rating scale shown below, rate each of the four students on the loop films

Subject: _____   Grade: _____

	1–2 Very poor	3–4 Poor	5–6 Fair	7–8 Good	9–10 Very good
1. Use of gravity (force)	Force swing, gravity not allowed	Too abrupt	Downswing good, extra "give" in end position on return swing	True swinging quality, gravity allowed to act	True swinging quality
2. Amplitude of the swing	Very narrow	Limited	Restrained in range backward	Adequate, consistent with use of gravity most of the time	Consistent with use of gravity

3. Time per period (round trip)	Slower than if gravity were allowed to act, extensive stops in end positions	Too slow	Not even in the two half-periods	Moderate, generally consistent with the length of lever	Consistent with use of gravity and length of lever
4. Speed at various points in the arc	Sustained, or fast throughout	Sustained rather than swinging, slow	Prolonged stops in end positions	Generally coordinated with use of gravity	Coordinated with use of gravity
5. Knee action (coordination)	Rigid or exaggerated or no knee action on the return swing	Decided knee action, but uneven	Not consistent with amplitude of the swing	Generally consistent with amplitude and force	Minor deviations but coordinated with the swing
6. Total body involvement	None, stiff back	Slight, stiff back	Limited range	Relaxed, but somewhat limited	Total body involvement, relaxed

Name _____   Date _____   Trial No. _____

these movements was balance and demonstration of an understanding of the concepts involved. Therefore, what is graded will depend on the teacher's philosophy which is reflected in the teaching methods used.

Subjective Assessment

Once the criteria have been determined and the meaning of the scores defined, the teacher plans for and observes his students to evaluate their performance. Many methods are available for determining the meaning of the different scores. One is by letting the class determine the standards. That is, poor, average, and good performances (or examples of all levels used) are demonstrated as the basis for each grade. This procedure is not only time-consuming but also might embarrass the students. Another difficulty is that classes vary from semester to semester and from year to year. Therefore, with this technique the standards would vary depending on the specific group being rated. To resolve this predicament, when developing such standards, a strong recommendation is to use an absolute which is tempered for the age or skill level (beginner, intermediate, advanced) of the group. Although this procedure is a bit more difficult to develop, it appears to be the most fair for the greatest number of students over the years, since a student who finds himself enrolled in a poor class will need to meet the same standards as a student in a well-skilled class, and vice versa.

One problem in applying this or any technique in subjective rating is that on occasion the teacher finds that for some reason he would like to change the criteria, standards, or points to be observed. Such changes should *never* be made during the evaluation sessions, since confusion will result. Teachers may forget which standards or criteria are currently being used, and therefore each student will not be evaluated on the same factors. Another problem would arise at the end of testing, when the meaning of the scores would be muddled by this change in midstream. Any necessary adjustments should be made at the end of the testing session and applied equally for all students.

In grading, care must be taken to score the sheets as the observations are made rather than relying on memory and grading at a later time. Reliance on memory leads to inaccuracy and confusion, since it is impossible to keep straight all the elements to be graded for each student. Also, reliance on memory increases the chance for the "halo effect" to encroach on a student's grade. This tends to invalidate the results, since the pupil would be graded on personality as well as execution rather than on execution alone.

Since students often have difficulty in deriving meaning from numbers but readily understand letter grades, a simple procedure can be followed to arrive at a composite grade when number values are given in scoring. Summate all scores, and divide by the number of parts graded. Example: A rating form has five parts, with each part receiving a maximum of 5 points. After his points have been added, Harry's score is 15. Divide this by five (the number of parts), and Harry's average is 3. Compare this grade to a preset scale which can be referred to whenever subjective evaluation is used. An example of such a scale would be:

A	4.1+
B	3.1–4.0
C	2.1–3.0
D	1.1–2.0
E	0–1.0

Therefore Harry's grade of 3 would be equal to a C.

Another aspect to be considered is whether each phase of the skill is equally important. In the previous example all five parts were of similar importance to the skill and therefore received the same weighting (all raw scores were summated). If, however, one aspect was more difficult or played a major role in the proper execution of the skill, it should receive additional weighting. Again using Harry's scores, let us assume that parts 1, 2, 4, and 5 are equally important and that part 3 is more important than any of the others. In this case, a higher weighting would be used for part 3:

Part	Grade	Weighting	Score
1	2	1	2
2	3	1	3
3	5	3	15
4	2	1	2
5	3	1	3
	—	—	—
	15	7	25

In this instance we divide by 7 (the sum of the weightings). There-fore, Harry's score would be $\frac{25}{7}$, or 3.57. According to our scale, Harry would receive a B.

Reliability and validity are also concerns in grading subjectively. An explanation of each as well as methods for determining each are found in Chapters 2 and 5.

Using More than One Rater

Often, more than one rater may be used. This is particularly true if subjective grading is being used in a research project, such as in validating an objective test. Ratings from three to five judges (ex-perts) may be used to determine the degree of similarity between the subjective ratings and objective test scores. When more than one rater is used, it would be advisable to standardize the techniques after judg-ing one performance. This procedure is observed in official gymnastic and diving competitions. After one performance the judges compare scores, and if a discrepancy is found they discuss the criteria until consensus is reached.

The important point in subjective ratings for grading purposes is *consistency* first, followed by agreement with experts. If Grader A is always 1 to 2 points higher than Grader B, consistency is maintained and therefore adjustments and interpretations can be made. If, however, each grader varies from subject to subject, it obviously would be difficult to interpret a student's grade.

In practicing subjective grading, the teacher should be concerned more with consistency rather than with agreement with a set standard. In grading as in other skills, it is "easier" to correct a consistent error than one that overshoots or undershoots indiscriminately. Wouldn't you rather correct someone who constantly shoots an arrow into the lower right-hand corner (cluster shoots) of the target than one who is all over the target face? The same principle may be applied to sub-jective evaluation. Once internal consistency is achieved, the rater should then strive for agreement with "experts."

Summary

As was mentioned in Chapter 1, every teacher carries the responsi-bility for making judgments. Chapter 2 discussed guidelines for selecting tests. Another aid the teacher has is reliance on his own training and experience to assist him in making subjective evaluations.

Subjective evaluation is a technique that complements objective evaluation. It may take many forms, but all have one thing in common. The key lies in the word evaluation—it is a judgment based on predetermined criteria. A phrase that aptly describes this aspect of · evaluation is "objective subjectivity." In developing the powers of observation necessary to grade a student accurately and subjectively, the teacher should first work for consistency and then toward agreement with a set standard.

Many forms for subjective evaluation are available. The type of form depends on (1) the teacher's experience, (2) the skill to be rated, and (3) the time to be devoted to rating. The teacher must have previously determined the criteria to be applied. Detailed organization is necessary to assess student performance accurately while giving other students meaningful experiences. Be certain to plan the timing of these rating opportunities as carefully and to have previously developed forms with which you are completely familiar. Do *not* alter your criteria once grading has begun, or it will be difficult if not impossible to interpret the grades.

Problems

1. Evaluate a performance of a "simple" skill which has been filmed or taped.
2. Rate a team during game play.
3. Develop a rating scale for a skill or routine which the students teach and evaluate. Include the preplanning phases as well as the development of criteria and grading form to be used.

References

Barrow, H., and McGee, R. *A practical approach to measurement in physical education.* Philadelphia, Pennsylvania: Lea and Febiger, 1964.

Scott, M. G., and French, E. *Measurement and evaluation in physical education.* Dubuque, Iowa: W. C. Brown, 1959.

CHAPTER 5

Interpretation of Test Scores

Normal Fluctuation?

Typical Score?

Relationship between Tests. . .between Groups?

HOW DO I EVALUATE
TEST SCORES???

What Am I Doing to the Students?

Difference between Groups?

Which
Method
Is Best?

The utilization of tests to fulfill their functions can be enhanced by the ability to quantify judgments concerning the following questions.

1. What is a typical score and normal fluctuation?
2. What is the relationship between different tests?
3. What is the difference between different groups?
4. What effects do various curriculums and teaching methods have on pupils?

Sampling

There are no absolute answers to the above questions in that each solution is found in terms of particular groups having specific characteristics. It may well be that the answer to any of these questions will be different for pupils of different age, sex, mental ability, physical condition, etc. It is essential that the answers to these questions be understood in terms of the groups (samples) used.

In statistical terms, a population is the entirety of something that is of interest. For example, our population might be Arkansas male tenth graders, or New York physical education teachers between 30 and 35 years of age who have had at least 5 years of teaching experience. A sample is part of the population that is chosen to be studied. If samples are properly selected, generalizations may be made back to the entire population. The procedure by which the sample is selected is important if we are going to have any confidence in the conclusions drawn for the population. One method is to select a *random sample*, which means that every member of the population has an equal chance of being selected. Drawing numbers from a hat that contained a slip for each member of the population would be an example of a random sample. Thus if we wanted a random sample of Arkansas male tenth graders, we could choose 100 names from a hat that contained the names of all Arkansas male tenth graders.

If we wanted to ensure, however, that we had subjects in our sample who came from different-size towns, then we might want to use a *stratified random sample*. For example, we could draw proportionate numbers of boys from towns larger than 20,000, from towns between 10,000 and 20,000, and from towns of less than 10,000. If the first group represented 60% of all tenth-grade boys, then 60% of our sample would come from that group.

Finally, we might want to ensure that each section of the state was represented so we could use a *cluster sample* and choose boys from different geographical regions. Thus we might end up with a clustered, stratified random sample, with 60 boys from towns over 20,000 (15 each from the eastern, western, southern, and northern parts of the state), 30 boys from towns of 10,000 to 20,000 (divided among all sections), and 10 from towns under 10,000 (from all areas).

If such a procedure were followed, it would allow the conclusions of the study to be generalized for the entire population of Arkansas tenth-grade boys based on a *probability statement* concerning the percent of time such results could be expected by chance for such a sample.* The conclusion could then be drawn for male tenth graders in Arkansas. Similar procedures could be used for larger samples (the United States, North America, etc.) or for smaller sections (Northwestern Arkansas, Washington County, a certain school system, a certain school, a certain class). The main point is that technically the conclusions are valid only for the population from which the samples are drawn.

Obviously, in most cases, physical education studies are limited to small populations; thus it is unlikely that any one study can be generalized to a large-enough population to be meaningful to the profession. The solution, however, is not to give up, but to replicate studies with different populations and then analyze the findings to determine similar and different results. Even though one may not be able to find a study that specifically applies to the population of interest, common findings from studies with similar populations can be of valuable assistance in making decisions.

Type of Statistical Method

Variables dealing with a whole population are called parameters. They are rarely measured directly. One of the traditional purposes of statistical methods is to estimate the population parameters by measuring random samples from the population. These statistical procedures are *parametric statistics*. They are based on certain mathematical and sampling prerequisites concerning the tests—the selection and nature of the samples. *Nonparametric* statistical procedures can be used with less precise tests and do not presuppose rigid sampling

---

* For example, suppose that a study has been conducted to determine the effects of six weeks of weight training on the strength of tenth-grade males. Suppose, further, that the sample assigned to the weight training was much stronger, as evidenced by scores on a battery of strength tests, following the six weeks than the sample that had participated in similar activities without the weight training. These results could be expressed in terms of probability; that is, we could say that the difference between these two groups was so large that, based on the sampling information, a difference this large would have occurred by chance (thus not due to the weight training) only 1% (.01) of the time, or one time out of one hundred. Thus the effects of the weight training would be significant at the .01 level of significance.

procedures. Although the nonparametric methods are less precise, they are easier to use and understand and are more appropriate for most nonlaboratory situations found in education.

It is more important to understand the reason for applying various statistical procedures than to become proficient in the computation of all the methods for answering a particular question. The *why* of statistical analysis is the same, even though the *how* ranges from relatively simple computations (as in nonparametric procedures) to very complex (as in some of the parametric methods).

Both the nonparametric (this chapter) and the parametric (Chapter 6) procedures to answer the questions raised earlier are included in this text. The teacher and class will need to choose which procedures are more appropriate for a specific class based on its background, vocational goals, and needs.

Test Scores

Test scores can be divided into two categories:* (1) equal interval and (2) rank order. The example shown will illustrate the difference.

Subject	600-yard run time (seconds)	Order of finish
A	110	2
B	129	8
C	119	4
D	127	7
E	97	1
F	122	5
G	113	3
H	123	6

The *time* for the run is an equal interval score, since 1 second is the

* There are various ways of classifying measurement scales, and there are more than two types of scale. Including the other scales does not substantially contribute to the understanding of this point, however.

same amount of time at any point on the scale. The *order of finish* ranks the pupils in order from the best to the poorest time. However, the difference between ranks is not equal. For example, there is a difference of 13 seconds between first and second but only 1 second between fifth and sixth. The rank order score is quicker and easier to use (the only possibility on some tests), but it does not give as much information as the equal interval measure.

An example of how to rank scores can be found in the first three steps of the computation of the Spearman Rank Order Correlation. The procedures for using a frequency distribution to handle large numbers of pupils are listed in Appendix A.

Typical Score and Range

A test score is not meaningful by itself. For example, John's parents will probably not be able to understand the meaning of running 600 yards in 110 seconds if that is all the information they are given. One of the ways of interpreting a particular test score is to compare it with scores made by similar pupils. The easiest way to do this is to rank the pupils. Since the importance of a particular rank depends on the size of the class (for example, a rank of 3 would be viewed differently in a class of 4 compared with a class of 1000), the rank can be expressed in terms of percent which allows comparison regardless of the size of the class. The rank of 3 would be better than 25% in a class of 4, whereas it would be better than 99.7% in a class of 1000. The rank expressed as percent is called the *percentile* and represents the percent of pupils below that score. Thus, in the 600-yard run, in Group 1, the percentiles would be as shown on page 55.

In this example, the 100th percentile is placed so that all the pupils (100%) scored worse than that time; each of the other percentiles is placed between pupils so that a certain number of pupils will score *below* that time. In this sample of 8, each pupil represents 12.5% (100/8).

The group can be divided into four equal groups (25% in each quartile). The 25th percentile is determined by finding the score that is better than 25% of the group; and the 75th percentile is better than 75% of the group. The 50th percentile, which divides the group into two equal parts, is also called the *median*. The *median* is the typical

Subject	600-yard run time (seconds)	Percentile	
		--------------------100[a]	
E	97		
		--------------------87.5	
A	110		
		--------------------75.0	Upper quartile
G	113		
		--------------------62.5	
C	119		
		--------------------50	Median
F	122		
		--------------------37.5	
H	123		
		--------------------25.0	Lower quartile
D	127		
		--------------------12.5	
B	129		
		-------------------- 0[a]	

[a] The 100th and 0th percentiles are obviously hypothetical scores, since if someone scored them, he would no longer be better than 100% or 0% of the pupils.

score for the group in that it divides the group into two equal groups. The median can be found by ranking the scores and locating the number that divides the group into two equal groups. If the number in the group is an even number (as in the example), then the median is between two real scores. If the number in the group is an odd number, then the median is the middle score. Thus, with 8 in the group, the median is between the fourth and fifth scores; if there had been 9 in the group, the median would have been the fifth score.

The range of scores for the test is found by subtracting the lowest score from the highest; thus in the example of the 600-yard run, the scores were from 97 to 129 seconds over a range of 32 seconds $(129 - 97)$.

Norms for test scores can be established by testing large groups of pupils for each age and sex. If norms are not available, a teacher can construct his own by combining scores from pupils over several years. It is then possible to tell a pupil what percent of pupils his age and sex did worse on the test than he did.

Percentiles are relatively easy to compute and are easily understood by pupils. One drawback is that they cannot be averaged, since (like ranked scores) there is not necessarily an equal distance between percentiles on different parts of the scale, and they depend on the size and distribution of the sample being used.

Relationship

One of the ways to understand a test is to know how it is related to other tests. The correlation coefficient gives a numerical value to represent the relationship between two tests. It ranges from -1.0 for a perfect negative correlation to 0 for no relationship to $+1.0$ for a perfect positive relationship. These relationships are illustrated in Fig. 5.1. If the correlation coefficient is $+1.0$ (as it is between A and B), the $+$ indicates that, the higher the score on A is, the higher the score on B. The 1.0 indicates that it is a perfect relationship. That is, if we know the value of A, we will know the value of B without measuring it. The relationship between height and weight is positive, in that taller pupils tend to be heavier; however, since it is not a perfect relationship, there would be some error involved if we predicted a person's weight from his height. The relationship between year of birth and age in the year 2000 illustrates a perfect negative relationship. The minus indicates that, the higher the score on one variable, the lower will be the score on the other. The number indicates the degree of relationship. Note that one can predict just as accurately from a correlation of -1.0 as from $+1.0$. The final example illustrates a zero correlation between Test C and Test D. There is no relationship between a pupil's score on Tests C and D. Knowing the results of Test C will not help us guess (predict) what his score would be on Test D.

A word of caution must be inserted about correlations. The correlation between two variables will change for different groups. A high correlation can be achieved for two tests that are not highly related to each other but are both related to a third factor that is not controlled. For example, reading ability and shoe size do not have a high relationship. However, if one used children aged 5 to 10, the correlation between reading ability and shoe size would probably be quite high because the age factor was not controlled (the older children have *both* larger feet and better reading ability). In this case, one would have to use the same age group to determine the relationship between shoe size and reading ability.*

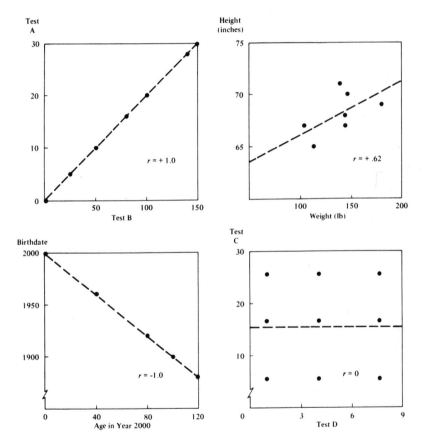

Fig. 5.1. Relationship between tests.

* There is a technique (partial correlation) for mathematically taking out the effect of a third variable.

It should also be noted that, although factors A and B are highly related (correlated), this does not mean that A *caused* or *was caused by* B. The fact that people with high blood pressure have more heart attacks than those with normal blood pressure does not mean that high blood pressure causes heart attacks. Both high blood pressure and heart attacks may be caused by other factors in the person's life.

USE OF CORRELATION

Correlation coefficients can be used to help establish reliability, objectivity, and validity. One of the methods used to determine the consistency (reliability) of a test is to give it twice to the same group of pupils in the same situation with a set period of time intervening. The correlation between these two testing sessions (on the same test) represents a *reliability coefficient*. The higher (positive) the correlation, the more consistent is the test.

The degree of objectivity of the scoring of a test can be established by determining the correlation between different scorers on the same group taking the same test. The scorers should arrive at their scores independently of each other.

Sometimes it is not possible to retest the pupils on the same test. In these cases, there are two ways of getting an estimate of reliability: (1) give an alternate test (designed to measure the same thing but with different test items) and correlate the scores between the two tests; or (2) divide the one test into two independent parts and correlate the two parts. The main problem in using alternate tests is to have two forms of the test that measure the same thing. Therefore, part of the lack of reliability may be due to the two forms measuring different things. When dividing a test into two parts, it is important to try to get two equal parts in terms of content and the difficulty of the items. The system of odd items versus even items has been used many times to divide a test into two parts.

Correlation can be used to determine one type of validity by correlating the new test with an accepted test of the same characteristic (criterion test). This correlation coefficient is referred to as a validity coefficient. The most important consideration is to have a good criterion test.

Another way to use correlation in understanding the meaning of a test is to correlate it with many other tests. This increases understanding of the test indirectly by showing relationships between tests (intercorrelations).*

SPEARMAN RANK ORDER CORRELATION COEFFICIENT, RHO (r')

One of the earlier methods for determining the relationship between rank order scores was developed by Spearman. The following example will illustrate how the relationship is determined.

Steps in Computation of Spearman Rank Order Correlation (r')

1. List all test scores in descending order (best to poorest scores)
2. Number these scores from 1 to 7 (or the total number of pupils)
3. Assign a rank to each score
   a. If there is only one pupil for a score, the rank is the same as the number
   b. If there is more than one pupil with the same score, assign all the pupils tied at that score the median (or average) rank
4. Take the difference between the ranks for the two scores for the same pupils (d)
5. Add d's ($\sum d$); they should equal 0 (check on Steps 1–4)
6. Square the individual differences (d^2)
7. Add the d^2's ($\sum d^2$)
8. Square the number of pupils (N^2)
9. Substitute in this formula†

$$r' = 1 - \frac{6 \sum d^2}{N(N^2 - 1)}$$

* Factor analysis of a battery of tests to determine what tests tend to relate to each other (load on the same factor) is a logical extension of this type of validity. A test of a particular trait should load on the same factor as tests of the same or highly related traits, have a negative loading on factors with tests that are inversely related, and have low factor loadings on factors of tests that are not related.

† If an odd number of pupils are tied, then the median is the middle number (for example, 6 is the median of 4, 5, 6, 7, 8). If an even number of pupils are tied, the median is between the two middle numbers (for example, 6.5 is the median of 5, 6, 7, 8).

Example

Step:	1	2	3	Step:	1	2	3
	Height				Weight		
	Inches	No.	Rank		Pounds	No.	Rank
	71	1	1		180	1	1
	70	2	2		146	2	2
	69	3	3		144	3	3
	68	4	4		138	4	4.5
	67	5	5.5		138	5	4.5
	67	6	5.5		113	6	6
	65	7	7		103	7	7

		Height		Weight	
	Pupil	Inches	Rank	Pounds	Rank
	I	67	5.5	103	7
	J	68	4	144	3
	K	71	1	138	4.5
	L	65	7	113	6
	M	69	3	180	1
	N	67	5.5	138	4.5
	O	70	2	146	2

		Rank		*Step 4* difference	*Step 6*
	Pupil	Height	Weight	d	d^2
	I	5.5	7	−1.5	2.25
	J	4.4	3	1	1
	K	1	4.5	−3.5	12.25
	L	7	6	1	1
	M	3	1	2	4
	N	5.5	4.5	1	1
	O	2	2	0	0

Step 5: $\sum d = 0$

Step 7:   Sum $(\sum d^2) = 21.5$

Step 8:   Number of pupils $(N) = 7$

$$N^2 = (7)^2 = 49$$

Step 9: $r' = 1 - \dfrac{6 \sum d^2}{N(N^2 - 1)} = 1 - \dfrac{6(21.5)}{7(49 - 1)} = 1 - \dfrac{129}{7(48)}$

$$r' = 1 - \frac{129}{336} = 1 - .38 = .62*$$

---

* A correction should be made in case of a large number of ties in rank. The formula is:

$$r' = \frac{\sum x^2 + \sum y^2 - \sum d^2}{2 \sqrt{\sum x^2 \sum y^2}}; \qquad \sum x^2 = \frac{N(N^2 - 1)}{12} - \sum T_x$$

$$\sum y^2 = \frac{N(N^2 - 1)}{12} - \sum T_y$$

$$\sum T_x = \text{sum of } \frac{t(t^2 - 1)}{12}; \qquad t = \text{number of pupils tied at one rank}$$

With the same example (where there was only one tie in each variable), the correlation coefficient would be as follows.

$$\sum T_x = \frac{2(4 - 1)}{12} = \frac{6}{12} = .5; \qquad t = 2; \qquad t^2 = 4$$

$$\sum T_y = \frac{2(4 - 1)}{12} = .5$$

$$\sum x^2 = \frac{N(N^2 - 1)}{12} - \sum T_x; \qquad N = 7; \qquad N^2 = 49$$

$$\sum x^2 = \frac{7(49 - 1)}{12} - .5 = \frac{336}{12} - .5 = 28 - .5 = 27.5$$

$$\sum y^2 = \frac{N(N^2 - 1)}{12} - \sum T_y$$

$$\sum y^2 = \frac{336}{12} - .5 = 28 - .5 = 27.5$$

The correlation has quantified the relationship between height and weight for this group by determining a numerical value. Thus on a scale from 0 (no relationship) to 1.00 (perfect relationship), the relationship is .62. The fact that the correlation is .62 tells us that there is a moderate relationship between these two variables. The fact that it is + means that there is a direct (positive) relationship, in that the larger one variable is, the larger the other tends to be.

Difference between Groups

One of the important functions of statistical procedures is to compare the performance of pupils in different classes and/or experimental treatments. The simplest way is to compare the group medians to see which group has the highest "typical score." The teacher who is knowledgeable about the test being used can then evaluate whether the differences are large enough to indicate that the groups are "really different." For example, a difference of 10 seconds on a two-mile run would be considered a small difference, whereas a difference of 10 seconds on a 220-yard run would be considerable. In general, one would evaluate the difference in terms of (1) the magnitude of a typical score (10 seconds would be a much smaller percentage of total time on the two-mile run than on the 220-yard dash); (2) the normal fluctuation on this test (due to measurement error, intraindividual variation, testing conditions, etc.); and (3) the number of pupils in the group (in general, larger groups lend more importance to the same amount of difference).

Since it would be difficult, if not impossible, for each teacher to be

---

$$ r' = \frac{\sum x^2 + \sum y^2 - \sum d^2}{2\sqrt{\sum x^2 \sum y^2}}; \qquad \sum d^2 = \text{see above} $$

$$ r' = \frac{27.5 + 27.5 - 21.5}{2\sqrt{(27.5)(27.5)}} = \frac{55 - 21.5}{2(27.5)} = \frac{33.5}{55} = .61 $$

Thus, in this case, there was little difference in the r' when correcting for ties. However, when there are large numbers of ties, the correction should be made, since the normal formula will overestimate the relationship (that is, the r' will be larger than it should be).

thoroughly familiar with every test, its typical score, normal fluctuation, and relation to sample size, there are significance tests that can be used to assist in the evaluation of group differences. Appropriate statistical tools permit the teacher to estimate the probability level of group differences. By taking into account the variation of the test and pupils used, one can then say that a certain difference between these groups could be expected to happen simply by chance (that is, because of these fluctuations rather than real differences) a certain percent of the time.

This probability statement is called the *level of significance*. Thus, if it were determined (by statistical procedure) that for two groups the difference of 5 seconds on the 600-yard run would occur by chance 90% of the time, it could be said that these groups differed at the .90 level of significance and one would *not* have any reason to conclude that the groups were different. It might be determined that a difference of 35 seconds on the 600-yard run between two other groups would have occurred by chance 1% of the time. Then this difference would be at the .01 level of significance and could be the basis for a conclusion that the two groups were different.

Two Independent Groups

To illustrate these points, let us compare two high school classes on the number of pull-ups after five weeks of calisthenics and volleyball (Group I) and after five weeks of volleyball only (Group II). The scores for the pupils prior to and after the five-week unit are shown on page 64.

The medians of the two groups are equal (2.5) prior to the unit. Each group had an increased number of pull-ups following the units. However, the group that included calisthenics along with volleyball increased more (median of 7 as compared with 4 for the volleyball-only group). The statistical question that can be asked is, What is the probability that the difference between the groups after the unit is due to normal fluctuations of the test and pupils? Several statistical tools can be employed to answer this question, one of which will be explained in detail.

Steps in Computation of Mann-Whitney U Test (to determine differ-

ence between two different and independent groups on a test which
has at least rank order scores)

Group I: Calisthenics and volleyball			Group II: Volleyball only		
	Pull-ups (maximum number)			Pull-ups (maximum number)	
Subject	Pre	Post	Subject	Pre	Post
A	6	9	P	1	4
B	1	7	Q	2	5
C	3	3	R	6	7
D	0	6	S	8	5
E	4	8	T	3	3
F	6	13	U	3	4
G	2	7	V	0	0
H	0	0	W	2	4
Median	2.5	7		2.5	4

1. Rank the scores for all the pupils (both groups, 1–16 in this
   case)
2. Sum the rank for Group I (R_I)
3. Total number of pupils (N_T) = number in Group I (N_I) +
   number in Group II (N_{II})
4. Find U (symbol for Mann-Whitney U Test)

$$U = N_I N_{II} + \frac{N_I(N_I + 1)}{2} - R_I$$

5. Find z (to determine probability)

$$z = \frac{U - \dfrac{N_I N_{II}}{2}}{\sqrt{\dfrac{(N_I N_{II})(N_I + N_{II} + 1)}{12}}}$$

6. Compare z to Appendix C for probability. (It should be noted that the z table is not appropriate for samples under 25 to 30. The small samples used in the examples are for ease of computation. It is assumed that most physical education classes will be dealing with larger groups.)

Example

Step 1:

Number	Score	Rank	Number	Score	Rank
1	13	1	9	5	8.5
2	9	2	10	4	11
3	8	3	11	4	11
4	7	5	12	4	11
5	7	5	13	3	13.5
6	7	5	14	3	13.5
7	6	7	15	0	15.5
8	5	8.5	16	0	15.5

Step 2:

	Group I			Group II	
Subject	Score	Rank	Subject	Score	Rank
A	9	2	P	4	11
B	7	5	Q	5	8.5
C	3	13.5	R	7	5
D	6	7	S	5	8.5
E	8	3	T	3	13.5
F	13	1	U	4	11
G	7	5	V	0	15.5
H	0	15.5	W	4	11
		$R_I = 52.0$			$R_{II} = 84.0$

Step 3: $N_T = N_I + N_{II} = 8 + 8 = 16$

Step 4: $U = N_I N_{II} + \dfrac{N_I(N_I + 1)}{2} - R_I$ *

$U = (8)(8) + \dfrac{8(8 + 1)}{2} - 52.0;$

$U = 64 + \dfrac{72}{2} - 52 = 64 + 36 - 52 = 100 - 52 = 48$

$U = 48$

Step 5:

$$z = \dfrac{U - \dfrac{N_I N_{II}}{2}}{\sqrt{\dfrac{(N_I)(N_{II})(N_I + N_{II} + 1)}{12}}}$$

$$z = \dfrac{48 - \dfrac{(8)(8)}{2}}{\sqrt{\dfrac{(8)(8)(8 + 8 + 1)}{12}}} = \dfrac{48 - \dfrac{64}{2}}{\sqrt{\dfrac{(64)(17)}{12}}} = \dfrac{48 - 32}{\sqrt{\dfrac{1088}{12}}}$$

$$= \dfrac{16}{\sqrt{90.67}} = \dfrac{16}{9.52}$$

$z = 1.68$†

Step 6: $p < .0465$

---

* Note that, if R_{II} is used in place of R_I, we have $U = 16$ instead of 48; when that is inserted into the formula for z, then the numerator becomes $16 - 32 = -16$ (instead of $48 - 32 = +16$). Therefore, the absolute value of z and the corresponding probability level remain the same. Thus it doesn't make any difference which group is used as Group I.

† In case of a large number of ties in scores, the following correction can be

made in the z formula:

$$z = \frac{U - \dfrac{N_I N_{II}}{2}}{\sqrt{\left(\dfrac{N_I N_{II}}{N_T(N_T - 1)}\right)\left(\dfrac{N_T^3 - N_T}{12}\right) - \Sigma T}}$$

$$T = \frac{t^3 - t}{12}$$

$t =$ number of pupils tied at any one rank

In this specific example:

Number of pupils	Tied score
3	7
2	5
3	4
2	3
2	0

$t = 3; 2; 3; 2; 2 \quad (3)^3 = 27 \quad (2)^3 = 8$

$$\Sigma T = \frac{(3)^3 - 3}{12} + \frac{(2)^3 - 2}{12} + \frac{3^3 - 3}{12} + \frac{2^3 - 2}{12} + \frac{2^3 - 2}{12}$$

$$\Sigma T = \text{sum of all } T\text{'s} = \frac{24}{12} + \frac{6}{12} + \frac{24}{12} + \frac{6}{12} + \frac{6}{12} = \frac{66}{12} = 5.5$$

$\Sigma T = 5.5$

$$z = \frac{48 - 32}{\sqrt{\left(\dfrac{64}{(16)(15)}\right)\left(\dfrac{16^3 - 16}{12}\right) - 5.5}} = \frac{16}{\sqrt{\dfrac{64}{240}\left(\dfrac{4080}{12}\right) - 5.5}}$$

$$= \frac{16}{\sqrt{(.27)(340) - 5.5}}$$

$$= \frac{16}{\sqrt{91.80 - 5.5}} = \frac{16}{\sqrt{86.30}} = \frac{16}{9.29} = 1.72$$

$$p < .0427$$

It should be noted that the correction for ties increases the z, although only slightly in spite of a large number of ties; therefore, for all practical purposes, there is no need to make a correction for ties except for very extreme cases.

It would then be concluded that Group 1 was better on ability to do pull-ups at the .05 level of significance, which means that a difference this large between the groups would occur by chance (with this test and these fluctuations) less than 5% of the time. Thus, the difference appears to be a real difference between the groups rather than normal or chance fluctuations.

Two Paired Groups

The Mann-Whitney U Test determines the differences between two independent groups. If one wants to compare two groups made up of matched pairs (each person in Group I is matched with one person in Group II), then the Wilcoxon Matched-Pairs Signed Rank Test (called by the misnomer One-Way Analysis of Variance) can be used. It can also be used to compare the same group at two different testing sessions (within-group comparison to test systematic changes in reliability, or changes due to a particular class or experimental treatment) in which each pupil is matched against himself. In most cases, the between-group comparison is more important than a within-group comparison. That is, the better question is, Did this group change more than a control group or a similar group with a different class, rather than, Did the group change? The disadvantage of a within-group comparison is that there are several possible reasons for any change that is found (was the change due to the class, or to retaking the test, or to a change in weather, or to a change in the way the test was administered, or to a normal change in growth? etc.). There is no way to attribute the change to the experimental treatment except by comparing the group to a similar group that was tested at the same time but did not have the same treatment. Therefore all factors are controlled except for one—the experimental variable.

To illustrate this significance test, pupils who scored the same from Groups I and II on pull-ups prior to the five-week unit are used as the pairs. The significance test will be used to determine if their scores *after* the five-week unit are significantly different after having been exposed to different classes.

Steps in Computation of Wilcoxon Matched-Pairs Signed Rank Test

(to determine difference between two groups consisting of paired pupils)

Group I: Calisthenics and volleyball			Group II: Volleyball only		
	Pull-ups (maximum number)			Pull-ups (maximum number)	
Subject	Pre	Post	Subject	Pre	Post
A	6	9	R	6	7
B	1	7	P	1	4
C	3	3	U	3	.4
G	2	7	Q	2	5
H	0	0	V	0	0
	—	—		—	—
Median	2	7		2	4

1. Determine the difference (d) between each pair (indicate $+$ or $-$ and always subtract Group II from Group I)
2. Rank the d's according to the size of the number (absolute value) without regard to the sign. In case of ties, use the median (or average)
3. Assign the appropriate sign ($+$ or $-$) to the ranks (taken from the sign of the d)
4. N = number of d's not equal to 0 (determined by counting all d's that have either $+$ or $-$ sign); in other words, *omit all d's $= 0$*
5. Sum the positive ($+$) and negative ($-$) ranks separately
6. T = the smaller sum, from step 5

7. $$z = \frac{T - \dfrac{N(N+1)}{4}}{\sqrt{\dfrac{N(N+1)(2N+1)}{24}}}$$

8. p determined from Appendix C

Example

				Step 1	Step 2	Step 3 +	Step 3 −
Subject	Pull-ups	Subject	Pull-ups	d	Ranks	Ranks	Ranks
A	9	R	7	+2	2.5	+2.5	
B	7	P	4	+3	1	+1.0	
C	3	U	4	−1	4		−4
G	7	Q	5	+2	2.5	+2.5	
H	0	V	0	0			

Step 4: Number of nonzero d's   4

Step 5: $\sum +$ ranks   6

  $\sum -$ ranks   4

Step 6: $T = 4.0$ (the smaller sum; note that sign is dropped)

Step 7:
$$z = \frac{4.0 - \dfrac{4(4+1)}{4}}{\sqrt{\dfrac{4(4+1)[2(4)+1]}{24}}} = \frac{4 - \dfrac{20}{4}}{\sqrt{\dfrac{20(9)}{24}}} = \frac{4-5}{\sqrt{\dfrac{180}{24}}}$$

$$= \frac{-1}{\sqrt{7.5}} = \frac{-1}{2.74} = -.365$$

$$z = -.365$$

Step 8: $p < .3575$

The probability of a difference this large occurring by chance between those two paired groups is about 36%. Thus, there is little evidence that these groups are different on pull-ups as a result of the addition of calisthenics for five weeks.

THREE OR MORE INDEPENDENT GROUPS

This same principle can be applied to different situations. For example, if one wanted to compare more than two independent groups, the following procedure could be used with the same Groups I and II, adding Group III which had calisthenics for the five-week unit.

Group I: Calisthenics and volleyball		Group II: Volleyball only		Group III: Calisthenics only	
Subject	Pull-ups post test (maximum number)	Subject	Pull-ups post test (maximum number)	Subject	Pull-ups post test (maximum number)
A	9	P	4	I	3
B	7	Q	5	J	12
C	3	R	7	K	4
D	6	S	5	L	6
E	8	T	3	M	13
F	13	U	4	N	6
G	7	V	0	O	9
H	0	W	4		
Median	7		4		6

Steps in Computation of Kruskal-Wallis Test (to determine differences in more than two independent groups on tests with at least rank order scores)

1. Rank the scores for all the subjects (from all the groups) (1–23 in this case)
2. Determine the sum of ranks (R) for each group
3. Determine R^2/N for each group
4. Add all the R^2/N:

$$\sum \frac{R_i^2}{N_i}$$

5. N_T = number of all subjects in all groups: $N_T = N_I + N_{II} + N_{III}$
6. Find H by this formula:

$$H = \frac{12}{N_T(N_T + 1)} \sum \frac{R_i^2}{N_i} - 3(N_T + 1)$$

7. Compare to chi-square table for significance level with degrees of freedom* = 1 less than number of groups ($k - 1$, where k = number of groups)

Example

Step 1:

Number (1–23)	Score (on pull-ups)	Rank	Number	Score	Rank
1	13	1.5	13	5	13.5
2	13	1.5	14	5	13.5
3	12	3	15	4	16.5
4	9	4.5	16	4	16.5
5	9	4.5	17	4	16.5
6	8	6	18	4	16.5
7	7	8	19	3	20
8	7	8	20	3	20
9	7	8	21	3	20
10	6	11	22	0	22.5
11	6	11	23	0	22.5
12	6	11			

* Degrees of freedom (df) is a term that is used with many statistical procedures in determining the probability of the statistical results occurring by chance. The degrees of freedom are determined by the restrictions placed on the observations; in the simpler procedures, there is only one restriction, so that the df = $k - 1$, or 1 less than the number of groups. The concept could be illustrated by saying that one had to choose two numbers whose sum was equal to 10. Obviously, any number could be chosen for the first number, but once the first number was chosen, there would be no choice for the second one (thus 1 degree of freedom).

Step 2:

Group I			Group II			Group III		
Subject	Score	Rank	Subject	Score	Rank	Subject	Score	Rank
A	9	4.5	P	4	16.5	I	3	20
B	7	8	Q	5	13.5	J	12	3
C	3	20	R	7	8	K	4	16.5
D	6	11	S	5	13.5	L	6	11
E	8	6	T	3	20	M	13	1.5
F	13	1.5	U	4	16.5	N	6	11
G	7	8	V	0	22.5	O	9	4.5
H	0	22.5	W	4	16.5			
R (sum of ranks)		81.5			127.0			67.5

Step 3:

Group	R	R^2	N	R^2/N
I	81.5	6642.25	8	830.3
II	127.0	16129.00	8	2016.1
III	67.5	4556.25	7	650.9

Step 4: $\sum R^2/N =$ 3497.3

Step 5: N_T (for all groups) $= 8 + 8 + 7 = 23$

Step 6: $H = [12/N(N+1)] \sum R^2/N - 3(N_T + 1)$

$H = [12/23(24)](3497.3) - 3(24) = 76.03 - 72 = 4.03*$

Step 7: The probability of H is found in chi square (χ^2) (see Appendix D). In this case, it is 4.03, $p < .20$, which means that a difference this large among these three groups could be expected to occur by chance less than 20% of the time.

---

* In case of a large number of ties, the following correction can be made in finding H, as shown on the following page:

$$H = \frac{\dfrac{12}{N_T(N_T + 1)} \sum \dfrac{Ri^2}{Ni} - 3 \ (N_T + 1)}{1 - \dfrac{\sum_T}{N_T{}^3 - N_T}}$$

$$T = t^3 - t$$

t = number of pupils tied at one score

In this specific case:

Number of pupils	Score
2	13
2	9
3	7
3	6
2	5
4	4
3	3
2	0

$t = 2; 2; 3; 3; 2; 4; 3; 2$

$T = 2^3 - 2; 2^3 - 2; 3^3 - 3; 3^3 - 3; 2^3 - 2; 4^3 - 4; 3^3 - 3; 2^3 - 2$

$T = 6 + 6 + 24 + 24 + 6 + 60 + 24 + 6$

$T = 156$

$$H = \frac{\dfrac{12}{23(24)} \ (3497.3) - 3 \ (24)}{1 - \dfrac{156}{23^3 - 23}} = \frac{\dfrac{1}{46} \ (3497.3) - 72}{1 - \dfrac{156}{12,144}}$$

$$H = \frac{76.03 - 72}{1 - 0.0128} = \frac{4.03}{.987} = 4.08$$

$$H = 4.08; \qquad p < .20$$

As in the Mann-Whitney U test, there was a very slight increase (4.03 to 4.08) in H after correcting for the ties. Therefore, the correction does not need to be used except in extreme cases.

In this case, one could conclude that the difference among the three groups occurred at the .20 level of significance, which means that one could expect a difference this large to occur by chance 20% of the time. Thus, we would not be as certain that the differences among the three groups were real differences as we could be concerning the difference between Groups I and II, which was significant at the .05 level.

Parametric versus Nonparametric Statistical Procedures

Parametric methods are based on *selecting* samples from populations that meet certain prerequisites. The populations are assumed to be normally distributed and to have similar variance. The samples are assumed to be randomly selected, and the tests are scored on an equal interval scale. If these assumptions are met, the parametric statistics are more precise than the nonparametric procedures and should be employed. In addition, many of the parametric statistical procedures appear to be quite good even when some of the basic assumptions are not met. Parametric statistical procedures (see Chapter 6) can be employed and are recommended if a computer and computer time are available, if fairly large groups of about equal size are used, and if the tests are measured by an equal interval scale. This situation exists in many research laboratories and physical education departments in universities.

Nonparametric procedures can be used with rank order data and do not presuppose rigid sampling procedures from populations who meet certain criteria. They are easier to use (without computer) and understand (without a good mathematics background) and appear to be more appropriate for most of the analyses done in education. Therefore if computer time is not available (or if there is no one who has time assigned to conduct statistical analyses on a desk calculator), if small and/or unequal groups are used, and if the measures are ranked, nonparametric statistical procedures are recommended. This situation exists in the majority of physical education situations and studies.

A summary of parametric and nonparametric statistics is given in Table 5.1.

TABLE 5.1

Summary of Parametric and Nonparametric Statistics

Statistical Topic	Parametric[a]	Nonparametric
Assumptions	Random sample from normally distributed population	
Scoring	At least equal interval	Rank order
Central tendency	Mean	Median
Variability	z, s.d.	Percentile, quartile
Correlation	Pearson r	Spearman rho, r'
Significance tests		
Two independent samples	t for independent groups	Mann-Whitney U
Two related samples	paired t	Wilcoxon Matched-Pairs Signed Rank
More than two independent samples	Analysis of variance (ANOVA)	Kruskal-Wallis
More than two related samples	Repeated measures ANOVA[b]	Friedman[b]
Conclusions	Back to population	Only for sample

[a] See Chapter 6.
[b] Not included in this book but available in statistical textbooks (see references for chapter 6).

Experimental Design

A more crucial problem to the importance of a study is the design used. It has to be set up so that there is some chance of answering the questions(s) being asked. For example, if one is interested in determining the cardiovascular changes made by a six-week unit of soccer, the first thought might be to simply measure a soccer class on a cardiovascular test prior to and at the conclusion of the unit, and then attribute any changes to the soccer unit. Unfortunately, in this type of design there is no way to discover what caused the change. It could have been due to soccer, to a change in testing conditions, to a change in weather, to the normal growth and development of the pupils, to simply being in group activity, to learning how to take the test (many physical education tests can show changes due to retaking the test), to improved motivation (many of the performance tests depend in part on will power), or to a combination of several of these components. How can that part of the change due to soccer be identified? One way is to test a group of similar pupils who do not take the soccer unit (control group). It would be advantageous if the control group could be involved in a team game (other than soccer). In other words, the control group could be expected to make changes due to weather, testing situation, retaking the test, group activity, etc., so that any change made by the soccer group that was greater than the change made by the control group could be attributed to the soccer unit. Thus, if the two-mile run was used for the cardiovascular test and the soccer group changed from 15:30 minutes to 13:00 minutes and the control group from 15:30 minutes to 14:30 minutes, we could conclude that 1 minute of improvement was due to a combination of factors not related to soccer (such as those listed above) and that $1\frac{1}{2}$ minutes of improvement was due to the soccer.*

In this example, the groups started at the same level on the two-mile run. In such a case, one can analyze the post test and attribute any differences to the difference in the treatment. If the groups are not equal at the beginning, then the initial differences must be taken into account in discussing the final differences. The more nearly the groups are equal at the beginning, the more confidence one can place in the results in that this is some evidence that the groups came from the same population. Some procedures to correct for initial differences are available (such as analysis of covariance), but they are beyond the scope of this text.

---

* This example is an oversimplification, since it disregards errors. A complete discussion of experimental design is beyond the scope of this book; however, many problems could be avoided if professional advice concerning design were solicited *prior* to the study being undertaken.

Summary

Statistical procedures are designed to assist evaluation by estimating typical score, normal fluctuation, relationship between tests, and difference between groups. These questions are always answered in terms of particular groups. Simple (nonparametric) statistical procedures are used to illustrate one of the ways these analyses of test scores can be accomplished. More precise, and more complex, statistical procedures (parametric) to answer *the same questions* are presented in Chapter 6. In general, the nonparametric statistical procedures are more appropriate for most physical education testing situations, whereas the parametric procedures are more often used in established research stations. Preplanning of the design to be used to answer these questions is essential.

Problems

1. Measure the weight of each class member.
2. Select a sample from the class that will be representative of different weights.
3. Determine the median and percentile scores for the entire class and for the sample. How well does the sample represent the class?
4. Determine reliability for the sample.
5. Measure the height of the sample. What is the relationship between height and weight?
6. Divide the class into half according to height. Take a random sample from each half. On the basis of these samples, what is the difference in body weight for persons of different height?

Reference

Blum, J. R., and Fattu, N. A. Nonparametric methods. *Review of Educational Research*, 1954, **24**, 476–487.

Page, E. B., and Marcotte, D. R. Nonparametric statistics. *Review of Educational Research*, 1966, **36**, 517–528.

Sawrey, W. L. A distinction between exact and approximate nonparametric methods. *Psychometrika*, 1958, **23**, 171–177.

Siegel, S. *Nonparametric statistics for the behavioral sciences*. New York: McGraw-Hill, 1956.

Walsh, J. E. *Handbook of nonparametric statistics*, Vols. I–III. Princeton, New Jersey: Van Nostrand-Reinhold, 1962.

CHAPTER 6

Optional Supplement to Interpretation of Test Scores

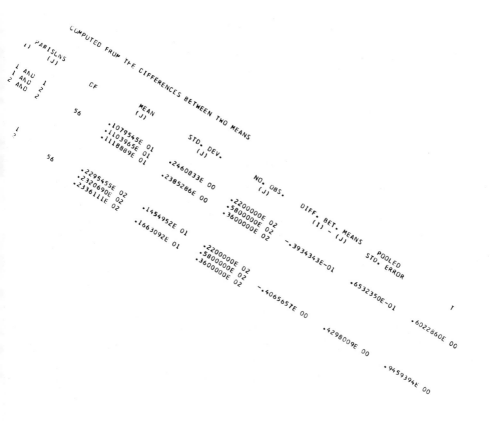

Parametric Statistics

The statistical procedures used in Chapter 5 (median, percentile, rank order correlation, Mann-Whitney U test, Wilcoxon Paired-Group test, and Kruskal-Wallis test) have all been nonparametric statistics. These statistical tools can be used with rank order data; they do not presuppose rigid sampling procedures from large populations or certain distributions of test scores. In general, they are more appropriate for the nonlaboratory situations generally found in education.

The more traditional approach to statistical analysis is based on selecting samples from a population that meet certain prerequisites. The populations used are assumed to be normally distributed and have similar variance. The groups are expected to be randomly selected and the tests to be scored in an equal interval scale. If these assumptions are met, the parametric statistics are more precise than the nonparametric procedures and should be employed. In addition, many of the parametric statistical procedures appear to be quite good even when some of the basic assumptions are not met.

Central Tendency and Variability

The parametric methods for determining the average score and degree of variability (fluctuation) are the mean ($\bar{X}$) and the standard deviation (s.d.), respectively. From the same example that was used for the nonparametric methods (median and percentile), the mean and standard deviation are as follows.

STEPS IN COMPUTATION OF THE MEAN ($\bar{X}$)

1. Sum all scores: ($\sum X$)
2. N = number of pupils
3. Divide sum of scores by number of pupils: $\bar{X} = \sum X / N$

Example

Pupil	600-yard run time (seconds) X
A	110
B	129
C	119
D	127
E	97
F	122
G	113
H	123

Step 1: $\sum X =$ 940

Step 2: $N = 8$

Step 3: $\bar{X} = \dfrac{\sum X}{N} = \dfrac{940}{8} = 117.5$

STEPS IN COMPUTATION OF THE STANDARD DEVIATION (s.d.)

1. Sum all scores: $(\sum X)$
2. Square $\sum X$: $(\sum X)^2$
3. Square each score: (X^2)
4. Add X^2: $(\sum X^2)$
5. N = number of pupils
6. Divide $(\sum X)^2$ by N: $(\sum X)^2/N$
7. Subtract $(\sum X)^2/N$ from $\sum X^2$: *Sum of squares (SS)* = $\sum X^2 - (\sum X)^2/N$
8. Divide sum of squares by $N - 1$: *Variance* (s^2) = $SS/(N-1)$
9. Find square root of variance: *Standard deviation* (s.d., or s) = $\sqrt{s^2}$

Example

	600-yard run time (seconds)	
Pupil	X	X^2 *(Step 3)*
A	110	12,100
B	129	16,641
C	119	14,161
D	127	16,129
E	97	9,409
F	122	14,884
G	113	12,769
H	123	15,129

Step 1: $\sum X =$ 940

Step 2: $(\sum X)^2 = (940)^2 = 883,600$

Step 4: $\sum X^2 =$ 111,222

Step 5: $N = 8$

Step 6: $\dfrac{(\sum X)^2}{N} = \dfrac{883{,}600}{8} = 110{,}450$

Step 7: Sum of squares $(SS) = \sum X^2 - \dfrac{(\sum X)^2}{N} = 111{,}222 -$

110,450 = 772

Step 8: Variance $(s^2) = \dfrac{SS}{N-1} = \dfrac{772}{7} = 110.29$

Step 9: Standard deviation (s.d.) $= \sqrt{s^2} = \sqrt{110.29} = 10.5$

Normal Curve

The probabilities used in connection with most statistical procedures are based on the assumption of a normal distribution (normal curve). Many variables do appear to be normally distributed in large groups. The table in Appendix C can be used to determine the probability of scores falling a certain number of standard deviations above or below the mean. Figure 6.1 illustrates a normal curve. It can be seen

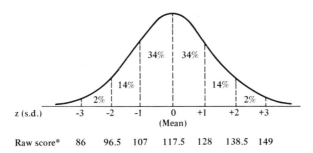

Fig 6.1. Normal curve based on mean and standard deviation for 600-yard run. It can be seen that in a normal curve 68% of the scores fall between -1 and $+1$ s.d.; about 96% between $+2$ and -2 s.d.; and over 99% between $+3$ and -3 s.d. * With a mean of 117.5 and a standard deviation of 10.5, 1 s.d. above the mean $= 117.5 + 10.5 = 128$; -1 s.d. $= 117.5 - 10.5 = 107$.

that about 68% of the pupils would normally be expected to fall between -1 and $+1$ s.d.; 69% between -2 and $+2$ s.d.; and almost 100% between -3 and $+3$ s.d.

Norms

The mean and standard deviation can be used to establish norms which express the test score from 0 to 100 (the parametric counterpart of percentiles). The mean is 50 on each norm table. Three of the norm tables are the Standard Score Table, which has 3 s.d. above and below the mean; the Hull Score Table, which has 3.5 s.d. above and below the mean; and the McCall T-Score Table, which has 5 s.d. above and below the mean. Extreme scores occasionally fall off the Standard Score and Hull Score tables, yet the McCall T-Score Table tends to group all the scores within a small range in the middle.

STEPS IN COMPUTATION OF STANDARD SCORE NORM TABLE

1. Determine $\bar{X}$ and s.d.
2. Assign $\bar{X}$ to be the 50 standard score
3. Determine 0 standard score ($\bar{X} - 3$ s.d. if lower score reflects poorer performance; $\bar{X} + 3$ s.d. if lower score reflects better performance, as in the example).
4. Determine 100 standard score ($\bar{X} + 3$ s.d. if higher score reflects better performance; $\bar{X} - 3$ s.d. if higher score reflects poor performance, as in the example).
5. Take difference between 100 and 0 standard scores (100 standard score $-$ 0 standard score, or $0 - 100$, depending on which is higher).
6. Divide this difference between 100 and 0 standard scores into the number of intervals between 0 and 100 desired. (In the example, the norm table is established in intervals of 10: $0, 10, 20, 30 \cdots 90, 100$. In that case the difference would be divided by 10.)
7. Begin at 0 standard score, and add (or subtract) the amount found in step 6 for each interval.

Example

Step 1: $\bar{X} = 117.5$; s.d. $= 10.5$ (see previous section of chapter for computation)

Step 2:   50 standard score $= 117.5$

Step 3:   0 standard score $= \bar{X} + 3$ s.d. (since lower score is better)
0 standard score $= 117.5 + 3(10.5) = 117.5 + 31.5 = 149.0$

Step 4:   100 standard score $= \bar{X} - 3$ s.d. $= 117.5 - 3(10.5) = 117.5 - 31.5 = 86.0$

Step 5:   0 standard score $-$ 100 standard score $= 149 - 86 = 63$

Step 6:   Number of intervals to be used $= 10$
Difference divided by number of intervals $= 63/10 = 6.3$

Step 7:

	Standard score	600-yard run time (seconds)	Computation
$\bar{X} - 3$ s.d.	100	86	$92.3 - 6.3$
	90	92.3	$98.6 - 6.3$
	80	98.6	$104.9 - 6.3$
	70	104.9	$111.2 - 6.3$
	60	111.2	$117.5 - 6.3$
$\bar{X}$	50	117.5	$123.8 - 6.3$
	40	123.8	$130.1 - 6.3$
	30	130.1	$136.4 - 6.3$
	20	136.4	$142.7 - 6.3$
	10	142.7	$149.0 - 6.3$
$\bar{X} + 3$ s.d.	0	149.0	$\bar{X} + 3$ s.d.

The same procedure would be used for the Hull Score and McCall T-Score tables except that, in steps 3 and 4, the standard deviation would be multiplied by 3.5 (for the Hull Score Table) or 5 (for the McCall T-Score Table). Each 10 units on the McCall T-Score Table is equal to 1 standard deviation.

With the same example, a comparison of the three types of norms would be as follows.

Standard score (6 s.d.)	600-yard run	Hull score (7 s.d.)	600-yard run	McCall T-score (10 s.d.)	600-yard run
100	86	100	80.7	100	65.0
90	92.3	90	88.1	90	75.5
80	98.6	80	95.4	80	86.0
70	104.9	70	102.8	70	96.5
60	111.2	60	110.1	60	107.0
50	117.5	50	117.5	50	117.5
40	123.8	40	124.8	40	128.0
30	130.1	30	132.2	30	138.0
20	136.4	20	139.5	20	149.0
10	142.7	10	146.9	10	159.5
0	149.0	0	154.2	0	170.0

Norms should, of course, be based on a much larger sample. However, it is clear that the norm used will cause the scores to be more spread out (standard score) or more bunched together (McCall) depending on which is used. In large samples, the percentile table will approach the Standard Score Table.

Errors

Any score on a person includes his "true" score + his own inconsistency (intraindividual variation) + error. The error may be caused by equipment, environment, psychological factors, or the tester. Some of the error may be constant (which can be corrected for) or random (cannot be predicted or corrected for).

The importance of correcting for constant errors depends on the nature of the study. For example, if scales consistently weighed five pounds too heavy, it would not change a study of the effects of training on weight or the correlation between weight and other variables. However, it would be essential to make the change (correction for constant error) before comparison with norms.

Random errors are not consistently in one direction (as are constant errors), and it is assumed that the random errors will tend to average out over several trials for an individual and for groups. One method for reporting error that can be used is the standard error of the mean, which is s.d./$\sqrt{N}$. Thus, in the above example, the standard error of the mean S.E.$_{\bar{x}}$ = 10.5/$\sqrt{8}$ = 3.71. A special case of the standard error of the mean is the standard error of measurement, which is s.d./$\sqrt{N}$ of a number of trials on the same test on the same individual instead of one test score for a group of subjects.

To express the error in terms of percent error for each test, the standard error of the mean (or measurement) is divided by the mean. In the example

$$\% \text{ error} = \frac{\text{S.E.}_{\bar{x}}}{\bar{X}} = \frac{3.71}{117.5} = .032 \text{ or } 3.2\% \text{ error}$$

Thus we would expect to have about 3% error in anyone's score on the 600-yard run given under the same conditions as used with the pupils in this example.

Correlation

The most commonly used correlation coefficient is the Pearson Product Moment Correlation Coefficient (the parametric counterpart to the Spearman Rank Order). This method assumes two equal interval scores and is illustrated by means of the same example that was used for the rank order coefficient.

STEPS IN COMPUTATION OF PEARSON PRODUCT MOMENT CORRELATION COEFFICIENT, r

1. List scores for both variables for each subject: X, Y
2. Multiply each subject's two scores: (XY)
3. Square each score: X^2, Y^2
4. Sum of all of above: $\sum X$ Square $\sum X$ and $\sum Y$: $(\sum X)^2$
   and $(\sum Y)^2$

$\sum Y$
$\sum X^2$
$\sum Y^2$
$\sum XY$

5. N = number of subjects
6. Substitute in this formula:

$$r = \frac{N \sum XY - (\sum X)(\sum Y)}{\sqrt{[N \sum X^2 - (\sum X)^2][N \sum Y^2 - (\sum Y)^2]}}$$

Example

Pupil	Height (inches)		Weight (pounds)		
	X *Step 1*	X^2 *Step 3*	Y *Step 1*	Y^2 *Step 3*	XY *Step 2*
I	67	4,489	103	10,609	6,901
J	68	4,624	144	20,736	9,792
K	71	5,041	138	19,044	9,798
L	65	4,225	113	12,769	7,345
M	69	4,761	180	32,400	12,420
N	67	4,489	138	19,044	9,246
O	70	4,900	146	21,316	10,220

Step 4: $\sum X$ $\sum X^2$ $\sum Y$ $\sum Y^2$ $\sum XY$
            = 477   = 32,529   = 962   = 135,918   = 65,772

$(\sum X)^2 = (477)^2 = 227,529$ $(\sum Y)^2 = (962)^2 = 925,444$

Step 5: $N = 7$*

Step 6:

$$r = \frac{7(65,722) - (477)(962)}{\sqrt{[7(32,529) - 227,529][7(135,918) - 925,444]}}$$

$$r = \frac{460,054 - 458,874}{\sqrt{(227,703 - 227,529)(951,426 - 925,444)}}$$

$$r = \frac{1180}{\sqrt{(174)(25,982)}} = \frac{1180}{\sqrt{4,520,868}} = \frac{1180}{2126.2}$$

$$r = .55$$

Although a probability statement can be made about correlation, significant at a certain level of significance, it is not very meaningful

* The means can be easily calculated at this point: $\bar{X} = \sum X/N$; $\bar{X}_x = 477/7 = 68.1$; $\bar{X}_y = 962/7 = 137.4$.

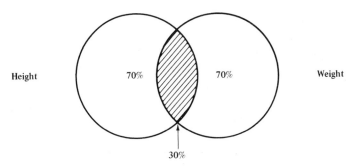

Fig. 6.2. Common variance (r^2) between height and weight.

in that it only means that the relationship is different from zero. A more meaningful evaluation of correlation is to determine the amount of common variance between the two tests, as determined by r^2.

In this sample, height and weight had 30.25% common variance (55^2). Another way of expressing the same point is to say that 69.75% of each variable was not accounted for by the other variable ($1 - r^2$), or that the variables were 69.75% specific. To illustrate the point, if all that is measured by height (100% variance) is represented by one circle and all that is measured by weight by another circle, the correlation indicates that they would overlap 30% (Fig. 6.2).

The amount of common variance gives a more accurate estimation of the relationship that exists between tests. It also shows how well one test can be predicted from another, or what degree of success one can expect when substituting one test for another one. For example, assume that maximum oxygen intake is a valid measure of cardiovascular fitness, but that we are measuring cardiovascular fitness with a 600-yard run. The correlation between the two squared (r^2) would indicate the degree to which the two tests measure the same thing.

Two Independent Groups

The t test for the difference between independent group means (a parametric statistic analogous to the nonparametric Mann-Whitney U Test) will be illustrated by using the same data for Groups I and II on the pull-up test.

STEPS IN COMPUTATION OF t TEST FOR INDEPENDENT GROUPS

1. Determine the mean $(\sum X/N)$ for the variable for each group: $\bar{X}_I$, $\bar{X}_{II}$
2. Determine the sum of squares $[\sum X - (\sum X)^2/N]$ for the variable for each group: SS_I, SS_{II}
3. Determine the number of subjects in each group: N_I, N_{II}
4. Substitute in this formula:

$$t = \frac{\bar{X}_I - \bar{X}_{II}}{\sqrt{\left(\dfrac{SS_I + SS_{II}}{N_I + N_{II} - 2}\right)\left(\dfrac{1}{N_I} + \dfrac{1}{N_{II}}\right)}}$$

Example

	Group I			Group II	
Pupil	X_I	$(X_I)^2$	Pupil	X_{II}	$(X_{II})^2$
A	9	81	P	4	16
B	7	49	Q	5	25
C	3	9	R	7	49
D	6	36	S	5	25
E	8	64	T	3	9
F	13	169	U	4	16
G	7	49	V	0	0
H	0	0	W	4	16
$\sum$	53	457	$\sum$	32	156

Step 1: $\quad \bar{X}_I = 53/8 = 6.6 \qquad \bar{X}_{II} = 32/8 = 4.0$

Step 3: $\quad N = 8$

Step 2: $\quad SS_I = 457 - \dfrac{(53)^2}{8} \qquad SS_{II} = 156 - \dfrac{(32)^2}{8}$

$$= 457 - \frac{2809}{8} \qquad\quad = 156 - \frac{1024}{8}$$

$$= 457 - 351 \qquad\qquad = 156 - 128$$

$$SS_I = 106 \qquad\qquad\quad SS_{II} = 28$$

Step 4: $t = \dfrac{6.6 - 4.0}{\sqrt{\dfrac{106 + 28}{8 + 8 - 2}\left(\dfrac{1}{8} + \dfrac{1}{8}\right)}} = \dfrac{2.6}{\sqrt{\dfrac{134}{14}\left(\dfrac{2}{8}\right)}} = \dfrac{2.6}{\sqrt{(9.57)(.25)}}$

$= \dfrac{2.6}{\sqrt{2.3925}} = \dfrac{2.6}{1.55} = 1.677$

$p < .10.*$

Thus the difference on pull-ups between Groups I and II after the five-week period was at the .10 level of significance.

Two Paired Groups

The parametric counterpart to the Wilcoxon Signed Ranks test for two paired groups is the t test for difference between *paired* groups. It is illustrated by using the same test scores that were used with the Wilcoxon Test. The pretest scores were used to pair individual pupils. The post test is used in the analysis of the data to determine the difference between the groups.

Steps in Computation of t Test for Paired Groups

1. Take difference (d) between each pair of scores
2. Square each difference: (d^2)
3. Sum of d: $\sum d$
4. Sum of d^2: $\sum d^2$
5. N = number of pupils in each group, or number of pairs
6. Determine mean of differences ($\bar{d}$): $\bar{d} = \sum d/N$
7. Substitute in this formula to determine t_{pr}:

$$t_{pr} = \dfrac{\bar{d}}{\sqrt{\dfrac{\sum d^2 - (\sum d)^2}{N\,(N-1)}}}$$

* The z table can be used for probabilities with large samples; for small samples, specific probabilities for the t test can be found in most statistical textbooks. To determine the probability from the z table, one should add the percent above and below the absolute value of t; in this case, the probability of scoring above 1.677 in the z table is .047. It is also .047 probability of scoring below -1.677; therefore the significance level of a $t = 1.677$ is $.047 + .047$, or .094, or less than 10%.

Example

	Pretest, paired subjects				Posttest						
	Group I		Group II		Group I (volleyball and calisthenics)		Group II (volleyball only)			Step 1	Step 2
	Pupil	Pull-up	Pupil	Pull-up	Pupil	Pull-up	Pupil	Pull-up		d	d^2
	A	6	R	6	A	9	R	7		2	4
	B	1	P	1	B	7	R	4		3	9
	D	3	U	3	D	3	U	4		-1	1
	G	2	Q	2	G	7	Q	5		2	4
	H	0	V	0	H	0	V	0		0	0

Step 3:　　　　　　　　　　　　　　　　　　　　　　　　$\sum d = 6$

Step 4:　　　　　　　　　　　　　　　　　　　　　　　　$\sum d^2 = 18$

Step 5: $N = 5$

Step 6:   Mean of $d = \bar{d} = \sum d/N = 6/5 = 1.2$

Step 7: $t_{\text{pr}} = \dfrac{1.2}{\sqrt{\dfrac{18 - \dfrac{(6)^2}{5}}{5(5-1)}}} = \dfrac{1.2}{\sqrt{\dfrac{18 - \dfrac{36}{5}}{5(4)}}} = \dfrac{1.2}{\sqrt{\dfrac{18 - 7.2}{20}}}$

$$= \frac{1.2}{\sqrt{\dfrac{10.8}{20}}} = \frac{1.2}{\sqrt{.54}} = \frac{1.2}{.735} = 1.6333$$

$t_{\text{pr}} = 1.633; \quad p < .20$

The parametric significance test was more precise. Therefore, conclusions about the differences would be more cautious with the nonparametric test (.36 level instead of .20 level). However, if some of the prerequisites for the t test have not been met, perhaps a more cautious conclusion is warranted.

More Than Two Independent Groups

This one-way analysis of variance (ANOVA) can be used to determine the difference among more than two groups (analogous to the Kruskal-Wallis Test). Once again, the same example will be used.

STEPS IN COMPUTATION OF ANALYSIS OF VARIANCE FOR INDEPENDENT GROUPS

1. Determine sum of squares $[\sum X^2 - (\sum X)^2/N]$ for all subjects in all groups: (SS_T)
2. Determine total number of subjects: (N_T)
3. Determine sum of scores for each group: $(\sum X_{\text{I}}, \sum X_{\text{II}} \cdots \sum X_k)$
4. Determine N for each group: $(N_{\text{I}}, N_{\text{II}} \cdots N_k)$
5. Determine sum of squares between groups (SS_B):

$$SS_B = \frac{(\sum X_I)^2}{N_I} + \frac{(\sum X_{II})^2}{N_{II}} + \frac{(\sum X_{III})^2}{N_{III}} \cdots \frac{(\sum X_k)^2}{N_k}$$

$$- \frac{(\sum X_T)^2}{N_T}$$

6. Determine sum of squares within groups: $(SS_W = SS_T - SS_B)$
7. k = number of groups
8. Determine degrees of freedom* for total group: $(\text{df}_T = N_T - 1)$
9. Determine degrees of freedom for between groups: $(\text{df}_B = k - 1)$
10. Determine degrees of freedom within groups: $(\text{df}_W = \text{df}_T - \text{df}_B)$
11. Determine mean square $(MS = SS/\text{df})$ for between, within, and total
12. Determine F ratio: $(F = MS_B/MS_W)$

Example

Group I: (Calisthenics and volleyball)			Group II: (Volleyball only)			Group III: (Calisthenics only)		
	Pull-ups (post)			Pull-ups			Pull-ups	
Subject	X_I	$(X_I)^2$	Subject	X_{II}	$(X_{II})^2$	Subject	X_{III}	$(X_{III})^2$
A	9	81	P	4	16	I	3	9
B	7	49	Q	5	25	J	12	144
C	3	9	R	7	49	K	4	16
D	6	36	S	5	25	L	6	36
E	8	64	T	3	9	M	13	169
F	13	169	U	4	16	N	6	36
G	7	49	V	0	0	O	9	81
H	0	0	W	4	16			

Step 3: $\sum X_I$			$\sum X_{II}$			$\sum X_{III}$		
= 53	457		= 32	156		= 53	491	

* Degrees of freedom (df) is a term that is used with many statistical procedures in determining the probability of the statistical result occurring by chance. The degrees of freedom are determined by the restrictions placed on the observations. There is only one restriction in the simpler procedures, so that df = $N - 1$, or $k - 1$. The concept could be illustrated by choosing two numbers whose sum is equal to 10. Obviously, any number could be chosen for the first number, but once the first number was chosen, there would be no choice for the second number (thus $N - 1$, or 1 degree of freedom).

Step 4: $\qquad N_I = 8 \qquad\qquad N_{II} = 8 \qquad\qquad N_{III} = 7$

$$\sum X_T = (53 + 32 + 53) = 138$$

$$\sum (X_T)^2 = (457 + 156 + 491) = 1104$$

Step 2: $\qquad N_T = (8 + 8 + 7) = 23$

Step 1: $\qquad SS_T = 1104 - \dfrac{(138)^2}{23} = 1104 - \dfrac{19{,}044}{23}$

$$= 1104 - 828 = 276$$

Step 5: $\qquad SS_B = \dfrac{(53)^2}{8} + \dfrac{(32)^2}{8} + \dfrac{(53)^2}{7} - \dfrac{(138)^2}{23}$

$$= \dfrac{2809}{8} + \dfrac{1024}{8} + \dfrac{2809}{7} - \dfrac{19094}{23}$$

$$SS_B = 351.1 + 128.0 + 401.3 - 828$$

$$= 880.4 - 828 = 52.4$$

Step 6: $\qquad SS_W = 276 - 52.4 = 223.6$

Step 7: $\qquad k = $ number of groups $= 3$

Step 8: $\qquad$ Degrees of freedom $= $ df; $\qquad$ df$_T = N - 1$;

$$N = \text{total number of pupils}$$

Step 9: $\qquad$ df$_B = k - 1$; $\qquad k = $ number of groups

Step 10: $\qquad$ df$_W = $ df$_T - $ df$_B$

ANOVA Summary

Source	SS	df	Step 11 $MS = SS/\text{df}$	Step 12 $F = MS_B/MS_W$
Between	52.4	2	26.2	2.34
Within	223.6	20	11.2	
Total:	276	22		

When this is compared with a probability table for F ratios (a probability table for the F ratio can be found in most statistical textbooks), the probability (p) would be less than the .25 level of significance. The F ratio represents an estimate of the variance between the groups over the variance within the groups. The larger the ratio (more variance between, less variance within), the more confident one would be that there were real differences among the groups.

Summary

Parametric statistical procedures for answering the questions raised in Chapter 5 are included as an option for those professors and/or students who choose to work their examples and/or problems with those methods rather than the simpler nonparametric methods presented in Chapter 5. This chapter may be omitted, or used instead of specific portions in Chapter 5.

Problems

The problems are the same as for Chapter 5. The option is whether to work them with the nonparametric statistical procedures given in Chapter 5 or the parametric statistical procedures given in this chapter.

References

Boneau, C. A. The effects of violation underlying the t test. *Psychological Bulletin*, 1960, **57**, 49–62.

Edwards, A. L. *Statistical methods for the behavioral sciences*. New York: Holt, 1964.

Ferguson, G. A. *Statistical analysis in psychology and education*. New York: McGraw-Hill, 1966.

Hays, W. L. *Statistics for psychologists*. New York: Holt, 1963.

Heusner, W. W. A method for evaluations the significance of difference observed in a case study. *Research Quarterly*, 1959, **30**, 363–365.

Manning, W. H., and DuBois, P. H. Correlational methods in research on human learning. *Perceptual and Motor Skills*, 1962, **15**, 287–321.

Nelson, R. C., and Morehouse, C. A. Statistical procedures used in multiple-group experiments. *Research Quarterly,* 1966, **37,** 3.

Snedecor, G. W. and Cochran, W. C. *Statistical methods.* (6th ed.) Ames, Iowa: Iowa State University Press, 1967.

Winer, B. J. *Statistical principles in experimental design.* New York: McGraw-Hill, 1962.

Wright, S. Correlation and causation. *Journal of Agricultural Research,* 1921, **20,** 557–585.

Evaluation of the Student

Objectives *Improvement* *Performance*

. . .Public Schools

Progress Report of_____ for School Year_____

Grade_____ Room _____   Teacher_____ ____

Report Periods

	1	2	3	4
Mathematics	____	____	____	____
Art	____	____	____	____
Health education	____	____	____	____
Language arts and speech	____	____	____	____
Reading	____	____	____	____
Written expression	____	____	____	____
Spelling	____	____	____	____
Handwriting	____	____	____	____
Music	____	____	____	____
Physical education	____	____	____	____
Science	____	____	____	____
Social studies	____	____	____	____

Teacher comments

Signature of parent

Promoted to grade _____

Rating Scale: A = Excellent
B = Good
C = Average
D = Slow progress
E = Unsatisfactory progress

One of the functions of testing is to determine the pupil's achievement of the objectives of a particular course. This evaluation of the pupil can enhance self-understanding, provide a means of evaluating the effectiveness of the teacher, as well as establish a basis for the pupil's grade.

Grading

The following questions need to be answered before any grading plan can be established for a class.

1. What are the objectives of the course?
2. What will be included in the physical education grade?
3. What grading system will be used?
4. Will grades be assigned on the basis of final performance or improvement?
5. Will performance (or improvement) be graded on the basis of set standards or the "curve"?
6. How will the handicapped be graded?
7. What will be done to achieve acceptance for the grading plan?

Objectives

Grades should be based on the achievement of the objectives of the course or unit being graded, with added weight given to the more important objectives. A prerequisite to the development of a sound grading plan is a value judgment made in terms of the importance of the objectives. The relative importance of the objectives will be determined by the priorities set by the department and by the individual teacher for the specific unit being taught. Although there will always be disagreement and debate on the relative importance of the objectives, it is generally accepted that a grading plan should be based on the objectives thought to be important.

Attending class, wearing a uniform in a certain way, having hair cut in a certain style, speaking politely, and smiling are not generally listed as objectives of physical education and therefore should *not* be used as basis for a grade. There may be certain school rules that apply to all classes (such as attending class) which carry administrative penalties for violation (such as temporary suspension); however, the physical education grade should be based solely on the pupil's performance related to *physical education* objectives.

Tests

The measuring devices used should be reliable, valid, easily understood and administered, and not too time-consuming. The test should consistently give the same results for the same performance (reliability). Inter- and intraindividual differences cannot be determined with unreliable tests, since the differences may be due to the normal fluctuations of the test rather than to variations between (inter) or within (intra) pupils. The test should measure the objective the teacher wants to test (validity). Invalid tests (even if reliable) lead to grading on irrelevant items. Tests that can be understood by the pupils aid the teacher in teaching about the objectives and in motivating pupils to work for greater achievement. The primary emphasis of the class must, of course, be aimed at activities designed to help pupils achieve the objectives; therefore, it is important to have tests that are easily administered in short periods of time.

Objectives versus Tests

Would that the objectives of physical education could be listed in one column, and reliable and valid tests that can be easily administered to large classes in short periods of time could be listed in another column. Until that time, there may be conflicts between (1) grading on the objectives and (2) using acceptable tests. The best test available should be used to evaluate each objective, but only those tests meeting acceptable standards should be used in grading. To illustrate this point, let us assume that we have a unit on endurance running, and the objectives are to (1) improve the pupil's attitude toward endurance running, (2) increase his cardiovascular fitness, and (3) improve his running skill. Assume further that the two-mile run has been found to be a reliable and valid test for cardiovascular fitness and that a rating scale for running skill has been developed which is reliable and has some support for its validity for this age group. Also assume that, after a thorough search of the literature, there does not seem to be an adequate test for the pupil's attitude toward endurance running, although one attitude inventory and a checklist of out-of-school participation have been suggested. In this situation, we recommend that the attitude inventory and checklist be used for information but that it not be used in the grading until there is more support for its reliability and validity. Further, we suggest that the grade for this unit be based on the two-mile run time and the rating scale for running (proportional to the relative importance placed on the two objectives). In this case, one of the most important objectives (development of a good attitude toward running) is not reflecetd in the grading plan because it cannot be adequately measured. The alternative appears to be to use unreliable and/or invalid tests or, worse, haphazard guesses, subjective feelings, or unacceptable measurement tools that have been included far too long in physical education grades!

This does not mean any decrease in emphasis on the development of good attitudes toward running achieved through the physical education class. It does mean that the grades should be based only on those objectives that can be adequately tested.

Grading System

There are legitimate differences of opinion concerning credit–no credit, pass–fail, letter grades, numerical grades, and other grading systems. Different schools adopt different grading systems, and there is no "right" one to be recommended for all schools. Within the same school, however, there is little justification for using one system in one subject and another system in another subject.* If letter grades are considered the best grading system for English, history, mathematics, and science, then letter grades should also be used for physical education.

Assignment of Grades

After deciding the tests to be used in the grading plan, the relative importance of each, and the grading system, one must then develop a specific grading plan for pupils in a specific class. There are basically two questions to be answered related to the assignment of grades: (1) Will the grade be based on final performance *or* on improvement? (2) Will the grade be assigned on the basis of comparison with a large sample of similar pupils (norms) *or* with the classmates ("curve")? Most of the controversy about grading involves these two questions. There is no general agreement or practice among schools or teachers.

PERFORMANCE

To assign grades on the basis of a person's performance involves testing his *achievement* at the end of the particular unit without regard to his potential, capabilities, or level of achievement at the beginning of the unit. This is the method normally used in other subjects at all levels and many times in university physical education

---

* An obvious exception to using the same grading system for the entire school system would be the practice in some universities of allowing courses outside the student's major to be graded pass–fail. In this case, the same physical education class might be graded with letter grades for majors and pass–fail for nonmajors.

theory classes. It obviously favors those who have a good background in the particular subject or unit.

IMPROVEMENT

To assign grades on the basis of a person's improvement involves testing the *change* that has taken place as a result of a particular unit (determined by the difference between a pretest and a post-test). This method is used many times in physical education activity classes. It favors those who make the greatest change from the pretest (prior to the unit) to the post-test (after the unit).

Pupils beginning at the lower end of the scale of a particular test have a greater potential for improvement than those who begin at a higher point on the scale. Three alternatives for compensating for this difference are:*

1. Develop separate norms for various levels of initial test performance.

2. Assign points for initial performance as well as amount of improvement (this alternative combines both performance and improvement in the grade).

3. Determine the maximum score for the test being used. Subtract the individual's percentage improvement by taking the difference between his initial and final scores and dividing by his potential. For example, the potential score on the Diagonal Wall Pass Test for college women may be 60. Sally's initial score was 20 and her final score was 40. Therefore, her potential for improvement was 40 $(60 - 20)$, while her actual improvement was 50% $[(40 - 20)/40]$. The percentages would then be used for the grade.

PERFORMANCE VERSUS IMPROVEMENT

The improvement a pupil makes as a result of a physical education class is very important for his self-understanding and for evaluating the effectiveness of the teacher. It can provide motivation for future physical activity in and out of school. However, it is very difficult, if

* Personal communication from Dr. Richard Pohndorf, Professor, University of Illinois, Urbana-Champaign.

not impossible, to establish a good grading plan based on improvement because it requires getting a valid initial score. Most of the tests used in physical education are influenced by a person's motivation to do well. It is difficult to motivate all pupils to do their best on an initial test when their grade is based on the amount of improvement they make. Grading on improvement may encourage pupils not to do their best on the pretest and thus reward those who intentionally did not do their best.

Another reason for grading on final performance is that this is consistent with the grading plans used in other subjects. This is not to suggest that the matter is closed and that further debate should not take place; however, it is suggested that it take place on a broader scale to include all classes—not just physical education activities. Most of the arguments made for and against grading on improvement apply equally well to mathematical skills as they do to physical skills.

SET STANDARD VERSUS CURVE

Regardless of whether a teacher decides to grade on final performance or on improvement, certain arbitrary decisions need to be made in the assignment of specific grades. The basic decision is whether to compare these pupils against a large sample of similar pupils (norms) or with each other (curve). The teacher then decides what final score or amount of improvement will be equal to a particular grade, or what percentage of the class will get particular grades. If norms for the same type of group are available on the tests used in the grading plan, there is some advantage in using this larger sample for the comparison. The advantage of using a larger sample rather than one class is that the abilities of individual classes vary; thus a person's grade may depend on which semester the course was taken rather than on his ability to achieve the objectives. If norms are not available, a teacher can develop his own by giving the same tests to several classes and revising the norms as he adds new pupils each year.

FLEXIBILITY

Although a specific grading plan should be worked out in detail in advance, the main criterion in assigning the final grade is that it should reflect the pupil's achievement of the objectives. Some feel that a combination of performance and improvement and/or a comparison with norms and the class is a more reasonable approach. For example, one might grade on improvement but give credit for the initial performance. Or one might set up tentative grades on the basis of norms, but modify them according to the distribution of scores within the specific class. The grading plan should be continually improved by use of more valid tests and by better arbitrary decisions about standards based on more information.

PHYSICALLY HANDICAPPED

There are no uniform practices in dealing with pupils with temporary or permanent physical handicaps. Regardless of whether the handicapped person is in the regular class or in a`separate class (depending largely on the handicap and the unit being conducted), there should be special consideration for grading on those tests that are affected by the particular handicap. For instance, a polio victim may be enrolled in a regular fencing class. When the teacher evaluates his skill, the pupil should be expected to exhibit all the points of the skill except those related to his handicap. If one leg is affected, the placement of that limb should be modified. Such modification should be preplanned according to sound principles so that the modified performance can be evaluated.

Acceptance of the Grading Plan

Acceptance of the grading plan by the parents, administration, and, most important, the pupils can be enhanced by communication before and after the course. Advance information concerning the basis for the grades will not only eliminate confusion concerning the method of grading but will also help explain the objectives of the class.

Proper follow-up of the testing can provide a meaningful learning experience as pupils discover their performance on these tests. The pupil should know the results of the tests as soon as possible, including a thorough discussion of correct and incorrect responses. The testing can provide a basis for guidance toward specific physical activities in and out of class.

It is difficult not to unconsciously favor pupils who are athletes, are polite, come from a friend's family, or are from the same socio-economic or racial group. If the grade is to be a reflection of the achievement of physical education objectives, it is imperative that the grading procedure be set up to eliminate possibilities for favoring pupils in these groups. This is the primary reason that the common practice of allowing a certain number of points for "attitude and participation" is not recommended, because these kinds of subjective items are most susceptible to discrimination for or against certain groups unrelated to their physical education performance.

Testing and grading can hinder the physical education teacher and program, depending on how well it is organized, administered, and communicated. If the testing is logically established to test the objectives and is carried out efficiently with an interest in individual pupils, and if its nature is explained in advance to all concerned, the testing and grading phases of the course can help educate the pupils and their parents concerning the overall class and be an important part of the course. If, on the other hand, it appears that the testing is simply thrown together with confusion about the objectives, and with no one understanding the basis for the grades, then questions will be raised not only about the tests and grades but about the entire course as well.

Example of Grading Plan*

The following example of a grading plan illustrates the steps to be followed in setting up a grading plan:

1. Grades will be based on three objectives; X, Y, and Z. The

* This is one method of grading the pupils in the class. How would you grade them? Compare the results of your grading system with these results.

relative importance of these three objectives is 40% for X, 30% for Y, and 30% for Z.

2. The pupils will be graded A–F.
3. The grades will be based on final performance.
4. The grades will be based on comparison with a norm, with slight adjustments made for class distribution.

Standards for Tests[a]

Given. Test A (possible 80 points) to measure objective X
Test B (possible 60 points) to measure objective Y
Test C (possible 15 points) to measure objective Z

Therefore: the score on A will be $\times.5$ (for possible 40%)
the score on B will be $\times.5$ (for possible 30%)
the score on C will be $\times 2$ (for possible 30%)

Grade	Test A Raw score	Test A corrected (Raw × .5)	Test B R	Test B C (Raw × .5)	Test C R	Test C C (Raw × 2)	Total (corrected)
Highest possible	80	40	60		15		100
A	78	39	44	22	9	18	79
B	70	35	40	20	7	14	69
C	50	25	34	17	4	8	50
D	40	20	30	15	2	4	39
F <							39

[a] Based on national norms.

Final Grades

Class distribution	Grade according to set set standard	Adjusted grade based on class distribution[a]
77	B	A
77	B	A
77	B	A
75	B	A
72	B	B
72	B	B
70	B	B
70	B	B
68	C	C
67	C	C
66	C	C
65	C	C
65	C	C
63	C	C
63	C	C
60	C	C
60	C	C
58	C	C
57	C	C
56	C	C
55	C	C
55	C	C
53	C	C
52	C	C
46	D	D

[a] Since the set standard for the grades is announced to the class prior to the unit, the adjustments in grade are made only to improve a pupil's grade (for example, if it is announced that a total score of 50 is equal to a C, then it would not be fair to assign pupils who scored 52 and 53 a D based on the class distribution).

Raw Data for Grading

| | Initial test | | | | | | | Final test | | | | | | | |
| | Raw score | Corrected score | | | | | | | | | | | | | |
Sub	A	A'	B	B'	C	C'	Total	A	A'	B	B'	C	C'	Total	Grade
1	66	33	42	21	6	12	66	66	33	38	19	9	18	70	
2	42	21	28	14	1	2	37	48	24	34	17	7	14	55	
3	50	25	34	17	3	6	48	56	28	38	19	3	6	53	
4	50	25	36	18	0	0	43	48	24	40	20	6	12	56	
5	66	33	38	19	4	8	60	80	40	42	21	8	16	77	
6	52	26	34	17	6	12	55	54	27	44	22	13	26	75	
7	56	28	36	18	2	4	50	62	31	40	20	7	14	65	
8	42	21	30	15	0	0	36	52	26	40	20	0	0	46	
9	70	35	34	17	7	14	66	80	40	42	21	8	16	77	
10	56	28	24	12	3	6	46	66	33	36	18	3	6	57	
11	52	26	34	17	4	8	51	58	29	38	19	6	12	60	
12	48	24	32	16	6	12	52	58	29	38	19	10	20	68	
13	46	23	30	15	5	10	48	56	28	34	17	10	20	65	
14	44	22	36	18	1	2	42	60	30	40	20	4	8	58	
15	60	30	36	18	1	2	50	72	36	44	22	7	14	72	
16	52	26	32	16	10	20	62	62	31	42	21	8	16	68	
17	40	20	38	19	3	6	45	64	32	50	25	3	6	63	
18	56	28	36	18	5	10	56	48	24	48	24	2	4	52	
19	58	29	42	21	3	6	56	80	40	42	21	8	16	77	
20	46	23	36	18	2	4	45	66	33	46	23	5	10	66	
21	60	30	32	16	3	6	52	56	28	40	20	6	12	60	
22	46	23	40	20	2	4	47	52	26	38	19	5	10	55	
23	58	29	24	12	10	20	61	62	31	38	19	5	10	70	
24	56	28	34	17	8	16	61	48	24	38	19	10	20	63	
25	58	29	34	17	5	10	56	70	35	35	18	7	14	67	
26	70	35	32	16	6	12	63	78	39	44	22	5	10	71	

Other Applications

The focus of this chapter has been on grading students, and the illustrations have implied a traditional class—that is, the teacher determines the objectives and tests and grades the students. The same questions and procedures would be used if students were grading themselves, their peers, or their professors. Many professors and classes are trying to include students in more of the decision-making for a particular course. The point we would make is simply that the evaluation should be done well, regardless of who evaluates whom. We believe that the questions raised in this chapter are essential ones to be answered before an adequate evaluation can be made.

Summary

Evaluation of a person's achievement is illustrated by dealing with one application of this process—namely, grading. The following questions need to be answered in order to evaluate a person's achievement.

1. What are the objectives and their relative importance? (Everyone agrees.)

2. What will be included in the evaluation (or grade)? We believe that only those objectives that can be validly measured should be used.

3. What grading system should be used? We evade this question by encouraging the physical education grading system to be consistent with others in the same school.

4. Will the grades be assigned on the basis of final performance or improvement? Although improvement is very important, we recommend grading on final performance because of the difficult task of getting valid pretest scores when grading on improvement. We also suggest that future debate of this topic include all classes, not just physical education activity classes.

5. Will the performance (or improvement) be graded on the basis of set standards or the "curve"? We recommend set standards (based on an appropriate sample), with some flexibility for class distribution.

Finally, it is suggested that this whole procedure be publicized and used to gain acceptance for the grading plan and physical education program.

Problem

Establish a specific grading plan for a physical education class.

References

American Association for Health, Physical Education, and Recreation. *Measurement and evaluation in health. physical education and recreation.* Washington, D.C.: AAHPER, 1950.

Grace, H. A. Meaning of grades. *Peabody Journal of Education*, 1959, **31**, 93.

Halladay, D. W. Marking in college physical education activities. *Research Quarterly*, 1948, **19**, 178.

McCormick, H. H. A grading procedure for physical education activities. *Journal of Health, Physical Education, and Recreation*, 1947, **18**, 716.

McGraw, L. E. Principles and practices for assigning grades in physical education. *Journal of Health, Physical Education, and Recreation*, 1964, **35**, 24.

Maxson, W. B. Grading—A serious matter. *National Education Association Journal*, 1964, **53**, 56.

Moriarty, M. J. How shall we grade them? *Journal of Health, Physical Education, and Recreation*, 1954, **25**, 27.

Rothney, W. *Evaluating and reporting pupil progress.* Washington, D.C.: National Education Association, 1963.

Shakweiler, J. F. Evaluation education by the individual produced. *Pennsylvania School Journal*, 1965, **113**, 262.

Tyler, R. W. Constructing achievement tests. Unpublished doctoral dissertation, Ohio State University, 1934.

Waglow, I. F. A measurement and evaluation manual for the Department of Required Physical Education at the University of Florida. Unpublished doctoral dissertation, New York University, 1964.

Weiss, R. A. The construction of achievement scales for the measurement of performance in selected physical education activities. Unpublished doctoral dissertation, New York University, 1949.

Wright, L., and Wright, P. K. An instrument for evaluation of skill in women's physical education classes. *Research Quarterly*, 1964, **35**, 69–74.

CHAPTER 8

Physical Performance and Fitness

Rating	Body Composition[a]	Efficiency	Endurance	Skills	Sociopsychological influences

Excellent

Good

Average

Fair

Poor

[a] These norms are based on the. . .sample, $N = \ldots$
□————□ is prior to the year's physical education program, September
x- - - - - -x is following the year's program, May.

Since man is a complex animal consisting of many and varied parts and functions, assessment of his performance efficiency is also a complex task. Man's systems allow for a virtually limitless array of responses which become even more numerous as they are combined in different ways. These different dimensions, functions, and abilities are not necessarily highly related. Therefore, an adequate total assessment of man's skills (physical performance in its broadest sense) and physical fitness (in its broadest sense) requires a battery of tests designed to measure each component of performance and fitness.

Basically the question being asked is: "What is physical performance and fitness?" This is a philosophical question which requires certain arbitrary value judgments and therefore negates the possibility of defining one answer that will meet the needs of all men for all time. In outlining a possible answer, many approaches might be used. At one extreme we might begin with specific test items and order them into different groupings involving common areas, reordering the groups into even larger units until we are able to identify the relatively few general components which clearly identify man's performance and fitness. At the other end of the continuum we might begin with identification of the larger components (general) and by constantly dividing and subdividing finally cull out the specific items that constitute the whole. We have used the latter approach—from the general to the specific—because it seems to offer a concise way of presenting the concept of the different levels in a model for physical performance and fitness and *not* because it was judged to be the only valid approach.

Hierarchical Model of Physical Performance and Fitness

The first priority for the student in this area is to develop an understanding of the magnitude of the concept of performance and fitness. The realization that physical performance and fitness is a multi-factored concept will allow us to make more intelligent decisions concerning evaluation, help us place research findings into proper perspective, and remind us of the limitations of any one study or test. We believe that understanding this concept is so important that we recommend that you deal generally with all the components of performance and fitness prior to selection of tests to measure specific levels of particular components of performance and fitness.

Since no one book, or course, can deal adequately with the whole of performance and fitness, the alternatives seem to be (1) to emphasize some of the aspects of performance and fitness in detail (in which the authors select certain areas to be covered—and certain ones not to be covered), or (2) to emphasize the overall scope of performance and fitness, expecting the student to select certain aspects to study in more depth (through additional courses, articles, books, etc.). We have clearly chosen the second route because we believe it is more important to begin with the overall scope, and because we realize that different individuals will decide to do their testing and research in different areas of performance and fitness. Thus, any selection we make will include irrelevant material and exclude relevant material. Furthermore, we have chosen to include an overview because presentation of the details of the tests (and controversies) in specific

TABLE 8.1

*Model for Physical Performance and Fitness**

General Factor

| Body composition | Efficiency | Endurance | Skills | Sociopsychological influences |

- - - - - - - - - - - - - -
- - - - - - Smaller group factor - - - - - -

- - - - - - - - - - - - - -
- - - - - - Smaller group factor - - - - - -

- - - - - - - - - - - - - -
- - - - - - Specific test items - - - - - -

---

* This heirarchical model emphasizes the different *levels* represented by components of performance and fitness. This type of model should help place different aspects of performance and fitness into proper perspective. Some of the components could be subdivided further, until separate test items for each segment of the body would be listed as a specific component (See Tables 8.2–8.6). The content of the model results from certain arbitrary value judgments; thus the specific content presented here must be viewed as one of many possibilities.

aspects of performance and fitness may hinder the understanding of the total concept much in the same way that studying the details of complex statistical procedures may hinder an understanding of the scope and reasons for these tools.

Although the model presented here (Table 8.1) is incomplete in that further subdivisions are possible, it does represent the various *levels* that are found within each major component in this type of model. Five major areas have been identified relative to performance and fitness: body composition, efficiency, endurance, skill, and sociopsychological influences.

Body Composition

Body composition is important for its contribution to the attractiveness of the appearance of the body, positive health, and physical performance. Some prefer to have body composition as a separate component above three of the major components of performance and fitness. It affects efficiency, endurance, and skills. In fact, many "fitness tests" are made up of test items that are administered and scored in such a way that obese persons are penalized in all the tests. For example, other things being equal, an obese person will be able to do fewer pull-ups and dips; will run more slowly in sprints, shuttle, and endurance runs; and will jump a shorter distance (vertically or horizontally). Thus if the body composition is not taken into consideration, one might be rated "poor" in power, muscular and cardiovascular endurance, speed, and agility simply as a result of obesity. In addition, many of the absolute measures of strength (for example, pounds of force for a particular muscle group), pulmonary function (for example, vital capacity in liters), and metabolism (for example, oxygen consumption in liters per minute) reflect primarily the size and composition of the person. Since body composition is such an influential component, we have chosen to separate it and recommend that other components of performance and fitness be scored in such a way as to partial out the effects of body composition when possible.

TABLE 8.2

Body Composition

Size		Weight		
Length	Circumference	Fat	Nonfat	Proportion
Whole body	Arms		Bones	Percent fat
Sitting	Lower		Muscle	Height/weight
Standing	Upper		Other	
	Wrist			
Arms	Legs			
Lower	Ankle			
Upper	Calf			
Hand	Thigh			
Legs				
Lower	Trunk			
Upper	Hips			
Foot	Abdomen			
	Chest			

SIZE

Two aspects of body composition are the length and circumference of various segments of the body. Length appears to be less susceptible to change by environmental stimuli, although activity in early childhood may have more effect than has been generally assumed. The circumference will reflect the size of the bones, muscles, or fat, depending on where it is taken. For example, the circumference of the wrist reflects the size of the bones; the upper arm, muscle; and the abdomen, fat.

WEIGHT

Weight and overweight are concepts that continue to be widely used. However, the division of weight into fat and nonfat weight would greatly enhance the interpretation of weight. The degree of overfatness (obesity) is more highly related to positive health than the degree of overweightness. The amount of lean body mass* (active tissue) is an important aspect of performance.

PROPORTION

In comparing the changes made by an individual, the measures of size and weight can be used directly. However, comparison of individual changes and their interpretation in regard to aspects of body composition may be enhanced by the use of various ratios based on these direct measurements. Percent fat (percent of total body weight that is fat) is easier to use and interpret than the number of pounds of fat, since the percent takes the total body weight into consideration. The same amount of fat weight might be 10% of the body weight for one person and 30% for another. A less informative ratio is the relation between height and weight—various indices involve this ratio. The length and circumference of various segments of the body are also more easily interpreted when viewed in terms of other segments. Thus the length of one part of a limb might be expressed in

---

* Since it is difficult to measure the amount of lean body mass, the usual procedure is to estimate the amount of fat and use the nonfat weight (total body weight − total fat weight) as an indication of the lean body mass.

terms of the length of the whole limb. The circumference of one portion of the trunk might be used in relation to the circumference of other portions of the trunk.

In other words, although size and weight are measured directly, it is easier to evaluate these measures by using ratios. One word of caution should be inserted about using ratios to evaluate changes in an individual. There are several possible reasons for a change or lack of change. For example, percent fat could be decreased by (1) an increase in lean body mass with no change in fat, (2) a decrease in fat with no change in lean body mass, or (3) an increase in lean body mass with a decrease in fat. The evaluation of the program that brought about the change would be different depending on which of the three combinations caused the decrease in percent of fat. Similarly, no change in percent fat could be caused by (1) no change in fat or lean body mass, (2) an increase in both, or (3) a decrease in both. Again the evaluation of the lack of change would depend on what actually happened to the fat and the lean body mass. If there are this many possibilities for a simple ratio involving only two variables, consider the number of possible explanations for more complex indices that combine several tests into one index!

Efficiency

The second major component of physical performance and fitness is the ability to function efficiently. Efficiency is defined as optimal performance with minimum effort. Although efficiency normally emphasizes the minimum effort (in terms of energy, movement, etc.), the performance cannot be ignored. For example, it would be tempting to say that person who ran 100 yards with less energy expenditure is a more efficient runner. However, if it took him 15 seconds longer to run it, it would hardly seem a desirable trait. Thus to measure efficiency, one normally tries to equalize the testing conditions.

REST

Lying in bed, sitting at a desk, and standing at a counter are not normally associated with "performance," but many internal activi-

TABLE 8.3

Efficiency

Rest	Response to stressors		
	Physical	Mental	Emotional
Circulatory	Circulatory	Circulatory	Circulatory
Hormonal	Hormonal	Hormonal	Hormonal
Neuromuscular	Neuromuscular	Neuromuscular	Neuromuscular
Respiratory	Respiratory	Respiratory	Respiratory

ties are going on continually in these situations. Since much of a person's time is spent in a relatively inactive state, the ability to function efficiently in a resting condition is an important part of one's health. One way to judge a person's efficiency at rest is to measure physiological functions while the person is in a resting state, by testing the circulatory, respiratory, hormonal, and nervous systems. Persons in physical education and medicine have long used tests taken in relatively inactive conditions as an indication of a person's health and fitness.

RESPONSE TO CHANGE

Another aspect of efficiency is the ability to adapt to external stimuli or stressors, whether physical, mental, or emotional. The same variables used at rest can be measured during and after standard amounts of stressors to determine change. This may be interpreted as the ability to adapt to that stressor. There is, of course, more involved in response to external changes than simply the physical condition of the person. The level of physical fitness, personality (for example, anxious persons tend to have a lower threshold to stress), and the nature of the situation (how threatening it is to the person) all interact in producing response to stressors. Although it can be stated that the most efficient person can accomplish whatever is required by the situation with the least change from resting conditions, we should account for all the factors that are present.

TABLE 8.4

Endurance

Muscular	Cardiovascular
Abdomen	With body weight supported
Arms	Supporting body weight
Back	
Hands	
Legs	

Endurance

One of the elements involved in success in many physical activities is the ability to continue to perform over a relatively long period of time. This involves a minimum decrease in the level of performance. Endurance can be divided into muscular and cardiovascular endurance.

MUSCULAR ENDURANCE

Muscular endurance is an important consideration for many tasks. The specific muscle group involved varies widely with different activities. The need for endurance is not all that is necessary for long-distance swimming, running, cycling, cross-country skiing, rowing, etc., but it is obviously a prerequisite for success in such activities. It would be much less important in running or swimming sprints. In general, its importance is directly proportional to the amount of time spent in the activity.

CARDIOVASCULAR ENDURANCE

Cardiovascular endurance is the ability to continue activities that tax the cardiac, circulatory, and respiratory functions. It is measured by two types of tests: (1) measurement of functions of the body related to the heart, lungs, and circulation during hard work; and (2) performance scores from endurance events (for example, time in a two-mile run). The first type of test has the advantage of measuring the functions related to cardiovascular function of the body, is generally less influenced by motivation, and can determine the various elements that contributed to the performance. The performance test assumes that persons who can perform better on endurance events do in fact have better cardiovascular endurance. This second type has the advantage of covering the whole performance; also it is easily administered and scored for large groups.

Two types of work tasks have been widely used in assessing cardiovascular endurance regardless of whether the function or performance is measured—namely, tasks where the body weight is supported, such as work done in supine or sitting positions, and tasks where the body weight must be supported during the work, such as running, bench stepping, and hopping.

The results of some tests have been expressed per unit of body weight or per unit of lean body mass. Although this helps in comparing and interpreting some measures whose absolute score reflects primarily body composition, the same precaution about ratios must again be stated. To illustrate the point, let us consider the commonly used maximum oxygen consumption, expressed in milliliters per kilogram of body weight. If we assume that we have considered the many factors that influence oxygen consumption (heart, lungs, oxygen transport, condition of the muscles involved, etc.) and the factors that influence body weight (fat and nonfat weight), there are still three possible causes for an increase, decrease, or lack of change in the ratio (ml/kg) that must be considered before evaluating the change: (1) The oxygen consumption may increase, with the body weight staying the same; (2) the oxygen consumption may stay the same, with a reduction of body weight; or (3) the oxygen consumption may increase and the body weight decrease.

Skills

Body consumption, efficiency, and endurance influence one's ability to perform various physical activities. There are additional underlying skills related to performance in many physical activities, such as agility, balance, flexibility, and strength. In addition, there are

TABLE 8.5

Skills

Underlying skills	Games
Agility	Individual versus
Balance	Self
Static	Other(s)
Dynamic	
Flexibility	Group versus
Static	Self
Dynamic	Others
Strength	
Static	
Dynamic	
Power	

specific skills that are part of any one physical activity or game. These involve interaction with various rules, facilities, equipment, cooperation, and/or competition with other individual(s). Another aspect of skill performance is the medium in which the skill is performed. Obviously, performing on land, performing in the water, and performing in the air (in or out of gravitational pull) are three very different "ballgames." Participation in some activities (such as most of the field events in track and field) require skills in more than one medium.

UNDERLYING SKILLS

We have grouped certain skills together that seem to influence many activities. However, these skills are relatively independent of each other, since they are not necessarily highly related. The skills included in this category are (1) agility—the ability to move quickly in different directions from different positions; (2) balance—the ability to maintain equilibrium at rest and during a series of prescribed movements; (3) flexibility—the range and ease of movement of joints; and (4) strength—the amount of force exerted.

Although we have used the term agility, a related concept is response time. Response time is the time it takes to perform a certain movement as quickly as possible after a certain stimulus. A dash in track would be one example of response time. It can be divided into premotor (time from stimulus until beginning of muscular action), motor (time from beginning of muscular action to beginning of movement), and movement time (time from beginning of movement until the desired response is accomplished). The first two parts of response time (premotor and motor) are also called reaction time. Thus response time equals reaction time plus movement time. In most cases, the movement time is the more critical. However, the reaction time obviously has a larger part in very short movements.

Static balance is the ability to remain in one position without moving, whereas dynamic balance is the ability to perform a series of movements in a prescribed way (walk a line, turn, jump, hop in a certain sequence). Static flexibility is simply the range of motion of a joint, whereas dynamic flexibility is the ease of movement within that range. Static strength is the amount of force that can be exerted from one position. Dynamic strength is the amount of force throughout a range of motion. Power is dynamic strength per unit of time.

GAMES

There are many ways to classify games: the number playing the game, the type of equipment used, the expected rewards from the game, the medium in which it is played, the caloric cost of playing it, the perceptions involved, the type of competition, etc. We have chosen to classify games according to whether they are played by individuals or by teams and according to how success is measured. Thus we have (1) the individual compared with himself (a world champion trying to beat his own record, or a week-end golfer trying to break 100 for the first time); (2) an individual compared with another individual (the world champion trying to win the event, or the golfer trying to beat an opponent); (3) a group compared with itself (a relay team trying to better its best time); (4) a group compared with others (a team trying to beat another team).

An almost limitless number of physical activities could be listed under each of these divisions. As illustrated in the golf and track examples above, some activities can appropriately be placed under more than one division, depending on the motives of the participant.

This component of a person's physical performance and fitness can be evaluated directly according to his ability to accomplish the goal for a specific activity. In addition, the elements involved in a good performance of a particular activity can be identified and measured (objective and/or subjective assessment).

Sociopsychological Influences

There are influences from outside and from within a person that determine much of his life style. These extra- and intraindividual influences may facilitate or hinder his physical performance and fitness. One of the recent advances in physical education research has been the attention given to the sociological and psychological aspects of performance and fitness.

Extraindividual Influences

The type of physical activity a person participates in appears to be highly related to his culture and various subcultures, such as family, peers, socioeconomic class, school, other institutions, and geographical location. Resultant differences in type and amount of physical activity affect body composition, efficiency, endurance, and skill.

Specific environmental conditions may also alter one's performance at any one time. Performance may be affected by such things as number and type of spectators, the reactions of others to one's performance, the nature of the contest or activity, and the ability of the opponent.

TABLE 8.6

Sociopsychological Influences

Extraindividual	Intraindividual	Interaction
Family	Drives	Situational
Peers	Goals	Long-term
Institutional		
representatives		
Others		

INTRAINDIVIDUAL INFLUENCES

All people have certain basic drives. Inability to fulfill any of these basic needs causes that need to become a primary goal for an individual. For example, food is the main focus of a person who is hungry. If the basic needs are fulfilled, then the person "selects" certain goals from his environment and internalizes them so that they become his goals. These goals are viewed as giving meaning to his life and are the criteria used for making decisions. The processes by which these goals are selected and the most important factors influencing such decisions have raised questions that have been and will continue to be widely debated. The life style that results from particular goals will be related to physical performance and fitness.

INTERACTION

These two influences (extra- and intraindividual) are not completely independent. Outside influences certainly affect the selection of the internalized goals. In addition, the extent of the extraindividual influences on a particular performance will depend on the type of intraindividual variables operating at the time.

The components of personality are good examples of the interaction between extra- and intraindividual influences. Personality is basically the interaction between a person's goals and his relation to other persons and situations. Many of the components of personality seem to include both situational and long-term aspects. For example, although a person may normally be somewhat withdrawn (introverted), in certain situations he will be quite outgoing (extroverted).

Application

The magnitude of the scope of physical performance and fitness makes it absurd to search for *one* test that will measure fitness. Many tests are needed to measure the various components of performance and fitness. It is therefore difficult for one person or one study to evaluate all these components. At least three options are open to persons interested in this area: (1) Measure the major components with gross tests that do not test the parts of each component; (2)

concentrate on one component by attempting to test its parts (or perhaps on one level of one component); (3) join with a team of testers—each one specializing in one of the components, so that together all the components can be tested. The conclusions of a particular battery of tests or a single study should not be generalized beyond the component(s) and sample(s) used. Thus the findings about the development and maintenance of static strength in one muscle group cannot be automatically generalized to other components of fitness.

Each component includes both fixed (inherited) and changeable (environmental) parts. It is helpful to compare a person's score with norms developed on persons as close to his inherited base as possible (same age, sex, body structure, etc.) to determine what his development has been in the various components. It is also interesting to compare a person's performance and fitness against the best that has been obtained. However, the most important comparison is to determine the *change* within a person that can be made as a result of regular, vigorous physical activities.

Again, we must emphasize that this is but one approach in the development of a model. An alternative approach is to identify the systems of the body and then determine which tests might be used in their assessment. Other approaches include identification of the needs of man as he exists within his environment and determination of tests that can adequately estimate his proficiency. Each approach has advantages and disadvantages which must be considered in their evaluation. Understanding the approach intended by any author or study permits one to more clearly put findings into perspective. Diversity in the literature results from differences in approach and different levels of the hierarchal model, as well as "true" discrepancies—those that result from differences in findings and require further study. Therefore, a clarification by the student of the model being used and the level being considered will be a valuable tool in enhancing his understanding of the findings and in resolving some of the seeming disagreements in the literature—those that result from different approaches and different levels. He would be in the advantageous position of being able to identify "real" differences rather than being caught in the maze of controversy due to differences in approach or level within the model of physical performance and fitness.

Summary

A multifactored hierarchical model of physical performance and fitness is proposed as a structure through which tests and research can be put into perspective. The major components of the model are body composition, efficiency, endurance, skills, and sociopsychological influences. It is impossible to deal with all aspects of physical performance and fitness with any one test, or in any one class; therefore, the need is to deal with the specific components directly.

Problems

1. Divide one of the five major components of performance and fitness into different subdivisions.
2. Select, or develop, a test for one level of one of the components of performance and fitness.
3. Analyze several "fitness tests" to determine what levels of what components are tested.
4. Using a hierarchal model similar to the one in this chapter, develop your own content for physical performance and fitness.

References

Adams, W. C., and McCrystal, K. J. *Foundations of physical activity*. Champaign, Illinois: Stipes, 1968.

Aierstock, B. Effects of exercise upon selected physiological responses to a psychic stressor in college women. Ed.D. dissertation, Temple University, 1972.

Altschule, M. D. Emotion and circulation. *Circulation*, 1951, **3**, 444–454.

American Association for Health, Physical Education, and Recreation. *Youth fitness test manual*. Washington, D.C.: AAHPER, 1950.

American Medical Association and American Association for Health, Physical Education, and Recreation. Exercise and fitness. *Journal of Health, Physical Education, and Recreation*, 1964, **35**, 42.

Anastasi, A. *Psychological testing*. (2nd ed.) New York: Macmillan, 1961.

Anthony, S. H. Anxiety as a function of psychomotor and social behavior. *British Journal of Psychology*, 1960, **51**, 141–152.

Asmussen, E., and Heeboll-Nielsen, K. A dimensional analysis of physical performance and growth in boys. *Journal of Applied Physiology*, 1955, 7, 593–603.

Åstrand, I. Aerobic work capacity in men and women with special reference to age. *Acta Physiologica Scandinavica*, 1960, **49**, Suppl. 169.

Åstrand, P. O., and Rodahl, K. *Textbook of work physiology.* New York: McGraw-Hill, 1970.

Athletic Institute. *Exercise and fitness.* Chicago, Illinois: Athletic Institute, 1960.

Athletic Institute. *Health and fitness in the modern world.* Chicago, Illinois: Athletic Institute, 1969.

Banister, E. W., Ribisl, P. M., Porter, G. H., and Cillo, A. R. The caloric cost of playing handball. *Research Quarterly,* 1964, **35,** 236–240.

Barry, A. J. Physical activity and psychic stress/strain. *Canadian Medical Association Journal,* 1967, **96,** 848–853.

Barry, A. J., and Cureton, T. K., Jr. Factorial analysis of physique and performance in pre-pubsecent boys. *Research Quarterly,* 1961, **32,** 282–300.

Barry, A. J., Steinmetz, J. R., and Page, H. F. The effects of physical conditioning on older individuals. II. Motor performance and cognitive function. *Journal of Gerontology,* 1966, **21,** 192–195.

Bauer, W. W. Facets of fitness. *Journal of Health, Physical Education, and Recreation,* 1960, **31,** 23–25.

Behnke, A. R. The estimation of lean body weight from "skeletal" measurements. *Human Biology,* 1959, **31,** 295–315.

Bendig, A. W. The development of a short form of the manifest anxiety scale. *Journal Consulting Psychology,* 1956, **20,** 384.

Bendig, A. W. Faster analyses of anxiety and neuroticism. *Journal Consulting Psychology,* 1960, **24,** 161–168.

Berger, R. A. Application of research finding to weight training. *Strength and Health,* 1965, 1–10.

Berger, R. A. Prediction of total dynamic strength from chinning and dipping strength. *Journal of the Association for Physical and Mental Rehabilitation,* 1965, **19,** 110–111.

Berger, R. A. Determination of a method to predict 1-RM chin and dip from repetitive chins. *Research Quarterly,* 1967, **38,** 330–335.

Booth, E. G. Personality traits of athletes. *Research Quarterly,* 1949, **20,** 296.

Buskirk, E., and Taylor, H. L. Maximal oxygen intake and its relation to body composition, with special reference to chronic physical activity and obesity. *Journal of Applied Physiology,* 1957, **11,** 72–78.

Campbell, D. E. Influence of several physical activities on serum cholesterol concentrations in young men. *Journal of Lipid Research,* 1965, **6,** 478–480.

Castandea, A., McCandless, B. R., and Palermo, D. S. The children's form of the Manifest Anxiety Scale. *Child Development,* 1956, **27,** 317–326.

Cattell, R. Some psychological correlates of physical fitness and physique. In *Exercise and fitness.* Chicago, Illinois: Athletic Institute, 1960.

Corbin, C. B. Standards of subcutaneous fat applied to percentile norms for elementary school children. *American Journal of Clinical Nutrition,* 1969, **22,** 836–841.

Corbin, C. B., and Pletcher, P. Diet and physical activity patterns of obese and nonobese elementary school children. *Research Quarterly,* 1968, **39,** 922–928.

Corral, V. A., and Cureton, T. K., Jr. Variabilité des mesures d'aptitudes phys-
ques dans différents groupes d'âge. *Biometrie Humaine*, 1967, **11**, 3–4.

Costill, D. L., Branam, G., Eddy, D. and Sparks, K. Determinants of marathon
running success. *Internationale Zeitschrift fuer Angewandte Physiologie*, 1971,
29, 249–254.

Crowne, D. P., and Marlowe, D. A new scale of social desirability independent of
psychopathology. *Journal Consulting Psychology* 1960, **24**, 349–354.

Cumming, G. R. Physical fitness and cardiovascular health. (Editorial) *Circulation*, 1968, **37**, 4–7.

Cureton, T. K., Jr. Elementary principles and technique of cinematographical
analysis as aids in athletics research. *Research Quarterly*, 1939, **10**, 3–24.

Cureton, T. K., Jr. *Physical fitness appraisal and guidance*. St. Louis, Missouri:
Mosby, 1947.

Cureton, T. K., Jr. *Physical fitness of champion athletes*. Urbana, Illinois: Univ. of
Illinois Press, 1951.

Cureton, T. K., Jr. The nature of cardiovascular fitness and its protection by exer-
cise-fitness programs. *Journal of Physical Education*, 1963, **61**, 30–34.

Cureton, T. K., Jr. *Improving the physical fitness of youth*. Washington, D.C.:
National Society for Research in Child Development, 1965.

Cureton, T. K., Jr. *Physical fitness and dynamic health*. New York: Dial, 1965.

Cureton, T. K., Jr. Comparison of various factor analyses of cardiovascular-
respiratory test variables. *Research Quarterly*, 1966, **37**, 317–325.

Cureton, T. K., Jr. *The physiological effects of exercise programs upon adults*.
Springfield, Illinois: Thomas, 1968.

Cureton, T. K., Jr., Huffman, W. S., Welser, L., and Kireilis, R. W. *Endurance
of young men*. Washington: Society for Research in Child Development, 1945.

Cureton, T. K., Jr., and Sterling, L. F. Factor analyses of cardiovascular test
variables. *The Journal of Sports Medicine and Physical Fitness*, 1963, **2**, 1–23.

Cureton, T. K., Jr., Welser, L., and Huffman, W. J. A short screen test for predicting motor fitness. *Research Quarterly*, 1945, **16**, 106–119.

Daly, J. W., Barry, A., and Birhead, N. C. The physical working capacity of older
individuals. *Journal of Gerontology*, 1968, **23**, 134–139.

deVries, H. A. *Physiology of exercise for physical education and athletes*. Dubuque,
Iowa: W. C. Brown, 1966.

Doroschuk, E. V. The physical working capacity of males as assessed by bicycle
ergometry. In B. D. Franks (Ed.), *Exercise and fitness—1969*. Chicago,
Illinois: Athletic Institute, 1969.

Doroschuk, E., Bernauer, E., Bosco, J., and Cureton, T. K., Jr. Prediction of all-
out treadmill running time in young boys in the sports-fitness school University of Illinois. *Australian Journal of Physical Education*, 1963, **29**, 36–40.

Duncan, C. H., Stevenson, I. P., and Woolf, H. G. Life situation emotions and
exercise tolerance. *Psychosomatic Medicine*, 1951, **13**, 36–50.

Enholm, O. G. The assessment of habitual activity. In K. Evang and K. Lange

Anderson (Eds.), *Physical activity in health and disease.* Oslo, Norway: University Press, 1966.

Espenschade, A. Motor development. In W. R. Johnson (Ed.) *Science and medicine of exercise and sports.* New York: Harper, 1960.

Falls, H. B., Ismail, A. H., MacLeod, D. F., Wiebers, J. E., Christian, J. E., and Kessler, M. V. Development of physical fitness test batteries by factor analysis techniques. *Journal of Sports Medicine and Physical Fitness,* 1965, **5,** 185–197.

Fascendelli, F. W., Cordova, C., Simons, D. G., Johnson, J., Pratt, L., and Lamb, L. Biomedical monitoring during dynamic stress testing: I. Instrumentation and normal values. *Aerospace Medicine,* 1966, **37,** 928–935.

Flanagan, L. Personality of physically active groups. *Research Quarterly,* 1951, **27,** 3–12.

Franks, B. D. Smoking and selected cardiovascular-respiratory measures. *Research Quarterly,* 1970, **41,** 140–144.

Franks, B. D., and Cureton, T. K., Jr. Orthogonal factors of cardiac intervals and their response to stress. *Research Quarterly,* 1968, **39,** 524–532.

Franks, B. D., and Franks, E. B. Effects of physical training on stuttering. *Journal of Speech and Hearing Research,* 1968, **11,** 767–776.

Franks, B. D., and Jetté, M. Manifest anxiety and physical fitness. *73rd Proceedings, National College Physical Education Association for Men.* 1969, Pp. 48–57.

Fulton, R. E., and Plunge, E. N. Motor learning of highly chosen and unchosen teammates. *Research Quarterly,* 1950, **21,** 126–131.

Giese, D., McAdam, R., Milton, G., and Wang, P. The role of exercise in the performance of a simple mental task (SMT). In B. D. Franks (Ed.), *Exercise and Fitness—1969.* Chicago, Illinois: Athletic Institute, 1969.

Glick, G., and Braunwald, E. Relative roles of the sympathetic and parasympathetic nervous systems in the reflex control of heart rate. *Circulation Research,* 1965, **16,** 363–375.

Gruber, J. J., and Kirkendall, D. R. Interrelationships among metal, motor personality, and social variables in low achieving high school students with high intelligence. *73rd National Physical Education Association for Men.* 1969. Pp. 35–42.

Hall, V. E. The relation of heart rate to exercise fitness: An attempt at physiological interpretation of the bradycardia of training. *Pediatrics,* Part II, 1963, 723–729.

Hammett, V. B. O. Psychological changes with physical fitness training. *Canadian Medical Association Journal* 1967, **96,** 764–769.

Hein, F. V., and Ryan, A. J. The contributions of physical ability to physical health. *Research Quarterly,* 1960, **31,** 263–285.

Hennis, G. M., and Ulrich, C. Effect of psychic stress on coordination. *Research Quarterly,* 1958, **29,** 172–179.

Henry, F. M. Independence of reaction and movement timer and equivalence of sensory motivation of fast response. *Research Quarterly,* 1952, **23,** 43–54.

Herron, R. E., Weissman, S., and Karara, H. M. A method of stereophotographic anthropometry for mentally handicapped children. *Digest of the 7th International Conference on Medical and Biological Engineering.* Stockholm, Sweden: 1967.

Holmes, H. Long-range effects of training on chronic complaints of middle-aged men. Unpublished doctoral dissertation, University of Illinois, 1967.

Howell, M. L., and Alderman, R. B. Psychological determinants of fitness. *Canadian Medical Association Journal*, 1967, **96**, 721–726.

Hunsicker, P. A., and Reiff, G. G. A survey and comparison of youth fitness 1958–1965. *Journal of Health, Physical Education, and Recreation*, 1966, **37**, 23.

Hurwitz, H. M. B., and Rowell, J. Drive strength and adaptation to stress. *British Journal of Psychology*, 1958, **49**, 335–338.

Jetté, M. Progressive physical training on anxiety in middle-aged men. Unpublished master's thesis, University of Illinois, 1967.

Jetté, M. The long-term effects of an exercise program on selected physiological and psychological measures in middle-aged men. Unpublished doctoral dissertation, University of Illinois, 1969.

Johnson, W. R. A study of emotion revealed in two types of athletic sports contests. *Research Quarterly*, **20**, 72–79, 1949.

Johnson, W. R. (Ed.) *Science and medicine of exercise and sports.* New York: Harper, 1960.

Kane, J. E. Personality and physical ability. In K. Kitsuo (Ed.), *Proceedings of International Congress of Sport Sciences.* Tokyo, Japan: Univ. of Tokyo Press, 1966. Pp. 36–43.

Katch, F. I. Pre- and post-test changes in the factors that influence computed body density changes. *Research Quarterly*, 1971, **42**, 280–285.

Kennedy, J. F. A presidential message to the schools on the physical fitness of youth. *Journal of Health, Physical Education, and Recreation*, 1961, **32**, cover.

Kenyon, G. S. (Ed.). Aspects of contemporary sport sociology. *Proceedings of C.I.C. Symposium on the Society of Sport.* Madison, Wisconsin: Univ. of Wisconsin Press, 1968.

Kramer, J. D., and Lurie, P. R. Maximal exercise tests in children. *American Journal of Diseases of Children*, 1964, **108**, 283–294.

Larson, L. A. A review of professional efforts on the measurement of physical fitness. In K. Kitsuo (Ed.), *Proceedings of International Congress of Sport Sciences.* Tokyo, Japan: Univ. of Tokyo Press, 1966.

Linde, Leonard M. An appraisal of exercise fitness test. *Pediatrics*, 1963, **32**, 656.

Liu, N. Effects of training on some selected physical fitness variables of middle-aged women. Unpublished doctoral dissertation, University of Illinois, 1970.

Lowe, B., Harrold, R. D., and Devitt, L. J. The relative importance of selected factors influencing attendance at college athletic contests. *Athletic Administration* 1972, **6**, 14.

Lowe, B. Sport sociology: A cosmopolitan perspective. Paper presented at World University Winter Games at Plattsburgh Conference, 1972.

Martens, R. Effect of an audience on learning and performance of a complex motor skill. *Journal of Personality and Social Psychology*, 1969. **12**, 252–260.

McCloy, C. H. A factor analysis of tests of endurance. *Research Quarterly*, 1956, **27**, 213–215.

McCurdy, J. H., and Larson, L. A. The measurement of organic efficiency for the prediction of physical condition in convalescent patients. *Research Quarterly*, 1935, **6**, 78–97.

Metz, K. F., and Alexander, J. F. An investigation of the relationship between maximum aeorbic work capacity and physical fitness in twelve- to fifteen-year old boys. *Research Quarterly*, 1969, **41**, 75–81.

Michael, E. D. Stress adaptation through exercise. *Research Quarterly*, 1957, **28**, 50–54.

Mitchell, J. C., and Tuttle, W. W. Magnitude of neuromuscular tremor due to exercise, emotional stress, and age. *Research Quarterly*, 1954, **25**, 65.

Molnar, S., Franks, B. D., Jette, M., and Cureton, T. K., Jr. Cardiac time components of boys 7–14 years of age. *Medicine and Science in Sports*, 1971, **3**, 12–17.

Montoye, H. J. Physical activity and risk factors associated with coronary heart disease. In B. D. Franks (Ed.), *Exercise and fitness—1969*. Chicago, Illinois: Athletic Institute, 1969.

Moore, R. D. The effect of velocity changes of selected hemodynamic parameters. In B. D. Franks (Ed.), *Exercise and fitness—1969*. Chicago: Athletic Institute, 1969.

Morgan, W. P. Psychological considerations. *Journal of Health, Physical Education, and Recreation*, 1968, **39**, 26–28.

Morgan, W. P. Physical working capacity in depressed and non-depressed psychiatric females: A preliminary study. *American Corrective Therapeutic Journal*, 1970, **24**, 14–16.

Morgan, W. P. Psychological effect of weight reduction in the college wrestler. *Medicine and Science in Sports*, 1970, **2**, 24–27.

Murray, M. P., Draught, A. B., and Kory, R. C. Walking patterns of normal men. *Journal of Bone and Joint Surgery*, 1964, **46A**, 335–360.

Oxendine, J. B. Social development: The forgotten objective? *Journal of Health, Physical Education, and Welfare*, 1966, **37**, 23.

Pascale, L., Grossman, M., Sloane, H., and Frankel, T. Correlations between thickness of skinfolds and body density in 88 soldiers. *Human Biology*, 1956, **28**, 165–176.

Physical activity and cardiovascular health. *Canadian Medical Association Journal*, 1967, **96**, 695–915.

Popejoy, D. I. The effects of a physical fitness program on selected psychological and physiological measures of anxiety. Unpublished doctoral dissertation, University of Illinois, 1967.

Raab, W. Civilization-induced neurogenic degenerative heart disease. *Cardiologia*, 1962, **41**, 129–143.

Raab, W. Training physical inactivity and the cardiac dynamic cycle. *Journal of Sports Medicine and Physical Fitness*, 1966, **6**, 38–47.

Raab, W., De Paula E Silva, P., Marchet, H., Kimura, E., and Starcheska, Y. K. Cardiac adrenergic preponderance due to lack of physical exercise and its pathogenic implications. *American Journal of Cardiology*, 1960, **5**, 300–329.

Rabb, W., and Krzywanek, H. J. Cardiovascular sympathetic tone and stress response related to personality patterns and exercise habits. *American Journal of Cardiology*, 1965, **16**, 42–53.

Reed, H. B., Jr. Anxiety: The ambivalent variable. *Harvard Education Review*, 1960, **30**, 141–153.

Ricci, B. For a moratorium on "physical fitness" testing. *Journal of Health, Physical Education, and Recreation*, 1970, **41**, 28–30.

Richards, J. N., Aurnhammer, W. L., Kawowith, I., Fleischman, S., Gurafola, G. A., Luffin, M. H. Aims and objectives of physical education activities. *Research Quarterly*, 1937, **8**, 103–122.

Russek, H. J. Emotional stress and the etiology of coronary artery disease. *American Journal of Cardiology*, 1958, **2**, 129–134.

Russels, H. I., and Zohman, B. L. Relative significance of heredity diet, and occupational stress in coronary heart disease of young adults. *American Journal of Medical Science*, 1958, **235**, 266–277.

Ryan, E. D. Effects of stress on water performance and learning. *Research Quarterly*, 1962, **33**, 111–119.

Selye, H. *The stress of life*. New York: McGraw-Hill, 1956.

Shephard, R. J. Physiological determinants of cardiorespiratory fitness. *Journal of Sports Medicine and Physical Fitness*, 1967, **7**, 111–134.

Shock, N. The physiology of aging. *Scientific American*, 1962, **106**, 110.

Skinner, J., Buskirk, E. R., and Borg, G. Physiological and perceptual characteristics of young men differing in activity and body composition. In B. D. Franks (Ed.), *Exercise and fitness—1969*. Chicago: Athletic Institute, 1969.

Smith, L. E. Relationship between muscular fatigue, pain tolerance, anxiety, extraversion-intraversion and neuroticism traits of college men. paper presented *2nd International Congress of Sport Psychology*, Washington, D. C.: 1968.

Spielberger, C. D. *Anxiety and behavior*. New York: Academic Press, 1966.

Strong, C. H. Motivation related to performance of physical fitness tests. *Research Quarterly*, 1963, **34**, 497–507.

Taylor, J. A. A personality scale of manifest anxiety. *Journal of Abnormal and Social Psychology*, 1953, **48**, 285–290.

Taylor, H. L., Buskirk, E., and Henschel, A. Maximal oxygen intake as an objective measure of cardio-respiratory performance. *Journal of Applied Physiology*, 1955, **8**, 73.

Time-Life, Inc. *The healthy life*. New York: Time-Life, 1966.

Ulrich, C. Stress and sport. In W. R. Johnson (Ed.), *Science and medicine of exercise and sports*. New York: Harper, 1960.

Ulrich, C., and Burke, R. K. Effect of motivational stress upon physical performance. *Research Quarterly*, 1957, **28**, 403.

Whipple, H. E. (Ed.) Body composition, part 1. *Annals of the New York Academy of Science*, 1963, **110**, 113–140.

Wilmore, J. H. The use of actual, predicted and constant residual volumes in the assessment of body composition by underwater weighing. *Medicine and Science in Sports*, 1969, **1**, 87–90.

Wilmore, J. H., and Behnke, Albert R. Predictability of lean body weight through anthropometric assessment in college men. *Journal of Applied Physiology*, 1968, **25**, 4.

Wilmore, J. H., and Behnke, A. R. An anthropometric estimation of body density and lean body weight in young women. *American Journal of Clinical Nutrition*, 1970, **23**, 267–274.

Wood, C. G., Jr., and Hokanson, J. E. Effects of induced muscular tension on performance and the inverted U function. *Journal of Personality and Social Psychology*, 1965, **1**, 506–510.

Zauner, C. W., and Swenson, E. W. Exercise, diet and other factors on blood lipids. *Journal of the Florida Medical Association*, 1970, **57**, 30–35.

CHAPTER 9

Written Tests

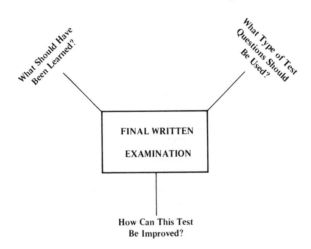

What Should Have Been Learned?

What Type of Test Questions Should Be Used?

FINAL WRITTEN

EXAMINATION

How Can This Test
Be Improved?

Evaluation in physical education must take many forms in order to effectively assess the many facets involved. In addition to objective motor tests and subjective evaluation of play and form, knowledge and understanding vital to physical education must also be evaluated. This is best obtained through the construction and proper administration of written tests.

There are several types of written test, including essay, short-answer completion, alternate response, multiple choice, and matching. Each has advantages as well as certain "rules" for construction. As with any type of testing or evaluation, the value and form depend on the objectives of the course, the age level of the students, and the type of material to be covered.

The following questions are related to the preparation of written tests.

1. What material is to be covered, and what is the relative importance of each aspect to be included?
2. What type of test questions will be used?
3. What precautions and instructions are appropriate for this type of question?
4. How can the test be evaluated and revised?

Test Preparation

There are *no short cuts* in the preparation of good written tests. The tester must consider the material that was covered and the time spent on each portion. These factors should reflect the objectives of the course and should be reflected in the test content. That is, each test should be weighted to reflect a balance in the content that was covered in class. For instance, if a course covered mechanical principles and rules and strategies equally, these parts should have similar importance (weightings) in a written test.

Similar importance does not necessarily mean the same number of questions for each area. Further consideration must be given to the difficulty of mastering the content. Obviously, areas of greatest difficulty require more instruction time and, therefore, may justifiably require more questions to properly evaluate that portion of the content.

The purpose of the test will also be influential in its construction. A final test as well as one used for demonstration of course proficiency should be comprehensive. A test used for drill or periodic assessment may be more limited in scope. Regardless of purpose, the aforementioned factors must be considered.

Test Forms

Once the content to be tested has been decided upon, the test form should be considered. If, in addition to content, the teacher desires to evaluate how the student organizes and expresses himself, essay or short-answer forms may be appropriate. Objective tests have the advantage of allowing a great deal of material to be covered in a relatively short time. Regardless of the form selected, much thought and energy must go into the development of the questions.

Essay

Since the essay test is more limited in scope than an objective test, the teacher must take care in the selection and wording of the questions. The scope must be clearly defined. Questions that have received greatest acceptance in physical education are those that require application of information rather than pure memory.

> *Example:* Discuss the factors that must be considered when selecting a skill test to be administered to a high school basketball class.

Short-answer questions are similar to essay questions except that space or sentence limits may be set by the teacher and the scope may also be more limited.

> *Example:* 1. Outline the steps involved in developing a frequency distribution.
> 2. (Basketball test) Define blocking.

In evaluating the answers, the teacher should outline the points to be covered as well as developing a rationale for granting or subtracting points. When grading papers, the teacher should read everyone's answer to the first question before going to the next question. These procedures have the advantage of maintaining standards and guarding against the familiar "halo effect."

OBJECTIVE TESTS

Objective tests are much more time-consuming to construct but have the advantage of greater reliability and ease of scoring. The level of question may vary from the purely factual, recall type to requiring the student to analyze and synthesize concepts. Since it takes only one to two minutes to read and answer each question, depending on the level being tested (see Bloom's taxonomies), more material can be covered.

In writing questions, avoid "textbook" language and opinion questions. When negatives are involved, they should be capitalized or underlined so that the reader's attention is drawn to them. Negative questions should be used sparingly. Questions should be written to the level of the student, and ambiguity must be avoided. To assist the teacher in obtaining these objectives, it is advisable to have someone else read the questions before giving the test to determine whether the purpose of the question is clear.

True–False

This type of test question should be used only when there are but two possible answers. Care must be taken to avoid giving clues such as using the words "always" or "never."

Be certain not to have a pattern of responses such as three "true" followed by a set number of "false." Since the letters T and F are similar, if an answer sheet is not used, be certain to have the students use a code (1 = true; 2 = false) or write the words in their entirety. This avoids errors in scoring.

One variation of a true–false test is to require all false statements to be corrected; another is a statement with a list of alternatives to which the student responds. The former is more complicated to grade and combines both short answer and true–false. The latter is a true–false question where an omission equals an error.

Example: True The mean is affected by extremes in scores.

Multiple Choice

This is the most versatile form of objective test question. It consists of the stem (in question or statement form) and three to five alternatives (called foils or distractors) from which the student must select the best answer. It is easily adapted to test degrees or depth of knowledge as well as the student's ability to discard incorrect answers while selecting the best answer. The degree of difficulty is increased by making the foils more homogeneous. Care must be taken to make each foil plausible and *not* to use synonyms, since, if the student does not select one, he automatically would not select the second, thus reducing the number of foils by two.

When writing multiple-choice questions, it is easier to use simple, direct questions or statements. This avoids giving grammatical clues in the foils. The foils should be similar in length (to avoid giving clues) and should be alphabetized or placed in random order to assure that there will be no patterning in the placement of the correct response. If the same terminology is repeated in all the foils, those words should be used in the stem so that the student will not have to spend time reading over the same material. Foils such as "all the above" and "none of the above" should be used sparingly. Do not make the answer of one question depend on a correct previous answer.

At times, the use of diagrams is advantageous, but they must be accurate and easily read.

Example:

1. How is the mean determined?

(a) $\dfrac{N}{2}$ (b) $\dfrac{\sum X}{2}$ (c) $\dfrac{\sum X}{N}$ (d) $\sum X$ (e) $N(\sum X)$

2. The scores from a test ranged from 90 (best) to 45. What is the real lower limit of the first interval?

(a) 42.5   (b) 43   (c) 44.5   (d) 45   (e) 90

Matching

Matching questions usually involve two lists—a column on the left with space provided for the answer to be selected from a right-hand column, known as the choices. There should be a minimum of two plausible choices for each. The right-hand column should include at least two choices more than the items ask for in the left-hand column.

Each list should be homogeneous to avoid boredom and to save time for the students. The tester must specify whether each choice may be used more than once. Each column should be in random order or alphabetized to avoid giving clues.

Example: Match the items in the right-hand column with those in the left-hand column, and place the appropriate letter in the space provided. Each choice may be used only once.

_____ 1. Archery
_____ 2. Badminton
_____ 3. Cardiovascular
_____ 4. Field hockey
_____ 5. Golf
_____ 6. Softball
_____ 7. Strength
_____ 8. Swimming
_____ 9. Tennis
_____10. Volleyball

(a) Columbia Round
(b) Distance Throw
(c) Dyer Backboard Test
(d) Fox Power Test
(e) Harvard Step Test
(f) Lockhart-McPherson Wall Volley Test
(g) Push-pull Test
(h) Russell-Lange Test
(i) Schmithals and French Fielding and Diving Test
(j) Scramble
(k) Vanderhoof Drive Test
(l) Vertical Jump Test
(m) Wall Pass

Compilation and Scoring

Using more than two different types of question in the same part of a test is a dubious practice which leads to confusion. Be certain to include specific instructions for each type of question used. These directions must include:

1. Whether there is but one correct choice (multiple choice)
2. Whether the *best* answer should be selected (multiple choice)
3. Whether an answer may be used more than once (matching)
4. What designation must be used for true and what for false
5. What to do if a question is partially true (true–false)

If the student may not write on the question paper, scratch paper should be provided and information to this effect must be included in the directions.

What is the penalty for omissions and errors? There has been a great deal of controversy on whether an error should be penalized more heavily than an omission. Often the score is calculated by subtracting the number wrong from the total number right. This practice is dubious, since often what may be perceived as a guess may actually be based on information. Therefore, this system of scoring may unduly penalize an informed but shy student.

The weighting of the question should be given to indicate its importance. This will guide the student in determining the length of time he should spend on each question.

For ease in scoring an objective test, a key should be prepared. This allows the tester to carefully proofread each question and also saves time. Preparation of a key involves using an answer sheet, marking the correct answers, and then cutting them out. When the key is placed over a completed answer sheet, wherever a mark does not appear in a space the answer is incorrect (multiple choice and true–false). Be sure, however, that only one answer has been selected per question. In establishing a key for matching questions be certain to leave room so that the student's answer will appear next to the keyed answer for each comparison.

Before administering a test, number all test papers consecutively and also number all answer sheets. When the papers are distributed, the students should receive a question paper and an answer sheet with the same number. Then, if a problem arises which may be due to a misprint or confusion resulting from unclear print, the teacher can consult the specific corresponding test paper.

If the test is to be timed, papers should be distributed face down to assure similar time lengths for all students. A signal to begin is then required. Students should also be kept informed as to the time the test ends and the time at various intervals. This is best achieved with a minimum of disturbance by writing on the blackboard.

Test Difficulty and Length

The problem of test difficulty and length is not easy to resolve. Many authorities believe that, in order to evaluate all levels properly, each test must challenge every student. Therefore, if a student receives full credits on a test (100 points out of 100), the teacher still does not know the extent of this student's knowledge. If this is the theoretical framework from which a teacher works, the student should be so informed to avoid undue frustration.

If the teacher has designed a lengthy test to measure speed as one factor, this should be made known to the student and accounted for in the scoring. One problem encountered with this technique is that of the slow reader. His score would be affected by this handicap as well as by his knowledge in the area being tested. However, this factor is present in any written test situation.

It would seem that, in addition to assessing how well the students have grasped the concepts being studied, written tests should indicate the different levels of achievement. How well a question "discriminates" and the difficulty of each question can be objectively evaluated by means of the item analysis to be covered in the next section. However, we must still consider the problem of whether *each* question should discriminate between the better and the poorer student. This is what is often referred to by students as trying to trick them. The problem the teacher faces is using time to best advantage. If he knows that all students have grasped a specific concept or technique, why should time be spent on testing this? However, if a concept is vital to a further understanding, how can the teacher know without testing?

Therefore, there may be instances when a question will not discriminate.

Item Analysis

An item analysis is a technique for analyzing test questions by means of statistics. It provides the teacher with objective information about the difficulty and validity or discrimination of each test question.

PREPARATION

After all the tests have been scored and ordered from best to poorest, the top 27% (high group) and the bottom 27% (low group) are selected for analysis, and the remainder are put aside. Depending on the number of papers, an equal number at each extreme close to 27% may provide similar results and may facilitate later computations. The technique of evaluating only the extremes is known as the Flanagan method.

Work sheets are prepared, listing question numbers in the left-hand margin, blocks divided in half corresponding to the number of foils used on the test, and five columns to the right of the blocks labeled Omit, DR, %, ID, and Revise (Chart 1). The block corresponding to

CHART 1

Item Analysis Work Sheets

Question	a	b	c	d	e	Omit	DR	%	ID	Revise
1										
2										
3										
4										
5										

CHART 2

Item Analysis Work Sheet

Question	a	b	c	d	e	Omit	DR	%	ID	Revise
1 (high)	|	|		|	|	1	50	$\frac{67}{33}$	35	
1 (low)	||	|		||	卌					
2 (high)		||	卌				33	$\frac{53}{13}$	46	
2 (low)	||	|||	卌	卌						
3 (high)	||			|	|	||	33	$\frac{67}{0}$	79	
3 (low)	卌		|||	|||	|||	1				
4 (high)	||	||	||	卌			43	$\frac{33}{53}$	21	ID
4 (low)	|	|	|	|||						
5 (high)		|||	|||				23	$\frac{33}{13}$	28	F
5 (low)		卌	卌							

the correct answer for each question is designated by drawing double lines, by shading, or by some other means. If some questions have fewer foils, the blocks not used are crossed out. It is important to have an omit column to provide a check after tabulating the papers, since some students inevitably omit questions.

To tabulate, the teacher takes the papers for the high group and records the students' answers to each question above the corresponding horizontal line (Chart 2). When all the papers from the high group have been tabulated, a similar procedure is followed with the papers for the low group. A color different from that used for the high group tabulation is used, and the tallies are made below the horizontal line. As a final check be certain that each question has the same number of tallies as papers used in the analysis. The number of students per group who selected the correct answer is circled in the appropriate section of the block.

DIFFICULTY RATING

To determine how easy or difficult a question is involves determining the proportion of students who answered the question correctly. The difficulty rating (DR) is calculated by dividing the number of correct responses by the total number of papers used in the analysis. Since the total number of papers in this example was 30 and the number of students correctly answering question 1 was 15, the DR is 50.

$$\text{DR} = \frac{\text{H} + \text{L}}{N} \qquad \text{DR} = \frac{10 + 5}{30} = \frac{15}{30} = .50$$

Thus 50% or one-half of the students answered question 1 correctly. The higher the DR, the easier the question is. Therefore, question 1 was the easiest and question 5 was the most difficult. The acceptable limits are 10 to 90, denoting questions that are too difficult or too simple, respectively. In these cases, the items should be revised.

For most tests in physical education a range of DR's is desirable to motivate the poorest student and to challenge the best. Most tests should have a mean (DR) of 50.

INDEX OF DISCRIMINATION

The Index of Discrimination (ID) is the term used to describe how well an item differentiates among the better and poorer students. The technique for determining the Index of Discrimination is based on correlation. Much of the work has been done and tabulated by Flanagan. To take advantage of his work, the teacher must do the following.

1. Determine the percentage of students in the high group who answered the question correctly.

2. Repeat the procedure for the low group.

$$\text{For question 1, H\%} = \frac{10}{15} = .67 \qquad \text{L\%} = \frac{5}{15} = .33$$

3. Place these findings in the column marked percent (%) with $\text{H/L} = 67/33$.

4. Convert the percentages into correlation coefficients by consulting Table 9.1. To read the table the proportion (percent) of

TABLE 9.1

Proportion of success in the 27% scoring highest on the continuous variable

	01	02	04	06	08	10	12	14	16	18	20	22	24	26	28	30	32	34	36	38	40	42	44	46	48
01	0	11	23	30	35	40	43	46	49	51	53	55	57	59	61	62	63	65	66	67	68	69	70	71	72
02	-11	0	12	19	25	30	34	37	40	43	46	48	50	51	53	55	56	58	59	61	62	63	64	66	67
04	-23	-12	0	08	14	19	23	26	30	33	36	38	40	42	44	46	48	49	51	53	54	56	57	58	60
06	-30	-19	-08	0	06	11	15	19	23	26	29	31	33	36	38	40	42	44	45	47	48	50	52	53	55
08	-35	-25	-14	-06	0	05	09	13	17	20	23	25	28	30	32	35	37	38	40	42	44	45	47	49	51
10	-40	-30	-19	-11	-05	0	04	08	12	15	18	21	23	26	28	30	32	34	36	38	40	41	43	45	47
12	-43	-34	-23	-15	-09	-04	0	04	07	11	13	16	19	21	24	26	28	30	32	34	36	38	39	41	43
14	-46	-37	-26	-19	-13	-08	-04	0	03	07	10	12	15	18	20	22	25	27	29	31	33	34	36	38	40
16	-49	-40	-30	-23	-17	-12	-07	-03	0	03	06	09	12	14	17	19	21	24	26	28	30	31	33	35	37
18	-51	-43	-33	-26	-20	-15	-11	-07	-03	0	03	06	08	11	13	16	18	20	23	25	27	28	30	32	34
20	-53	-46	-36	-29	-23	-18	-13	-10	-06	-03	0	03	06	08	11	13	15	17	19	22	24	26	27	29	31
22	-55	-48	-38	-31	-25	-21	-16	-12	-09	-06	-03	0	03	06	08	10	12	15	17	19	21	23	25	27	29
24	-57	-50	-40	-33	-28	-23	-19	-15	-12	-08	-06	-03	0	03	05	08	10	12	14	16	18	20	22	24	26
26	-59	-51	-42	-36	-30	-26	-21	-18	-14	-11	-08	-06	-03	0	02	05	07	09	12	14	16	18	20	22	24
28	-61	-53	-44	-38	-32	-28	-24	-20	-17	-13	-11	-08	-05	-02	0	02	04	07	09	11	13	15	17	19	21
30	-62	-55	-46	-40	-35	-30	-26	-22	-19	-16	-13	-10	-08	-05	-02	0	02	04	07	09	11	13	15	17	19
32	-63	-56	-48	-42	-37	-32	-28	-25	-21	-18	-15	-12	-10	-07	-04	-02	0	02	04	07	09	11	13	15	17
34	-65	-58	-49	-44	-38	-34	-30	-27	-24	-20	-17	-15	-12	-09	-07	-04	-02	0	02	04	06	09	11	13	15
36	-66	-59	-51	-45	-40	-36	-32	-29	-26	-23	-19	-17	-14	-12	-09	-07	-04	-02	0	02	04	06	08	11	13
38	-67	-61	-53	-47	-42	-38	-34	-31	-28	-25	-22	-19	-16	-14	-11	-09	-07	-04	-02	0	02	04	06	08	11
40	-68	-62	-54	-48	-44	-40	-36	-33	-30	-27	-24	-21	-18	-16	-13	-11	-09	-06	-04	-02	0	02	04	06	08
42	-69	-63	-56	-50	-45	-41	-38	-34	-31	-28	-26	-23	-20	-18	-15	-13	-11	-09	-06	-04	-02	0	02	04	06
44	-70	-64	-57	-52	-47	-43	-39	-36	-33	-30	-27	-25	-22	-20	-17	-15	-13	-11	-08	-06	-04	-02	0	02	04
46	-71	-66	-58	-53	-49	-45	-41	-38	-35	-32	-29	-27	-24	-22	-19	-17	-15	-13	-11	-08	-06	-04	-02	0	02
48	-72	-67	-60	-55	-51	-47	-43	-40	-37	-34	-31	-29	-26	-24	-21	-19	-17	-15	-13	-11	-08	-06	-04	-02	0
50	-72	-68	-61	-56	-52	-48	-45	-42	-39	-36	-33	-31	-28	-26	-23	-21	-19	-17	-15	-13	-10	-08	-06	-04	-02
52	-73	-69	-62	-57	-53	-50	-46	-43	-40	-38	-35	-33	-30	-28	-26	-23	-21	-19	-17	-15	-12	-10	-08	-06	-04
54	-74	-70	-63	-59	-55	-51	-48	-45	-42	-39	-37	-34	-32	-30	-27	-25	-23	-21	-19	-16	-14	-12	-10	-08	-06
56	-75	-71	-64	-60	-56	-53	-49	-47	-44	-41	-39	-36	-34	-32	-29	-27	-25	-23	-21	-18	-16	-14	-12	-10	-08
58	-76	-72	-66	-61	-58	-54	-51	-48	-45	-43	-40	-38	-36	-33	-31	-29	-27	-25	-22	-20	-18	-16	-14	-12	-10
60	-77	-73	-67	-62	-59	-56	-52	-50	-47	-45	-42	-40	-37	-35	-33	-31	-29	-27	-25	-22	-21	-18	-16	-14	-12
62	-78	-73	-68	-64	-60	-57	-54	-51	-49	-47	-44	-42	-39	-37	-35	-33	-31	-29	-27	-25	-22	-20	-18	-16	-15
64	-78	-74	-69	-65	-61	-58	-55	-53	-50	-48	-46	-43	-41	-39	-37	-35	-33	-31	-29	-27	-25	-22	-21	-19	-17
66	-79	-75	-70	-66	-63	-60	-57	-54	-52	-49	-47	-45	-43	-41	-39	-37	-35	-33	-31	-29	-27	-25	-23	-21	-19
68	-80	-76	-71	-67	-64	-61	-58	-56	-53	-51	-49	-47	-45	-42	-40	-38	-37	-35	-33	-31	-29	-27	-25	-23	-21
70	-81	-77	-72	-68	-65	-63	-60	-57	-55	-53	-51	-49	-46	-44	-42	-40	-38	-37	-35	-33	-31	-29	-27	-25	-23
72	-82	-78	-73	-70	-66	-64	-61	-59	-57	-54	-52	-50	-48	-46	-44	-42	-40	-39	-37	-35	-33	-31	-29	-27	-26
74	-82	-79	-74	-71	-68	-65	-63	-60	-58	-56	-54	-52	-50	-48	-46	-44	-42	-41	-39	-37	-35	-33	-32	-30	-28
76	-83	-80	-75	-72	-69	-67	-64	-62	-60	-58	-56	-54	-52	-50	-48	-46	-45	-43	-41	-39	-37	-36	-34	-32	-30
78	-83	-80	-76	-73	-70	-68	-66	-63	-61	-60	-57	-56	-54	-52	-50	-49	-47	-45	-43	-42	-40	-38	-36	-34	-33
80	-84	-81	-77	-74	-72	-70	-67	-65	-63	-61	-60	-57	-56	-54	-52	-51	-49	-47	-46	-44	-42	-40	-39	-37	-35
82	-85	-82	-78	-76	-73	-71	-69	-67	-65	-63	-61	-60	-58	-56	-54	-53	-51	-49	-48	-47	-45	-43	-41	-39	-38
84	-86	-83	-80	-77	-75	-72	-70	-68	-67	-65	-63	-61	-60	-58	-57	-55	-53	-52	-50	-49	-47	-45	-44	-42	-40
86	-87	-84	-81	-78	-76	-74	-72	-70	-68	-67	-65	-63	-62	-60	-59	-57	-56	-54	-53	-51	-50	-48	-47	-45	-43
88	-87	-85	-82	-80	-77	-76	-73	-72	-70	-69	-67	-66	-64	-63	-61	-60	-58	-57	-55	-54	-52	-51	-49	-48	-46
90	-88	-86	-83	-81	-79	-77	-76	-74	-72	-71	-70	-68	-67	-65	-64	-63	-61	-60	-58	-57	-56	-54	-53	-51	-50
92	-89	-87	-84	-82	-81	-79	-77	-76	-75	-73	-72	-70	-69	-68	-66	-65	-64	-63	-61	-60	-59	-58	-56	-55	-53
94	-90	-88	-86	-84	-82	-81	-80	-78	-77	-76	-74	-73	-72	-71	-70	-68	-67	-66	-65	-64	-62	-61	-60	-59	-57
96	-91	-90	-88	-86	-84	-83	-82	-81	-80	-78	-77	-76	-75	-74	-73	-72	-71	-70	-69	-68	-67	-66	-64	-63	-62
98	-92	-91	-90	-88	-87	-86	-85	-84	-83	-82	-81	-80	-80	-79	-78	-77	-76	-75	-74	-73	-73	-72	-71	-70	-69
99	-93	-92	-91	-90	-89	-88	-87	-87	-86	-85	-84	-83	-83	-82	-82	-81	-80	-79	-78	-78	-77	-76	-75	-74	-73

Proportion of success in the 27% scoring lowest on the continuous variable

[a] A table of the values of the product moment coefficient of correlation in a normal bivariate population corresponding to given proportions of successes.

Indices of Discrimination[a,b]

Proportion of success in the 27% scoring highest on the continuous variable

50	52	54	56	58	60	62	64	66	68	70	72	74	76	78	80	82	84	86	88	90	92	94	96	98	99
72	73	74	75	76	77	78	78	79	80	81	82	82	83	83	84	85	86	87	87	88	89	90	91	92	93
68	69	70	71	72	73	73	74	75	76	77	78	79	80	80	81	82	83	84	85	86	87	88	90	91	92
61	62	63	64	66	67	68	69	70	71	72	73	74	75	76	77	78	80	81	82	83	84	86	88	90	91
56	57	59	60	61	62	64	65	66	67	68	70	71	72	73	74	76	77	78	80	81	82	84	86	88	90
52	53	55	56	58	59	60	61	63	64	65	66	68	69	70	72	73	75	76	77	79	81	82	84	87	89
48	50	51	53	54	56	57	58	60	61	63	64	65	67	68	70	71	72	74	76	77	79	81	83	86	88
45	46	48	49	51	52	54	55	57	58	60	61	63	64	66	67	69	70	72	73	76	77	80	82	85	87
42	43	45	47	48	50	51	53	54	56	57	59	60	62	63	65	67	68	70	72	74	76	78	81	84	87
39	40	42	44	45	47	49	50	52	53	55	57	58	60	61	63	65	67	68	70	72	75	77	80	83	86
36	38	39	41	43	45	47	48	49	51	53	54	56	58	60	61	63	65	67	69	71	73	76	78	82	83
33	35	37	39	40	42	44	46	47	49	51	52	54	56	57	60	61	63	65	67	70	72	74	77	81	84
31	33	34	36	38	40	42	43	45	47	49	50	52	54	56	57	60	61	63	66	68	70	73	76	80	83
28	30	32	34	36	37	39	41	43	45	46	48	50	52	54	56	58	60	62	64	67	69	72	75	80	83
26	28	30	32	33	35	37	39	41	42	44	46	48	50	52	54	56	58	60	63	65	68	71	74	79	82
23	26	27	29	31	33	35	37	39	40	42	44	46	48	50	52	54	57	59	61	64	66	70	73	78	82
21	23	25	27	29	31	33	35	37	38	40	42	44	46	49	51	53	55	57	60	63	65	68	72	77	81
19	21	23	25	27	29	31	33	35	37	38	40	42	45	47	49	51	53	56	58	61	64	67	71	76	80
17	19	21	23	25	27	29	31	33	35	37	39	41	43	45	47	49	52	54	57	60	63	66	70	75	79
15	17	19	21	22	25	27	29	31	33	35	37	39	41	43	46	48	50	53	55	58	61	65	69	74	78
13	15	16	18	20	22	25	27	29	31	33	35	37	39	42	44	47	49	51	54	57	60	64	68	73	78
10	12	14	16	18	21	22	25	27	29	31	33	35	37	40	42	45	47	40	52	56	59	62	67	73	77
08	10	12	14	16	18	20	22	25	27	29	31	33	36	38	40	43	45	48	51	54	58	61	66	72	76
06	08	10	12	14	16	18	21	23	25	27	29	32	34	36	39	41	44	47	49	53	56	60	64	71	75
04	06	08	10	12	14	16	19	21	23	25	27	30	32	34	37	39	42	45	48	51	55	59	63	70	74
02	04	06	08	10	12	15	17	19	21	23	26	28	30	33	35	38	40	43	46	50	53	57	62	69	73
0	02	04	06	08	10	13	15	17	19	21	23	26	28	31	33	36	39	42	45	48	52	56	61	68	72
-02	0	02	04	06	08	11	13	15	17	19	21	24	26	29	31	34	37	40	43	47	51	55	60	67	72
-04	-02	0	02	04	06	08	11	13	15	17	19	22	24	27	29	32	35	38	41	45	49	53	58	66	71
-06	-04	-02	0	02	04	06	08	11	13	15	17	20	22	25	27	30	33	36	39	43	47	52	57	64	70
-08	-06	-04	-02	0	02	04	06	09	11	13	15	18	20	23	26	28	31	34	38	41	45	50	56	63	69
-10	-08	-06	-04	-02	0	02	04	06	09	11	13	16	18	21	24	27	30	33	36	40	44	48	54	62	68
-13	-11	-08	-06	-04	-02	0	02	04	07	09	11	14	16	19	22	25	28	31	34	38	42	47	53	61	67
-15	-13	-11	-08	-06	-04	-02	0	02	04	07	09	12	14	17	19	23	26	29	32	36	40	45	51	59	66
-17	-15	-13	-11	-09	-06	-04	-02	0	02	04	07	09	12	15	17	20	24	27	30	34	38	44	49	58	65
-19	-17	-15	-13	-11	-09	-07	-04	-02	0	02	04	07	10	12	15	18	21	25	28	32	37	42	48	56	63
-21	-19	-17	-15	-13	-11	-09	-07	-04	-02	0	02	05	08	10	13	16	19	22	26	30	35	40	46	55	62
-23	-21	-19	-17	-15	-13	-11	-09	-07	-04	-02	0	02	05	08	11	13	17	20	24	28	32	38	44	53	61
-26	-24	-22	-20	-18	-16	-14	-12	-09	-07	-05	-02	0	03	06	08	11	14	18	21	26	30	36	42	51	59
-28	-26	-24	-22	-20	-18	-16	-14	-12	-10	-08	-05	-03	0	03	06	08	12	15	19	23	28	33	40	50	57
-31	-29	-27	-25	-23	-21	-19	-17	-15	-12	-10	-08	-06	-03	0	03	06	09	12	16	21	25	31	38	48	55
-33	-31	-29	-27	-26	-24	-22	-19	-17	-15	-13	-11	-08	-06	-03	0	03	06	10	13	18	23	29	36	46	53
-36	-34	-32	-30	-28	-27	-25	-23	-20	-18	-16	-13	-11	-08	-06	-03	0	03	07	11	15	20	26	33	43	51
-39	-37	-35	-33	-31	-30	-28	-26	-24	-21	-19	-17	-14	-12	-09	-06	-03	0	03	07	12	17	23	30	40	49
-42	-40	-38	-36	-34	-33	-31	-29	-27	-25	-22	-20	-18	-15	-12	-10	-07	-03	0	04	08	13	19	26	37	46
-45	-43	-41	-39	-38	-36	-34	-32	-30	-28	-26	-24	-21	-19	-16	-13	-11	-07	-04	0	04	09	15	23	34	43
-48	-47	-45	-43	-41	-40	-38	-36	-34	-32	-30	-28	-26	-23	-21	-18	-15	-12	-08	-04	0	05	11	19	30	40
-52	-51	-49	-47	-45	-44	-42	-40	-38	-37	-35	-32	-30	-28	-25	-23	-20	-17	-13	-09	-05	0	06	14	25	35
-56	-55	-53	-52	-50	-48	-47	-45	-44	-42	-40	-38	-36	-33	-31	-29	-26	-23	-19	-15	-11	-06	0	08	19	30
-61	-60	-58	-57	-56	-54	-53	-51	-49	-48	-46	-44	-42	-40	-38	-36	-33	-30	-26	-23	-19	-14	-08	0	12	23
-68	-67	-66	-64	-63	-62	-61	-59	-58	-56	-55	-53	-51	-50	-48	-46	-43	-40	-37	-34	-30	-25	-19	-12	0	11
-72	-72	-71	-70	-69	-68	-67	-66	-65	-63	-62	-61	-59	-57	-55	-53	-51	-49	-46	-43	-40	-35	-30	-23	-11	0

[b]Used by permission of John C. Flanagan. From "Calculating Correlation Coefficients," American Institute of Research, Pittsburgh, Pennsylvania, 1962.

students in the high group who answered the question correctly is read along the horizontal while the percent of students in the low group answering correctly is read along the vertical. Where these two percentages meet in the table is the number that corresponds to the Index of Discrimination. For question 1, look along the horizontal axis for **67** and along the vertical axis for **33**. Since these numbers are odd, and only the even numbers are tabulated, you must interpolate. Therefore, the ID entered in the column for question 1 is 35. Follow the same procedure for each question.

The higher the ID, the greater is the discriminatory power of the item. A negative ID denotes that more students in the low group

---

CHART 3

Name of test_____   Class_____   Date_____

Total number taking test____   Number and percent of incomplete papers_____

Total number of questions_____

Mean_____   Standard deviation_____

Test analyzed by_____

Difficulty	Number	Percent	Decision
Above 90			
10–90			
Below 10			
Discrimination			
Above 90			
10–90			
Below 10			
Nonfunctioning foils			
1			
2			
3			
Comments			

---

answered the question correctly than in the high group. Such questions should be marked for revision. An ID higher than 20 is good; one between 15 and 20 is acceptable. An item with an ID below 15 should be discarded or revised.

RESPONSE REVISION

Any foils not used by at least 3% of the students taking the test should be considered for revision. By examining all the blocks, it becomes evident that in question 5 foil "a" was not used and should therefore be revised. This is noted in the appropriate column (revise).

SUMMARY SHEET

The item analysis is then reviewed and a summary sheet is prepared (Chart 3).

Test reliability should also be determined. This requires a form of correlation, some of which are mentioned in Chapter 4. More complex forms are given in the statistics books listed in the references.

Summary

Suggestions for essay, true-false, multiple-choice, and matching test questions are presented. Methods are included to determine the difficulty and discrimination of specific test items so that the test can be revised.

Problems

1. Have the student write one question for each form described. Then have the class evaluate and correct the questions.

2. Have the students develop, administer, analyze, and interpret the test results and analysis.

References

Barrow, H. M., and McGee, R. *A practical approach to measurement in physical measurement in physical education*. Philadelphia, Pennsylvania: Lea and Febiger, 1964.

Ebel, R. L. *How to judge the quality of a classroom test.* The Examination Service of the State University of Iowa, Technical Bulletin No. 7, 1954.

Scott, M. G., and French, E. *Measurement and evaluation in physical education.* Dubuque, Iowa: W. C. Brown Co., 1959.

Wood, D. A. *Test construction.* Columbus, Ohio: C. E. Merrill, 1960.

CHAPTER 10

Conclusion

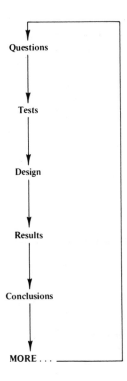

Testing in physical education is almost infinite in scope. The physical educator must be able to select, construct, administer, score, record, interpret, and evaluate tests of knowledge, attitudes, and psychological and sociological aspects of activity, as well as the major and minor components of physical performance and fitness. He must learn not only from colleagues in physical education but also from those in computer science, education, medicine, physiology, psychology, sociology, and statistics. Seldom can information from others be applied without modification and adaptation to his specific situation.

This final chapter attempts to put the material covered in this book into perspective by asking these two questions:

1. What two factors are most important in evaluation?
2. What are some of our limitations?

Importance of Testing

Testing is essential for all phases of physical education. How else can one evaluate the pupil, the teacher, the program? How else does one find better methods? How else does one resolve theoretical conflicts? How else does one test theories and hypotheses? No grade, evaluation, or research can be any better than the tests being used. The *importance of the validity* of tests can hardly be overemphasized. Yet there are too few concentrated efforts to establish valid tests in all areas of performance and fitness.

Limitations of Testing

Let us be honest enough to admit that evaluating performance through testing in physical education as currently practiced has many limitations. The tests may not measure precisely what we want to measure. They may not be as consistent as desired. They may be influenced by other factors not directly connected with physical education or our objectives. Time, personnel, facilities, and equipment to measure the individuals in our classes with a comprehensive battery of tests may be inadequate. Neither is there enough time or assistance to interpret the scores in terms of the class, much less compare different classes (treatments) or write up the findings for the benefit of others. The statistical procedures may be based on mathematical models that do not fit our situation; thus it is not a question of violating assumptions, but rather of which ones are violated. Grading is based on irrelevant and unreliable data, including a portion of—at best—haphazard guesses and—at worst—prejudice for or against certain pupils.

Objective and subjective evaluations presuppose that one knows what elements constitute successful performance and that these elements can be clearly defined. In addition, objective evaluation assumes that these elements can be objectively measured, and subjective evaluation assumes that the elements can be identified through observation.

We are hopeful that significant advances in evaluating performance will be forthcoming soon and that these advances will be *used* throughout physical education. Assuming that we will have highly valid tests and the time, personnel, and facilities to conduct an adequate testing program, there is the danger of testing's being elevated out of perspective. Tests should remain a *means* of evaluating the achievement of particular goals. It is much more important to attain the goals (for example, changes in attitudes, physical activity habits, performance, and fitness) than to administer a good testing program.

Importance of Design

There are two main and necessary ingredients to evaluation, whether within one physical education class or in a large interdisciplinary research project—namely, *valid tests* and *proper evaluative design*. Obviously, if one does not measure the variables being studied, there is little use in conducting the evaluation. A less obvious but equally important aspect is to design the evaluation in such a way that the results of the testing will answer the questions that are being asked.

Some of the problems in answering the questions being asked have already been mentioned. In studying the relationship among variables, one must be careful to control those variables that might affect the ones being studied but are not of primary interest to the study (age is an obvious one; however, there are many others that are less obvious). In studies designed to determine cause and effect, it is important to have control groups that are treated like the experimental groups except in the treatments being studied so that changes caused by other factors can be identified and partialed out.

A more difficult problem is that there are no simple answers to the questions physical educators are asked and are asking. For example, how does one answer the "simple" question: What activities should I do to be fit? Assuming that one can define and measure what it means to be "fit," there are still many factors that interact in determining the answer. What body composition, endurance, efficiency, and skill does the person now possess? What is his age, current activity habits, diseases? How much time, facilities, and interest in particular activities does he have? What kind of personality does he have and how will he interact with other persons? Assuming that these questions can be answered, then the prescription of physical activities must be made in terms of type, frequency, intensity, and duration, in addition to certain safety precautions and means of progressively increasing the activities. Then we must be able to determine when the person has reached the desired level. Experts from cardiology, physical activity, physiology, psychology, pulmonary function, and recreation are needed before one can even begin to deal with this question. In spite of some progress in research in this area, we are a long way from answering these and related questions. One of the difficulties is that one cannot look at any single factor by itself. The question of frequency of activity cannot be answered *except as it is related to* and *interacts with* questions of type, intensity, and duration of activities for persons of different age, body composition, endurance, efficiency, skill, personality, activity habits, etc. The scope of studies designed to examine several of these variables quickly increases beyond the ability of one person, or even one research station, to deal with it effectively. The same complexity is involved in all areas of physical education—how administrative decisions are made, how performance is analyzed, how skill is taught and learned, and any of the other aspects of physical education.

Summary

The most important factors in evaluation are *valid tests* and *evaluative design* that will answer the questions being asked. Evaluation in physical education is hampered by many practical considerations and by lack of knowledge in many areas. This book has attempted to provide the primary questions that need to be asked, with some suggestions concerning where to start to find answers.

No one book (or course) can hope to deal in depth with the entire area of testing and evaluation. This book should be viewed as only the beginning of the search for ways of evaluating performance. Additional growth can come about in many ways—additional courses (many graduate courses are primarily advanced test and measurement courses in specific areas of performance and fitness); individual and group research; reading in the literature; and conferences and informal contacts with colleagues.

This discussion of the limitations under which we all work is not intended to dampen one's enthusiasm for testing in physical education, nor to belittle past and present research efforts of limited scope. It is intended to point out the need for continued learning in this area and to help put these matters into some kind of perspective. It is also a plea for recognition of the fact that none of us can cope with the testing and research needed for our field unless we do it together.

Problem

Select an important question that needs to be answered in our field. How would you answer it.

References

Asmussen, E., and Phil, D. Exercise: General statement of unsolved problems. *Circulation Research*, 1967, **20,** 1.

Barry, A. J., Daly, J. W., Pruett, E. D. R., Steinmetz, J. R., Page, H. F., Birkhead, N. C., and Rodahl, K. The effects of physical conditioning on older individuals. I. Work capacity, circulatory, respiratory function, and work electrocardiogram. *Journal of Gerontology*, 1966, **21**, 2.

Bird, P. J., and Alexander, J. F. Effects of an individually geared exercise program on physical fitness of adult men. *Research Quarterly*, 1968, **39**, 4.

Bosco, J. S., Greenleaf, J. E., Kaye, R. L., and Averkin, E. G. The effects of acute and chronic exercise on serum uric acid concentration. In B. D. Franks (Ed.), *Exercise and fitness—1969*. Chicago, Illinois: Athletic Institute, 1969.

Campbell, D. T., and Stanley, J. C. *Experimental and quasi-experimental designs for research on teaching.* Chicago, Illinois: McNally, 1967.

Chinnici, J. C., and Zauner, C. W. The effect of two intensities of exercise on the magnitude and duration of postprandial lipemia. *Journal of Sports Medicine and Physical Fitness*, 1971, **11**, 36–41.

Cochran, W. C., and Cox, G. M. *Experimental designs.* (2nd ed.) New York: Wiley, 1957.

Costill, D. L. *What research tells the coach about distance running.* Washington, D.C.: American Association for Health, Physical Education, and Recreation, 1968.

Cureton, T. K. Anatomical, physiological and psychological changes induced by exercise programs in adults. In *Exercise and Fitness*. Chicago, Illinois: Athletic Institute, 1960.

Cureton, T. K. *The physiological effects of exercise programs on adults.* Springfield, Illinois: Thomas, 1969.

Cureton, T. K. The relative value of various exercise programs to protect adult human subjects from degenerative heart disease. In W. Raab (Ed.), *Prevention of ischemic heart disease: principles and practice.* Springfield, Illinois: Thomas, 1966.

Doroschuk, E. V. The physical working capacity of males as assessed by bicycle ergometry. In B. D. Franks (Ed.), *Exercise and fitness—1969*. Chicago, Illinois: Athletic Institute, 1969.

Elder, H. P. Effects of training of middle-aged men. In B. D. Franks (Ed.), *Exercise and fitness—1969*. Chicago, Illinois Athletic Institute, 1969.

Exercise in the prevention, in the evaluation, and in the treatment of heart disease. *Journal of the South Carolina Medical Association*, 1969, **65**: Suppl.

Fabricuis, H. Effect of added calisthenics on the physical fitness of fourth grade boys and girls. *Research Quarterly*, 1964, **35**, 135–140.

Faulkner, J. A. *What research tells the coach about swimming.* Washington, D.C.: American Association for Health, Physical Education, and Recreation, 1967.

Franks, B. D. Effects of different types and amounts of training on selected fitness measures. In B. D. Franks (Ed.), *Exercise and fitness—1969*. Chicago, Illinois: Athletic Institute, 1969.

Franks, B. D. Effects of training on selected cardiovascular parameters. *Oregon Association of Health, Physical Education, and Recreation Journal*, 1968, **2**, 13–15.

Franks, B. D., and Cureton, T. K. Effects of training on time components of the left ventricle. *Journal of Sports Medicine and Physical Fitness*, 1969, **9**, 80–88.

Franks, B. D., and Moore, G. C. Effects of calisthenics and volleyball on the AAHPER fitness test and volleyball skill. *Research Quarterly*, 1969, **40**, 2.

Garrett, L., Sabie, M., and Pangle, R. Four approaches to increasing cardiovascular fitness during volleyball instruction. *Research Quarterly*, 1965, **36**, 496–499.

Hilsendager, D. Comparison of a calisthenic and a noncalisthenic physical education program. *Research Quarterly*, 1966, **37**, 148–150.

Hunsicker, P. Future directions in physical research. In B. D. Franks (Ed.), *Exercise and fitness—1969*. Chicago, Illinois: Athletic Institute, 1969.

Kendrick, Z. V., Pollock, M. L., Hickman, T. N., and Miller, H. S., Jr. Effects of training and retraining on cardiovascular efficiency. *American Corrective Therapeutic Journal*, 1971, **25**, 79–83.

Knowlton, R. G., and Weber, H. Effects of progressive endurance training on metabolic and cardiorespiratory adaptations in markedly obese subjects. In B. D. Franks (Ed.), *Exercise and fitness—1969*. Chicago, Illinois: Athletic Institute, 1969.

Linquist, E. F. *Design and analysis of experiments in psychology and education.* Boston, Massachusetts: Houghton, 1953.

Metivier, G. Blood biochemical changes in man associated with physical training. In B. D. Franks (Ed.), *Exercise and fitness—1969*. Chicago, Illinois: Athletic Institute, 1969.

Murphy, H. F., Lohman, T., Oscai, L., and Pollock, M. The potassium scintillator as a measurer of fat in physical education research. In B. D. Franks (Ed.), *Exercise and fitness—1969*. Chicago, Illinois: Athletic Institute, 1969.

Noble, B. J. Problematology of exercise prescription. In B. D. Franks (Ed.), *Exercise and fitness—1969*. Chicago, Illinois: Athletic Institute, 1969.

Olson, A. L., and Edelstein, E. Spot reduction of subcutaneous adipose tissue. *Research Quarterly*, 1968, **39**, 647–652.

Oscai, L. B., and Hooloszy, J. O. Effects of weight changes produced by exercise, food restriction, or overeating on body composition. *Journal of Clinical Investigation*, 1969, **48**, 2124–2128.

Plowman, S. A comparison of Cureton's low and middle gear training program and Cooper's aerobics and young adult women. Doctoral dissertation, University of Illinois, 1970, microcard.

Pollock, M. L. Sports-fitness school for boys. *Journal of Health, Physical Education, and Recreation*, 1967, **38**, 38–40.

Pollock, M. L., Janeway, R., and Lofland, H. B. Effects of frequency of training on serum lipids, cardiovascular function and body composition. In B. D. Franks (Ed.), *Exercise and fitness—1969*. Chicago, Illinois: Athletic Institute, 1969.

Rasch, P., and Kroll, W. *What research tells the coach about wrestling.* Washington, D.C.: American Association for Health, Physical Education, and Recreation, 1964.

Rothermel, B. L., Pollock, M. L., and Cureton, T. K., Jr. AAHPER physical
fitness test score changes resulting from an eight-week sport and physical
fitness program. *Research Quarterly,* 1968, **39,** 1134.

Scott, R. S. A comparison of teaching two methods of physical education with
grade one pupils. *Research Quarterly,* 1968, **38,** 151–154.

Sherman, M. A. Development of a mechanized system for retrieving physical activity information. In B. D. Franks (Ed.), *Exercise and fitness—1969.* Chicago,
Illinois: Athletic Institute, 1969.

Stoedefalke, K. G., and Balke, B. The effect of dynamic physical activity on handicapped university students. In B. D. Franks (Ed.), *Exercise and fitness—1969.*
Chicago, Illinois: Athletic Institute, 1969.

Taddonio, D. A. Effect of daily fifteen-minute periods of calisthenics upon physical
fitness of fifth grade boys and girls. *Research Quarterly,* 1966, **37,** 267–281.

Van Huss, W. D., Heusner, W. W., and Michelsen, O. Effects of prepubertal exercise on body composition. In B. D. Franks (Ed.), *Exercise and fitness—1969.*
Chicago, Illinois: Athletic Institute, 1969.

Wilmore, J. H., Royce, J., Girandola, R. N., Katch, F. I., and Katch, V. L. Body
composition changes with a 10-week program of jogging. *Medicine and Science
in Sports,* 1970, **2**(3), 113–117.

Winer, B. *Statistical principles in experimental design.* New York: McGraw-Hill,
1962.

Wireman, E. O. Comparison of four approaches to increasing physical fitness.
Research Quarterly, 1960, **31,** 658–666.

Procedure for Large Groups

If you have large groups and do not have access to a calculator, a procedure for grouping data will facilitate calculations of measures of central tendency, variability, and Pearson Product Moment Correlation Coefficient. In working with grouped data some accuracy is lost, but, depending on the size of the group (N) and the interval size (i), differences may be minimized. The larger the i, the greater will be the loss of identity of each score, since the midpoint of the interval is considered representative of all scores within that interval, and the scores within the interval are considered to be equally distributed.

Below is an example of the steps involved in setting up a frequency distribution and calculating various measures of interest. The data are from college women who took the Diagonal Wall Pass Test. Although only 50 scores are used for ease of computation, this procedure may be used with any number of scores.

Frequency Distribution

Although the precise decisions necessary in developing a frequency distribution are arbitrary, the steps and procedures given below should be followed for ease and consistency.

The following outline assumes an understanding of the meanings of the terms such as measures of central tendency and variability. Students who are uncertain of their meaning should review Chapter 4.

The following steps are used (see Table A.1 for raw data).

1. Determine the range:

$$\text{High score} - \text{low score} = \text{range}; \quad 60 - 15 = 45$$

2. Determine the size of the interval (i).

Since most biological data can be handled satisfactorily with 10 to 20 intervals (unless norms are to be developed, in which case more intervals are desirable), we divide the range by 15 (halfway between 10 and 20) to estimate the size of the interval.

$$\text{Interval } (i) = \frac{\text{range}}{15} ; \quad i = \frac{45}{15} = 3$$

An odd-number interval size is desirable, since the midpoint (repre-

TABLE A.1

Diagonal Wall Pass—Raw Data[a]

Subject	Score	Subject	Score	Subject	Score	Subject	Score	Subject	Score
1	25	11	21	21	22	31	23	41	39
2	25	12	23	22	45	32	25	42	37
3	15	13	35	23	34	33	27	43	35
4	30	14	38	24	38	34	22	44	32
5	45	15	42	25	43	35	18	45	26
6	35	16	42	26	48	36	48	46	36
7	37	17	60	27	35	37	35	47	34
8	40	18	58	28	34	38	33	48	24
9	28	19	33	29	32	39	29	49	22
10	18	20	22	30	30	40	28	50	38

[a] Sum of three 30-second trials.

senting all the scores in that interval) of the interval would be divisible by i.

Alternative method for determining i: Decide on the number of intervals needed and divide the range by that number.

Example: If we decide to use 10 intervals, we divide the range by 10 ($45/10 = 4.5$). Then i will be 5 (rounded).

Note: The larger the i, the greater will be the loss of identity of each score, since, once the data have been tabulated, the midpoint of each interval represents the scores in that interval.

3. Determine the lower and upper limits of the first interval. Take the lowest score and find the whole number closest to that score that is divisible by i. This becomes the midpoint of our lowest interval. To determine the lower limit and upper limits, add one-half of i to and subtract one-half of i from the midpoint.

Example: Low score $= 15$: 15 is divisible by $i = 3$; Therefore 15 is the midpoint of the lowest interval. Add 1.5 to and subtract 1.5 from the midpoint:

$$15 + 1.5 = 16.5; \quad 15 - 1.5 = 13.5$$

Alternative method: Many books recommend the same procedure but beginning with the best score. Another procedure recommends making the lower limit divisible by i. The specific procedure selected is immaterial, provided that consistency is achieved.

Note: The *real* limits of the interval in question are 13.5 and 16.5. With $i = 3$, the *apparent* limits of the lowest interval are 14 and 16. The real limits of a number are $\frac{1}{2}$ plus and minus a decimal more than the raw score data. Therefore, if the test scores are taken to the nearest whole number, a score of 15 represents a number between 14.5 and 15.5. If a test score is 15.5, the real limits of that score would be 15.45 and 15.55. To avoid confusion due to seeming overlap, that is, the real limits of 15 are 14.5 and 15.5, and for 16 they are 15.5 and 16.5, the upper limit in the last decimal is changed from 5 to 4. Therefore, in our examples, the limits for recording purpose are written as

TABLE A.2

Diagonal Wall Pass—
Frequency Distribution

Interval	Tally		f
58.5–61.4	I		1
55.5–58.4	I		1
52.5–55.4			
49.5–52.4			
46.5–49.4	II		2
43.5–46.4	II		2
40.5–43.4	III		3
37.5–40.4	ⅢⅡ		5
34.5–37.4	ⅢⅡ	III	8
31.5–34.4	ⅢⅡ	II	7
28.5–31.4	III		3
25.5–28.4	IIII		4
22.5–25.4	ⅢⅡ	I	6
19.5–22.4	ⅢⅡ		5
16.5–19.4	II		2
13.5–16.4	I		1
			——
			50

follows: for 15 they are 14.5 and 15.4, and for 15.5 they are 15.45 and 15.54.

4. Record all the limits for each and every interval, beginning with the lowest interval. Do *not* skip any interval.

5. Tally all the raw scores (Table A.2).

6. Count the number of tally marks and convert them to arabic numbers for easier calculation. They should total N. In our example, $N = 50$.

Measures of Central Tendency

We shall use the same data to determine the mean, median, and mode.

MODE

The most frequent score is determined by inspection of the frequency distribution. The interval from 34.5 to 37.4 contains the greatest number of scores. Since the midpoint of the interval represents all the scores in that interval, the *mode* of this distribution is *36*.

MEAN

The determination of the "average" is more complicated. Following are the steps involved.

$$\bar{X} = \text{A.M.} + \left(\frac{\sum fd}{N}\right) i$$

1. Designate an interval as the assumed mean (A.M.). This may be done arbitrarily, since the formula is designed to correct itself. We have designated the interval 31.5–34.4 to contain our assumed mean (Table A.3).

2. Designate a deviation column. Each interval above the mean is labeled as a positive number equal to the number of intervals above the designated assumed mean. Intervals below the assumed mean are similarly labeled but are negative. In essence the student counts by one's in each direction.

TABLE A.3

Diagonal Wall Pass—Assumed Mean

	Interval	f	d	fd	cf
	58.5–61.4	1	9	9	50
	55.5–58.4	0	8	8	49
	52.5–55.4	0	7	0	48
	49.5–52.4	0	6	0	48
	46.5–49.4	2	5	10	48
	43.5–46.4	2	4	8	46
	40.5–43.4	3	3	9	44
	37.5–40.4	5	2	10	41
	34.5–37.4	8	1	8	36
A.M.	31.5–34.4	7	0	0	28
	28.5–31.4	3	−1	−3	21
	25.5–28.4	4	−2	−8	18
	22.5–25.4	6	−3	−18	14
	19.5–22.4	5	−4	−20	8
	16.5–19.4	2	−5	−10	3
	13.5–16.4	1	−6	−6	1
		$N = 50$		−3	

Rationale:

$$d = \frac{X - \text{A.M.}}{i}$$

Therefore

$$d = \frac{36 - 33}{3} = \frac{3}{3} = 1$$

$$d = \frac{18 - 33}{3} = \frac{-15}{3} = -5$$

3. Multiply the f times the d columns. Be certain to include the signs.

Example: $(5)(0) = 0;$ $(3)(1) = 3;$ $(5)(-6) = -30$

4. In the column marked fd add all the positive numbers (62) and all the negative numbers (-65). Then take the difference and give it the sign of the larger value.

$$-65 + 62 = -3$$

5. Divide $\sum fd$ by N.

$$\frac{-3}{50} = -.06$$

6. Multiply by i to decode (convert into raw score units).

$$(-.06)(3) = -.18$$

7. Add algebraically to the assumed mean: $33 + (-.18) = 32.82$. Therefore:

$$\bar{X} = \text{A.M.} + \left(\frac{\sum fd}{N}\right)i$$

$$\bar{X} = 33.0 + \left(\frac{-3}{50}\right)3 = 33.0 + (-.06)3$$

$$= 33.0 + (-.18) = 32.82$$

MEDIAN

The median is that score above and below which 50% of the scores appear. The formula is

$$\text{Median} = ll + \left(\frac{(N/2) - \sum f_b}{f_W}\right)i$$

The following steps are used in determining the median.

1. Determine the cumulative frequency (cf) column by adding the frequencies for each interval consecutively beginning with the lowest interval.

Example: $1 + 2 + 5 + \cdots + 1 = 50$

To check, be certain that the cf of the top interval equals N.

2. Since you are dividing the distribution into two equal parts, divide N by 2.

Example: $\dfrac{N}{2} = \dfrac{50}{2} = 25$

This tells you that the 25th number in the distribution is the median.

3. To determine the value of the median:

(a) Look for the interval that contains the median. In this example we note that there are 28 (cf) scores accounted for within and below the 31.5–34.4 interval. Twenty-one of these scores are accounted for within and below the interval containing the median. Therefore, subtract the number that represents our median from the sum of the frequencies below.

$$\text{Example: } \frac{N}{2} - \sum f_b; \qquad \frac{50}{2} - 21; \qquad 25 - 21 = 4$$

(b) Divide the result in 3a by the frequencies within the interval containing the median.

$$\text{Example: } \frac{4}{f_W} = \frac{4}{7} = .57$$

(c) Convert this result into raw score units by multiplying by the interval size.

$$\text{Example: } (.57)(3) = 1.71$$

(d) To finish decoding, add these units to the real lower limit (ll) of the interval that contains the median.

$$\text{Example: } 31.5 + 1.71 = 33.21 = \text{median}$$

$$\text{Median} = ll + \left(\frac{(N/2) - \sum f_b}{f_W} \right) i$$

$$= 31.5 + \left(\frac{(50/2) - 21}{7} \right) 3$$

$$= 31.5 + \left(\frac{25 - 21}{7} \right) 3$$

$$= 31.5 + \left(\frac{4}{7} \right) 3$$

$$= 31.5 + (.57)3$$

$$= 31.5 + 1.71$$

$$= 33.21$$

Measures of Variability

The two measures of variability of concern, in addition to the range, are the quartile (Q) and the standard deviations(s). Since procedures for determining quartiles, the basis for finding the quartile deviation, are so similar to the ones used in determining the median, only a résumé of the steps is given below. However, the procedure for calculating the standard deviation is covered in detail.

QUARTILE DEVIATION

The quartile deviation (Q) represents one-half of the middle 50% of the scores. The formula is

$$Q = \frac{Q_3 - Q_1}{2}$$

To determine Q_1 (first quartile), use the formula for finding the median, but since the distribution is divided into four parts rather than two, divide N by 4. Proceed, following the steps outlined for calculating the median. To find Q_3 (third quartile), multiply N by 3 and then divide by 4.

$$\textit{Formula: } Q_3 = ll + \left(\frac{(3N/4) - \sum f_b}{f_w} \right) i$$

Note: The same formula is used in determining deciles and centiles, but with the appropriate correction.

STANDARD DEVIATION

The standard deviation is the square root of the squares of the deviations from the mean. To calculate the standard deviation, we already have the d and fd columns. The remaining steps are as follows.

1. Determine the frequencies times the deviations squared (fd^2) by multiplying each fd by its respective deviation. (Table A.4).

Example: $(-6)(-6) = 36;$ $(-10)(-5) = 50$

Alternative method: Square the deviations and multiply by f.

Example: $(-6^2)(1) = (36)(1) = 36;$ $(-5^2)(2) = (25)(2) = 50$

TABLE A.4

Diagonal Wall Pass—Standard Deviation

Interval	f	d	fd	fd^2
58.5–61.4	1	9	9	81
55.5–58.4	1	8	8	64
52.5–55.4	0	7	0	0
49.5–52.4	0	6	0	0
46.5–49.4	2	5	10	50
43.5–46.4	2	4	8	32
40.5–43.4	3	3	9	27
37.5–40.4	5	2	10	20
34.5–37.5	8	1	8	8
31.5–34.4	7	0	0	0
28.5–31.4	3	−1	−3	3
25.5–28.4	4	−2	−8	16
22.5–25.4	6	−3	−18	54
19.5–22.4	5	−4	−20	80
16.5–19.4	2	−5	−10	50
13.5–16.4	1	−6	−6	36
	50		−3	521

2. Summate the fd^2 column.

   Example: $36 + 50 + \cdots + 81 = 521$

3. Divide $\sum fd^2$ by N.

$$\frac{521}{50} = 10.42$$

4. Divide $\sum fd$ by N.

$$\frac{-3}{50} = (-.06)$$

Note: We have already computed this in calculating the mean.

5. Square the results from step 4.

$$(-.06)^2 = .0036$$

6. Subtract the result in step 5 from the result in step 3.

$$10.42 - .0036 = 10.4164$$

7. Take the square root of step 6.

$$\sqrt{10.4164} = 3.23$$

8. Decode by multiplying by the size of the step interval.

$$(3.23)(3) = 9.69$$

$$S = i \sqrt{\frac{\sum fd^2}{N} - \left(\frac{\sum fd}{N}\right)^2}$$

$$= 3 \sqrt{\frac{521}{50} - \left(\frac{-3}{50}\right)^2}$$

$$= 3 \sqrt{10.42 - (-.06)^2}$$

$$= 3 \sqrt{10.42 - .0036}$$

$$= 3 \sqrt{10.4164}$$

$$= 3 (3.23)$$

$$= 9.69$$

Pearson Product Moment Correlation Coefficient (r)

In seeking relationships, one needs one group but two test scores for each person within the group. Therefore, to the raw data previously used, we now add the results from the Vertical Jump Test. When correlating, you have two axes (X—horizontal; Y—vertical). Designate one test as the X (DWP) and the second test as the Y (VJ). Following are the steps involved in plotting the scattergram and computing the correlation (Table A.5).

1. Develop a frequency distribution for each test. You do *not* need the same i for each. Since we have already grouped the data for the

TABLE A.5

Pearson Product Moment Correlation Coefficient—Raw Data

Subject	DWP	VJ	Subject	DWP	VJ	Subject	DWP	VJ
1	25	15	18	58	20.5	35	18	12
2	25	10	19	33	15	36	48	19.5
3	15	7	20	22	12.5	37	35	15
4	30	13	21	22	15	38	33	11
5	45	20	22	45	21	39	29	15
6	33	14	23	34	15	40	28	14.5
7	37	16	24	38	18	41	39	17
8	40	19	25	43	17	42	37	19
9	28	20	26	48	17.5	43	35	16
10	18	12.5	27	35	14	44	32	16.5
11	21	13	28	34	16	45	26	15
12	23	14	29	32	13	46	36	18
13	35	19	30	30	13.5	47	34	17
14	38	16	31	23	12	48	24	13
15	42	19	32	25	15	49	22	14
16	42	20	33	27	15	50	38	22
17	60	23	34	22	11			

results from the Diagonal Wall Pass, we need only group the data from the Vertical Jump Test.

2. Plot the intervals along the respective axis going from left to right (poorest to best score) along the X-axis and from the bottom to the top (poorest to best score) on the Y-axis (Table A.6).

3. Plot the data, accounting for each subject's X and Y values simultaneously. Where the two intervals intersect, place a tally.

Example: Subject 1: $X = 25$; $Y = 15$

Look along the X-axis for the interval containing 25. Then go down within this interval until you come to the interval along the Y-axis containing the number 15. Place your tally (we have used the symbol + for clarity).

4. Summate the frequencies along the X- and Y-axes, heading each column appropriately. For f_x in our first interval we account for all the tallies in the 13.5–16.4 interval (1); in the next interval, add 1 +

1 = 2. For f_y, summate the tallies per interval beginning either at the top or bottom and counting across the interval. f_y = 1; 1; 2.

5. Add the f_y column and then add the f_x column. The f_y should equal the f_x and should be equal to N. In our example N is 50. If an error has been made, replot the data.

6. Determine an assumed mean (just as was done previously in calculating the mean) along each axis. These should be designated in some manner. (We have done this by drawing heavy lines.)

7. Assign deviation values as before in columns marked d with the appropriate subscript. For d_y, any interval above the assumed mean is positive, and any below is negative. For d_x, intervals to the left of the assumed mean are negative, and those to the right are positive. Remember to begin with ± 1 at the intervals closest to the assumed mean which is equal to 0 along each axis.

8. Compute the following along each axis and then summate each: (a) fd; (b) fd^2.

9. Two steps must be followed to calculate the product moment values of each cell that contains a tally.

(a) Determine the deviation cross products of each cell involved.

Example: The cell X = 37.5–40.4, Y = 16.5–17.4, d_x = 1, and d_y = 2 has a value of $(2)(1)$ = 2; this is placed in the upper right-hand corner. The cell x = 19.5–22.4, y = 12.5–13.4, d_x = −5, d_y = −2 has a value of $(-5)(-2)$ = 10, which is placed in the upper right-hand corner of that cell.

(b) The product moment value of each cell is the result of step 9a, times the number of tallies appearing in that cell.

Example: With the same cells as in 9a, the first cell value was 2 with 1 tally. Therefore, the product moment value is 2. This number is placed in the lower right-hand corner and circled. The value of the second example was 10 but it had 2 tallies. Therefore, the product moment value is $(10)(2)$ = 20.

Note: As you gain experience, steps 9a and b can be combined.

10. Summate under a column marked $x'y'$ along each axis. Be certain to watch the signs.

Example: Along the Y-axis for the interval 19.5–20.4, there are values of $-15 + 10 + 15 + 20 = -15 + 45 = 30$. This is placed in the appropriate column. The value of the interval 22.5–25.4 is $4 + 8 + 12 + 20 = 44$.

TABLE A.6
Pearson Product Moment Correlation – Scattergram
Diagonal Wall Pass

	13.5-16.4	16.5-19.4	19.5-22.4	22.5-25.4	25.5-28.4	28.5-31.4	31.5-34.4	34.5-37.4	37.5-40.4	40.5-43.4	43.5-46.4	46.5-49.4	49.5-52.4	52.5-55.4	55.5-58.4	58.5-61.4	f_y	d_y	fd_y	fd_{y^2}	$x'y'$
22.5-23.4																64 / (64)	1	8	8	64	64
21.5-22.4									7 / (7)								1	7	7	49	7
20.5-21.4											18 / (18)				42 / (42)		2	6	12	72	60
19.5-20.4					-15 / (15)					10 / (10)	15 / (15)	20 / (20)					4	5	20	100	30
18.5-19.4								0	4 / (4)	8 / (8)							4	4	16	64	12
17.5-18.4								0	3 / (3)			12 / (12)					3	3	9	27	15
16.5-17.4							1-2 / (-4)		2 / (2)	4 / (4)							4	2	8	16	2
15.5-16.4							-1 / (-1)	0	1 / (1)								4	1	4 / (84)	4	0
14.5-15.4			0	0	0	0	0	0									10	0	0	0	0
13.5-14.4		12 / (12)	15 / (5)	4 / (4)		2 / (2)	1 / (1)										5	-1	-5	5	12
12.5-13.4		12 / (12)	10 / (20)	8 / (8)		4 / (4)	2 / (2)										6	-2	-12	24	46

Vertical Jump Test

Correlation computation table (values as shown; variable x along columns with deviations d_x, variable y along rows with deviations d_y).

Row (y-class) margins

y interval	cell products	f_y	d_y	fd_y	fd_{y^2}	$\Sigma x'y'$
11.5–12.4	$\mid 18$ ⑱	2	−3	−6	18	30
10.5–11.4	$\mid 12$ ⑫ $\mid 20$ ⑳	2	−4	−8	32	24
9.5–10.4	$\mid 20$ ⑳ $\mid 20$ ⑳	1	−5	−5	25	20
8.5–9.4		0	−6	0	0	0
7.5–8.4		0	7	0	0	0
6.5–7.4	$\mid 56$ 56 $\mid 4$ ④	1	−8	−8 (−44)	64	56
		50 = N		40 Σfd_y	564 Σfd_{y^2}	378 $\Sigma x'y'$

Column (x-class) margins

																	Total
f_x	1	2	5	6	4	3	8	7	5	3	2	2	0	0	1	1	50 = N
d_x	−7	−6	−5	−4	−3	−2	−1	0	1	2	3	4	5	6	7	8	
fd_x	−7	−12	−25	−24	−12	−6	−8 (−94)	0	5	6	6	8	0	0	7	8 (40)	−54 Σfd_x
fd_{x^2}	49	72	125	96	36	12	8	0	5	18	12	32	0	0	49	64	578 Σfd_{x^2}
$x'y'$	56	30	45	44	−15	6	2	0	17	33	22	32	0	0	42	64	393 −15 = 378 $\Sigma x'y'$

11. Compute $\sum x' y'$ along each axis. Note that they should be equal. If they do not agree, an error has been made and the addition should be checked. If you do not discover the error, begin with step 9.

12. You are now ready to calculate the Pearson Product Moment Correlation Coefficient by following these simple steps.

(a) Divide the $\sum f d_x$ by N.

$$Example: \quad \frac{\sum f d_x}{N} = \frac{-54}{50} = -1.08$$

(b) Divide the $\sum f d_y$ by N.

$$Example: \quad \frac{\sum f d_y}{N} = \frac{40}{50} = .8$$

(c) Multiply the results from steps a and b.

$$Example: \ (-1.08)(.8) = -.864$$

(d) Divide $\sum x' y'$ by N.

$$Example: \quad \frac{378}{50} = 7.56$$

(e) Subtract the result of step c from that of step d.

$$Example: \ 7.56 - (-.864) = 8.424$$

(f) Divide $\sum f d_x^2$ by N.

$$Example: \quad \frac{578}{50} = 11.56$$

(g) Square the results from step a.

$$Example: \ (-1.08)^2 = 1.1664$$

(h) Subtract the result obtained in step g from that of step f.

$$Example: \ 11.56 - 1.1664 = 10.3936$$

(i) Divide $\sum f d_y^2$ by N.

$$Example: \quad \frac{564}{50} = 11.28$$

(j) Square the results from step b.

$$Example: (.8)^2 = .64$$

(k) Subtract the result obtained in step j from that of step i.

$$Example: 11.28 - 0.64 = 10.64$$

(l) Multiply the results from steps h and k.

$$Example: (10.3936)(10.64) = 110.587904$$

(m) Take the square root of the result from step l.

$$Example: \sqrt{110.587094} = 10.516$$

(n) Divide the result from step m into the result from step e. This will give *r*.

$$Example: \frac{8.424}{10.516} = .80$$

Following is a summary of the formula and steps involved in calculating *r*.

$$r = \frac{\dfrac{\sum x'y'}{N} - \left(\dfrac{\sum f\,d_x}{N}\right)\left(\dfrac{\sum f\,d_y}{N}\right)}{\sqrt{\left[\dfrac{\sum f\,d_x{}^2}{N} - \left(\dfrac{\sum f\,d_x}{N}\right)^2\right]\left[\dfrac{\sum f\,d_y{}^2}{N} - \left(\dfrac{\sum f\,d_y}{N}\right)^2\right]}}$$

$$= \frac{\dfrac{378}{50} - \left(\dfrac{-54}{50}\right)\left(\dfrac{40}{50}\right)}{\sqrt{\left[\dfrac{578}{50} - \left(\dfrac{-54}{50}\right)^2\right]\left[\dfrac{564}{50} - \left(\dfrac{40}{50}\right)^2\right]}}$$

$$= \frac{7.56 - (-1.08)\,(.8)}{\sqrt{[11.56 - (-1.08)^2]\,[11.28 - (.8)^2]}}$$

$$= \frac{7.56 - (-.864)}{\sqrt{(11.56 - 1.1664)(11.28 - .64)}}$$

$$= \frac{8.424}{\sqrt{(10.3036)(10.64)}}$$

$$= \frac{8.424}{\sqrt{110.587904}}$$

$$= \frac{8.424}{10.516}$$

$r = .80$

Note: The respective means and standard deviations can be easily obtained by decoding. Coding in no way affects the correlation. Its advantage lies in working with smaller numbers.

You should estimate the sign and degree of relationship from the scattergram before doing your calculations.

Raw Score Values for Examples Used in the Appendix

Diagonal Wall Pass: $N = 50$

$$\sum X = 1642$$
$$\sum X^2 = 58532$$

Mode: 22.35

Median: 33.0

Mean: 32.84

Standard deviation: $9.697 = 9.70$

Vertical Jump: $N = 50$

$$\sum Y = 786$$
$$\sum Y^2 = 12,885$$
$$\sum XY = 27,064$$
$$r = .80$$

Problems

1. Have students develop a frequency distribution for data which they have gathered.
2. Determine the (a) mode, (b) median, (c) mean, (d) standard deviation, and (e) quartile deviation.
3. Determine the same five statistics (a–e) from the raw scores.
4. Have students explain the findings.
5. Have the students correlate two sets of data using the raw score and grouped score procedures. Explain the results.
6. Determine the square root of a random number. It is often interesting to use a student's social security number.

References

Barrow, H. M., and McGee, R. *A practical approach to measurement in physical education.* Philadelphia, Pennsylvania: Lea and Febiger, 1964. P. 560.

Edwards, A. L. *Statistical methods.* (2nd ed.) New York: Holt, 1967. P. 462.

Runyan, R. P., and Haber, A. *Fundamentals of behavioral statistics.* Reading, Massachusetts: Addison-Wesley, 1967. P. 304.

Scott, M. G., and French, E. *Measurement and evaluation in physical education.* Dubuque, Iowa: W. C. Brown, 1959. P. 493.

Squares, Square Roots, and Reciprocals of Numbers

N	N²	√N	1/N	N	N²	√N	1/N	N	N²	√N	1/N
1	1	1.0000	1.000000	56	3136	7.4833	.017857	111	12321	10.5357	.00900901
2	4	1.4142	.500000	57	3249	7.5498	.017544	112	12544	10.5830	.00892857
3	9	1.7321	.333333	58	3364	7.6158	.017241	113	12769	10.6301	.00884956
4	14	2.0000	.250000	59	3481	7.6811	.016949	114	12996	10.6771	.00877193
5	25	2.2361	.200000	60	3600	7.7460	.016667	115	13225	10.7238	.00869565
6	36	2.4495	.166667	61	3721	7.8102	.016393	116	13456	10.7703	.00862069
7	49	2.6458	.142857	62	3844	7.8740	.016129	117	13689	10.8167	.00854701
8	64	2.8284	.125000	63	3969	7.9373	.015873	118	13924	10.8628	.00847458
9	81	3.0000	.111111	64	4096	8.0000	.015625	119	14161	10.9087	.00840336
10	100	3.1623	.100000	65	4225	8.0623	.015385	120	14400	10.9545	.00833333
11	121	3.3166	.090909	66	4356	8.1240	.015152	121	14641	11.0000	.00826446
12	144	3.4641	.083333	67	4489	8.1854	.014925	122	14884	11.0454	.00819672
13	169	3.6056	.076923	68	4624	8.2462	.014706	123	15129	11.0905	.00813008
14	196	3.7417	.071429	69	4761	8.3066	.014493	124	15276	11.1355	.00800452
15	225	3.8730	.066667	70	4900	8.3666	.014286	125	15625	11.1803	.00800000
16	256	4.0000	.062500	71	5041	8.4261	.014085	126	15876	11.2250	.00793651
17	289	4.1231	.058824	72	5184	8.4853	.013889	127	16129	11.2694	.00787402
18	324	4.2426	.055556	73	5329	8.5440	.013699	128	16384	11.3137	.00781250
19	361	4.3589	.052632	74	5476	8.6023	.013514	129	16641	11.3578	.00775194
20	400	4.4721	.050000	75	5625	8.6603	.013333	130	16900	11.4018	.00769231
21	441	4.5826	.047619	76	5776	8.7178	.013158	131	17161	11.4455	.00763359
22	484	4.6904	.045455	77	9296	8.7750	.012987	132	17424	11.4891	.00757576
23	529	4.7958	.043478	78	6084	8.8318	.012821	133	17689	11.5326	.00751880
24	576	4.8990	.041667	79	6241	8.8882	.012658	134	17956	11.5758	.00746269
25	625	5.0000	.040000	80	6400	8.9443	.012500	135	18225	11.6190	.00740741
26	676	5.0990	.038462	81	6561	9.0000	.012346	136	18406	11.6619	.00735294
27	729	5.1962	.037037	82	6724	9.0554	.012195	137	18769	11.7047	.00729927
28	784	5.2915	.035714	83	6889	9.1104	.012048	138	19044	11.7473	.00724638
29	841	5.3852	.034483	84	7056	9.1652	.011905	139	19321	11.7898	.00719424
30	900	5.4772	.033333	85	7225	9.2195	.011765	140	19600	11.8322	.00714286
31	961	5.5678	.032258	86	7396	9.2736	.011628	141	19881	11.8743	.00709220
32	1024	5.6569	.031250	87	7569	9.3274	.011494	142	20164	11.9164	.00704225
33	1089	5.7446	.030303	88	7744	9.3808	.011364	143	20449	11.9483	.00699301
34	1156	5.8310	.029412	89	7921	9.4340	.011236	144	20736	12.0000	.00694444
35	1225	5.9161	.028571	90	8100	9.4868	.011111	145	21025	12.0416	.00689655
36	1296	6.0000	.027778	91	8281	9.5394	.010989	146	21316	12.0830	.00684932
37	1396	6.0828	.027027	92	8464	9.5917	.010870	147	21609	12.1244	.00690272
38	1444	6.1644	.026316	93	8649	9.6437	.010753	148	21904	12.1655	.00674676
39	1521	6.2450	.025641	94	8836	9.6954	.010638	149	22201	12.2066	.00671141
40	1600	6.3246	.025000	95	9025	9.7468	.010526	150	22500	12.2474	.00666667
41	1681	6.4031	.024390	96	9216	9.7980	.010417	151	22801	12.2882	.00662252
42	1764	6.4807	.023810	97	9409	9.8489	.010309	152	23104	12.3288	.00657895
43	1849	6.5574	.023256	98	9604	9.8995	.010204	153	23409	12.3693	.00653595
44	1936	6.6332	.022727	99	9801	9.9499	.010101	154	23716	12.4097	.00649351
45	2025	6.7082	.022222	100	1000	10.0000	.010000	155	24025	12.4499	.00645161
46	2116	6.7823	.021739	101	10201	10.0499	.00990099	156	24336	12.4900	.00641026
47	2209	6.8557	.021277	102	10404	10.0995	.00980392	157	24649	12.5300	.00636943
48	2304	6.9282	.020833	103	10609	10.1489	.00970874	158	24964	12.5698	.00632911
49	2401	7.0000	.020408	104	10816	10.1980	.00961538	159	25281	12.6095	.00628931
50	2500	7.0711	.020000	105	11025	10.2470	.00952381	160	25600	12.6491	.00625000
51	2601	7.1414	.019608	106	11236	10.2956	.00943396	161	25921	12.6886	.00621118
52	2704	7.2111	.019231	107	11449	10.3441	.00923479	162	26244	12.7279	.00617284
53	2809	7.2801	.018868	108	11664	10.3923	.00925926	163	26569	12.7671	.00613497
54	2916	7.3485	.018519	109	11881	10.4403	.00917431	164	26896	12.8062	.00609756
55	3025	7.4162	.018182	110	12100	10.4881	.00909091	165	27225	12.8452	.00606061

N	N^2	$\sqrt{N}$	$1/N$	N	N^2	$\sqrt{N}$	$1/N$	N	N^2	$\sqrt{N}$	$1/N$
166	27556	12.8841	.00602410	221	48841	14.8661	.00452489	276	76176	16.6132	.00362319
167	27889	12.9228	.00598802	222	49284	14.8997	.00450450	277	76729	16.6433	.00361011
168	28224	12.9615	.00595238	223	49729	14.9332	.00448430	278	77284	16.6733	.00359712
169	28561	13.0000	.00591716	224	50176	14.9666	.00446429	279	77841	16.7033	.00358423
170	28900	13.0384	.00588235	225	50625	15.0000	.00444444	280	78400	16.7332	.00357143
171	29241	13.0767	.00584795	226	51076	15.0333	.00442478	281	78961	16.7631	.00355872
172	29584	13.1149	.00581395	227	51529	15.0665	.00440529	282	79524	16.7929	.00354610
173	29929	13.1529	.00578035	228	51984	15.0997	.00438596	283	80089	16.8226	.00353357
174	30276	13.1909	.00574713	229	52441	15.1327	.00436681	284	80656	16.8523	.00352113
175	30625	13.2288	.00571429	230	52900	15.1658	.00434783	285	81225	16.8819	.00350877
176	30976	13.2665	.00568182	231	53361	15.1987	.00432900	286	81796	16.9115	.00349650
177	31329	13.3041	.00564972	232	53824	15.2315	.00431034	287	82369	16.9411	.00348432
178	31684	13.3417	.00571798	233	54289	15.2643	.00429185	288	82944	16.9706	.00347222
179	32041	13.3791	.00558659	234	54756	15.2971	.00427350	289	83521	17.0000	.00346021
180	32400	13.4164	.00555556	235	55225	15.3297	.00425532	290	84100	17.0294	.00344828
181	32761	13.4536	.00552486	236	55696	15.3623	.00423729	291	84681	17.0587	.00343643
182	33124	13.4907	.00549451	237	56169	15.3948	.00421941	292	84264	17.0880	.00342466
183	33489	13.5277	.00543478	238	56644	15.4272	.00420168	293	85849	17.1172	.00341297
184	33856	13.5647	.00432378	239	57121	15.4596	.00418410	294	86436	17.1464	.00340136
185	34225	13.6015	.00540541	240	57600	15.4919	.00416667	295	87025	17.1756	.00338983
186	34596	13.6382	.00527634	241	58081	15.5242	.00414938	296	87616	17.2047	.00337838
187	34969	13.6748	.00534759	242	58564	15.5563	.00413223	297	88209	17.2337	.00336700
188	35344	13.7113	.00531915	243	59049	15.5885	.00411523	298	88804	17.2627	.00335570
189	35721	13.7477	.00529101	244	59536	15.6205	.00409836	299	89401	17.2916	.00334448
190	36100	13.7840	.00526316	245	60025	15.6525	.00408163	300	90000	17.3205	.00333333
191	36481	13.8203	.00523560	246	60516	15.6844	.00406504	301	90601	17.3494	.00332226
192	36864	13.8564	.00520833	247	61009	15.7162	.00404858	302	91204	17.3781	.00331126
193	37249	13.8924	.00518135	248	61504	15.7480	.00403226	303	91809	17.4069	.00330033
194	37636	13.9284	.00515464	249	62001	15.7797	.00401606	304	92416	17.4356	.00328047
195	38025	13.9642	.00512821	250	62500	15.8114	.00400000	305	93025	17.4642	.00328947
196	38416	14.0000	.00510204	251	63001	15.8430	.00398406	306	93636	17.4929	.00326797
197	38809	14.0357	.00507614	252	63504	15.8745	.00396825	307	94249	17.5214	.00325733
198	39204	14.0712	.00505051	253	64009	15.9060	.00395257	308	94864	17.5499	.00321675
199	39601	14.1067	.00502513	254	64516	15.9374	.00393701	309	95481	17.5784	.00323625
200	40000	14.1421	.00500000	255	65025	15.9687	.00392157	310	96100	17.6068	.00322581
201	40401	14.1774	.00497512	256	65536	16.0000	.00390625	311	96721	17.6352	.00321543
202	40804	14.2127	.00495050	257	66049	16.0312	.00389105	312	97344	17.6635	.00320513
203	41209	14.2478	.00492611	258	66564	16.0624	.00387597	313	97969	17.6918	.00319489
204	41616	14.2829	.00490196	259	67081	16.0935	.00386100	314	98596	17.7200	.00318471
205	42025	14.3178	.00487805	260	67600	16.1245	.00384615	315	99225	17.7482	.00317460
206	42436	14.3527	.00485437	261	68121	16.1555	.00382142	316	99856	17.7764	.00316456
207	42849	14.3875	.00483092	262	68644	16.1864	.0038167	317	100489	17.8045	.00315457
208	43264	14.4222	.00480769	263	69169	16.2173	.00380228	318	101124	17.8326	.00314465
209	43681	14.4568	.00478469	264	69696	16.2481	.00378788	319	101761	17.8606	.00313480
210	44100	14.4914	.00476190	265	70225	16.2788	.00377358	320	102400	17.8885	.00312500
211	44521	14.5258	.00473934	266	70756	16.3095	.00375940	321	103041	17.9165	.00311526
212	44944	14.5602	.00471698	267	71289	16.3401	.00374532	322	103684	17.9444	.00310559
213	45369	14.5945	.00469484	268	71824	16.3707	.00373134	323	104329	17.9722	.00309598
214	45796	14.6287	.00467290	269	72361	16.4012	.00371747	324	104976	18.0000	.00308642
215	46225	14.6629	.00465116	270	72900	16.4317	.00370370	325	105625	18.0278	.00307692
216	46656	14.6969	.00462963	271	73441	16.4621	.00369004	326	106276	18.0555	.00306748
217	47089	14.7309	.00460829	272	73984	16.4924	.00367647	327	106929	18.0831	.00305810
218	47524	14.7648	.00458716	273	74529	16.5227	.00366300	328	107584	18.1108	.00304878
219	47961	14.7986	.00456621	274	75076	16.5529	.00364964	329	108241	18.1384	.00303951
220	48400	14.8324	.00454545	275	75625	16.5831	.00363636	330	108900	18.1659	.00303030

N	N²	√N	1/N	N	N²	√N	1/N	N	N²	√N	1/N
331	109561	18.1934	.00302115	386	148996	19.6469	.00259067	441	194481	21.0000	.00226757
332	110224	18.2209	.00301205	387	149769	19.6723	.00258398	442	195364	21.0238	.00226244
333	110889	18.2483	.00300300	388	150544	19.6977	.00257732	443	196249	21.0476	.00225734
334	111556	18.2757	.00299401	389	151321	19.7231	.00257069	444	197136	21.0713	.00225225
335	112225	18.3030	.00298507	390	152100	19.7484	.00256410	445	198025	21.0950	.00224719
336	112896	18.3303	.00297619	391	152881	19.7737	.00255754	446	198916	21.1187	.00224215
337	113569	18.3576	.00296736	392	153664	19.7990	.00255102	447	199809	21.1424	.00223714
338	114244	18.3848	.00295858	393	154449	19.8242	.00254453	448	200704	21.1660	.00223214
339	114921	18.4120	.00294985	394	155236	19.8494	.00253807	449	201601	21.1896	.00222717
340	115600	18.4391	.00294118	395	156025	19.8746	.00253165	450	202500	21.2132	.00222222
341	116281	18.4662	.00293255	396	156816	19.8997	.00252525	451	203401	21.2368	.00221729
342	116964	18.4932	.00292398	397	157609	19.9249	.00251889	452	204304	21.2603	.00221239
343	117649	18.5203	.00291545	398	158404	19.9499	.00251256	453	295209	21.2838	.00220751
344	118336	18.5472	.00290698	399	159201	19.9750	.00250627	454	206116	21.3073	.00220264
345	119025	18.5742	.00289855	400	160000	20.0000	.00250000	455	207025	21.3307	.00219870
346	119716	18.6011	.00289017	401	160801	20.0250	.00249377	456	207936	21.3542	.00219298
347	120409	18.6279	.00288184	402	161604	20.0499	.00248756	457	208849	21.3776	.00218818
348	121104	18.6548	.00287356	403	162409	20.0749	.00248139	458	209764	21.4009	.00218341
349	121801	18.6815	.00286533	404	163216	20.0998	.00247525	459	210681	21.4243	.00217865
350	122500	18.7083	.00285714	405	164025	20.1246	.00246914	460	211600	21.4476	.00217391
351	123201	18.7350	.00284900	406	164836	20.1494	.00246305	461	212521	21.4709	.00216920
352	123904	18.7617	.00284091	407	165649	20.1742	.00245700	462	213444	21.4942	.00216450
353	124609	18.7883	.00283286	408	166464	20.1990	.00245098	463	214369	21.5174	.00215983
354	125316	18.8149	.00282486	409	167281	20.2237	.00244499	464	215296	21.5407	.00215517
355	126025	18.8414	.00281690	410	168100	20.2485	.00243902	465	216225	21.5639	.00215054
356	126736	18.8680	.00280899	411	168921	20.2731	.00243309	466	217156	21.5870	.00214592
357	127499	18.8944	.00280112	412	169744	20.2978	.00242718	467	218089	21.6102	.00214133
358	128164	18.9209	.00279330	413	170569	20.3224	.00242131	468	219024	21.6333	.00213675
359	128881	18.9473	.00278552	414	171396	20.3470	.00241546	469	219961	21.6564	.00213220
360	129600	18.9737	.00277778	415	172225	20.3715	.00240964	470	220900	21.6795	.00212766
361	130321	19.0000	.00277000	416	173056	20.3961	.00240385	471	221841	21.7025	.00212314
362	131044	19.0263	.00276243	417	173889	20.4206	.00239808	472	222784	21.7256	.00211864
363	131769	19.0526	.00275482	418	174724	20.4450	.00239234	473	223729	21.7486	.00211416
364	132496	19.0788	.00274725	419	175561	20.4695	.00238663	474	224676	21.7715	.00210970
365	133225	19.1050	.00273973	420	176400	20.4939	.00238095	475	225625	21.7945	.00210526
366	133956	19.1311	.00273224	421	177241	20.5183	.00237530	476	226576	21.8174	.00210084
367	134689	19.1572	.00272480	422	178084	20.5426	.00236967	477	227529	21.8403	.00209644
368	135424	19.1833	.00271739	423	178929	20.5670	.00236407	478	228484	21.8632	.00209205
369	136161	19.2094	.00271003	424	179776	20.5913	.00235849	479	229441	21.8861	.00208768
370	136900	19.2354	.00270270	425	180625	20.6155	.00235294	480	230400	21.9089	.00208333
371	137641	19.2614	.00269542	426	181476	20.6398	.00234742	481	231361	21.9317	.00207900
372	138384	19.2873	.00268817	427	182329	20.6640	.00234192	482	232324	21.9545	.00207469
372	139129	19.3132	.00268097	428	183184	20.6882	.00233645	483	233289	21.9773	.00207039
374	139876	19.3391	.00267380	429	184041	20.7123	.00233100	484	234256	22.0000	.00206612
375	140625	19.3649	.00266667	430	184900	20.7364	.00232558	485	235225	22.0227	.00206186
376	141376	19.3907	.00265957	431	185761	20.7605	.00232019	486	236196	22.0454	.00205761
377	142129	19.4165	.00265252	432	186624	20.7846	.00231481	487	237169	22.0681	.00205339
378	142884	19.4422	.00264550	433	187489	20.8087	.00230947	488	238144	22.0907	.00204918
379	143641	19.4679	.00263852	434	188356	20.8327	.00230415	489	239121	22.1133	.00204499
380	144400	19.4936	.00263158	435	189225	20.8567	.00229885	490	240100	22.1359	.00204082
381	145161	19.5192	.00262467	436	190096	20.8806	.00229358	491	241081	22.1585	.00203666
382	145924	19.5448	.00261780	437	190969	20.9045	.00228833	492	242064	22.1811	.00203252
383	146689	19.5704	.00261097	438	191844	20.9284	.00229311	493	243049	22.2036	.00202840
384	147456	19.5959	.00260417	439	192721	20.9523	.00227790	494	244036	22.2261	.00202429
385	148225	19.6214	.00259740	440	193600	20.9762	.00227273	495	245025	22.2486	.00202020

N	N^2	$\sqrt{N}$	$1/N$	N	N^2	$\sqrt{N}$	$1/N$	N	N^2	$\sqrt{N}$	$1/N$
496	246016	22.2711	.00201613	551	303601	23.4734	.00181488	606	367236	24.6171	.00165017
497	247009	22.2935	.00201207	552	304704	23.4947	.00181159	607	368449	24.6374	.00164745
498	248004	22.3159	.00200803	553	305809	23.5160	.00180832	608	369664	24.6577	.00164474
499	249001	22.3383	.00200401	554	306916	23.5372	.00180505	609	370881	24.6779	.00164204
500	250000	22.3607	.00200000	555	308025	23.5584	.00180180	610	372100	24.6982	.00163934
501	251001	22.3830	.00199601	556	309136	23.5797	.00179856	611	373321	23.7184	.00163666
502	252004	22.4054	.00199203	557	310249	23.6008	.00179533	612	374544	24.7386	.00163399
503	253009	22.4277	.00198807	558	311364	23.6220	.00179211	613	375769	24.7588	.00163132
504	254016	22.4499	.00198413	559	312481	23.6432	.00178891	614	376996	24.7790	.00162866
505	255025	22.4722	.00298020	560	313600	23.6643	.00178571	615	378225	24.7992	.00162602
506	256036	22.4944	.00197628	561	314721	23.6854	.00178253	616	379456	24.8193	.00162338
507	257049	22.5167	.00197239	562	315844	23.7065	.00177936	617	380689	24.8395	.00162075
508	258064	22.5389	.00196850	563	316969	23.7276	.00177620	618	381924	24.8596	.00161812
509	259081	22.5610	.00196464	564	318096	23.7487	.00177305	619	383161	24.8797	.00161551
510	260100	22.5832	.00196078	565	319225	23.7697	.00176991	620	384400	24.8998	.00161290
511	261121	22.6053	.00195695	566	320356	23.7908	.00176678	621	385641	24.9199	.00161031
512	262144	22.6274	.00195312	567	321489	23.8118	.00176367	622	386884	24.9399	.00160772
513	263169	22.6495	.00194932	568	322624	23.8328	.00176056	623	388129	24.9600	.00160514
514	264196	22.6716	.00194553	569	323761	23.8537	.00175747	624	389376	24.9800	.00160256
515	265225	22.6936	.00194175	570	324900	23.8747	.00175439	625	390625	25.0000	.00160000
516	266256	22.7156	.00193798	571	326041	23.8956	.00175131	626	391876	25.0200	.00159744
517	267289	22.7376	.00193424	572	327184	23.9165	.00164825	627	393129	25.0400	.00159490
518	268324	22.7596	.00193050	573	328329	23.9374	.00174520	628	394384	25.0599	.00159236
519	269361	22.7816	.00192678	574	329476	23.9583	.00174216	629	395641	25.0799	.00158983
520	270400	22.8035	.00192308	575	330625	23.9792	.00173913	630	396900	25.0998	.00158730
521	271441	22.8254	.00191939	576	331776	24.0000	.00173611	631	398161	25.1197	.00158479
522	272484	22.8473	.00191571	577	332929	24.0208	.00173310	632	399424	25.1396	.00158228
523	273529	22.8692	.00191205	578	334084	24.0416	.00173010	633	400689	25.1595	.00157978
524	274576	22.8910	.00190840	579	335241	24.0624	.00172712	634	401956	25.1794	.00157729
525	275625	22.9129	.00190476	580	336400	24.0832	.00172414	635	403225	25.1992	.00157480
526	276676	22.9347	.00190114	581	337561	24.1039	.00172117	636	404496	25.2190	.00157233
527	277729	22.9565	.00189753	582	338724	24.1247	.00171821	637	405769	25.2389	.00156986
528	278784	22.9783	.00189394	583	339889	24.1454	.00171527	638	407044	25.2587	.00156740
529	279841	23.0000	.00189036	584	341056	24.1661	.00171233	639	408321	25.2784	.00156495
530	280900	23.0217	.00188679	585	342225	24.1868	.00170940	640	409600	25.2982	.00156250
531	281961	23.0434	.00188324	586	343396	24.2074	.00170648	641	410881	25.3180	.00156006
532	283024	23.0651	.00187970	587	344569	24.2281	.00170358	642	412164	25.3377	.00155763
533	284089	23.0868	.00187617	588	345744	24.2487	.00170068	643	413449	25.3574	.00155521
534	285156	23.1084	.00187266	589	346921	24.2693	.00169779	644	414736	25.3772	.00155280
535	286225	23.1301	.00186916	590	348100	24.2899	.00169492	645	416025	25.3969	.00155039
536	287296	23.1517	.00186567	591	349281	24.3105	.00169205	646	417316	25.4165	.00154799
537	288369	23.1733	.00186220	592	350464	24.3311	.00168919	647	418609	25.4362	.00154560
538	289444	23.1948	.00185874	593	351649	24.3516	.00168634	648	419904	25.4558	.0015432!
539	290521	23.2164	.00185529	594	352836	24.3721	.00168350	649	421201	25.4755	.00154083
540	291600	23.2379	.00185185	595	354025	24.3926	.00168067	650	422500	25.4951	.00153846
541	292681	23.2594	.00184843	596	355216	24.4131	.00167785	651	423801	25.5147	.00153610
542	293764	23.2809	.00184502	597	356409	24.4336	.00167504	652	425104	25.5343	.00153374
543	294849	23.3024	.00184162	598	357604	24.4540	.00167224	653	426409	25.5539	.00153139
544	295936	23.3238	.00183824	599	358801	24.4745	.00166945	654	427716	25.5734	.00152905
545	297025	23.3452	.00183486	600	360000	24.4949	.00166667	655	429025	25.5930	.00152672
546	298116	23.3666	.00183150	601	361201	24.5153	.00166389	656	430336	25.6125	.00152439
547	299209	23.2880	.00182815	602	302404	24.5357	.00166113	657	431649	25.6320	.00152207
548	300304	23.4094	.00182462	603	363609	24.5561	.00165837	658	432964	25.6515	.00151976
549	301401	23.4307	.00183149	604	364816	24.5764	.00165563	659	434281	25.6710	.00151745
550	302500	23.4521	.00181818	605	366025	24.5967	.00165289	660	435600	25.6905	.00151515

N	N²	√N	1/N	N	N²	√N	1/N	N	N²	√N	1/N
661	436921	25.7099	.00151286	716	512656	26.7582	.00139665	771	594441	27.7669	.00129702
662	438244	25.7294	.00151057	717	514089	26.7769	.00139470	772	595984	27.7849	.00129534
663	439569	25.7488	.00150830	718	515524	26.7955	.00139276	773	597529	27.8029	.00129366
664	440896	25.7682	.00150602	719	516961	26.8142	.00139082	774	599076	27.8209	.00129199
665	442225	25.7876	.00150376	720	518400	26.8328	.00138889	775	600625	27.8388	.00129032
666	443556	25.8070	.00150150	721	519841	26.8514	.00138696	776	602176	27.8568	.00128866
667	444889	25.8263	.00149925	722	521284	26.8701	.00138504	777	603729	27.8747	.00128700
668	446224	25.8457	.00149701	723	522729	26.8887	.00138313	778	605284	27.8927	.00128535
669	447561	25.8650	.00149477	724	524176	26.9072	.00138122	779	606841	27.9106	.00128370
670	448900	25.8844	.00149254	725	525625	26.9258	.00137931	780	608400	27.9285	.00128205
671	450241	25.9037	.00149031	726	527076	26.9444	.00137741	781	609961	27.9464	.00128041
672	451584	25.9230	.00148810	727	528529	26.9629	.00137552	782	611524	27.9643	.00127877
673	452929	25.9422	.00148588	728	529984	26.9815	.00137363	783	613089	27.9821	.00127714
674	454276	25.9615	.00148368	729	531441	27.0000	.00137174	784	614656	28.0000	.00127551
765	455625	25.9808	.00148148	730	532900	27.0185	.00136986	785	616225	28.0179	.00127389
676	456976	26.0000	.00147929	731	534361	27.0370	.00136799	786	617796	28.0357	.00127226
677	458329	26.0192	.00147710	732	535824	27.0555	.00136612	787	619369	28.0535	.00127065
678	459684	26.0384	.00147493	733	537289	27.0740	.00136426	788	620944	28.0713	.00126904
679	461041	26.0576	.00147275	734	538756	27.0924	.00136240	789	622521	28.0891	.00126743
680	462400	26.0768	.00147059	735	540225	27.1109	.00136054	790	624100	28.1069	.00126582
681	463761	26.0960	.00146843	736	541696	27.1293	.00135870	791	625681	28.1247	.00126422
682	465124	26.1151	.00146628	737	543169	27.1477	.00135685	792	627264	28.1425	.00126263
683	466489	26.1343	.00146413	738	544644	27.1662	.00135501	793	628849	28.1603	.00126103
684	467856	26.1534	.00146199	739	546121	27.1846	.00135318	794	630436	28.1780	.00125945
685	469225	26.1725	.00145985	740	547600	27.2029	.00135135	795	632025	28.1957	.00125786
686	470596	26.1916	.00145773	741	549081	27.2213	.00134953	796	633616	28.2135	.00125628
687	471969	26.2107	.00145560	742	550564	27.2397	.00134771	797	635209	28.2312	.00125471
688	473344	26.2298	.00145349	743	552049	27.2580	.00134590	798	636804	28.2489	.00125313
689	474721	26.2488	.00145138	744	553536	27.2764	.00134409	799	638401	28.2666	.00125156
690	476100	26.2679	.00144928	745	555025	27.2947	.00134228	800	640000	28.2843	.00125000
691	477481	26.2869	.00144718	746	556516	27.3130	.00134048	801	641601	28.3019	.00124844
692	478864	26.3059	.00144509	747	558009	27.3313	.00133869	802	643204	28.3196	.00124688
693	480249	26.3249	.00144300	748	559504	27.3496	.00133690	803	644809	28.3373	.00124533
694	481636	26.3439	.00144092	749	561001	27.3679	.00133511	804	646416	28.3549	.00124373
695	483025	26.3629	.00143885	750	562500	27.3861	.00133333	805	648025	28.3725	.00124224
696	484416	26.3818	.00143678	751	564001	27.4044	.00133156	806	649636	28.3901	.00124069
697	485809	26.4008	.00143472	752	565504	27.4226	.00132979	807	651249	28.4077	.00123916
698	487204	26.4197	.00143266	753	567009	27.4408	.00132802	808	625864	28.4253	.00123762
699	488601	26.4386	.00143062	754	568516	27.4591	.00132626	809	654481	28.4429	.00123609
700	490000	26.4575	.00142857	755	570025	27.4773	.00132450	810	656100	28.4605	.00123457
701	491401	26.4764	.00142653	756	571536	27.4955	.00132275	811	657721	28.4781	.00123305
702	492804	26.4953	.00142450	757	573049	27.5136	.00132100	812	659344	28.4956	.00123153
703	494209	26.5141	.00142248	758	574564	27.5318	.00131926	813	660969	28.5132	.00123001
704	495616	26.5330	.00142045	759	576081	27.5500	.00131752	814	662596	28.5307	.00122850
705	497025	26.5518	.00141844	760	577600	27.5681	.00131579	815	664225	28.5482	.00122699
706	498436	26.5707	.00141643	761	579121	27.5862	.00131406	816	665856	28.5657	.00122549
707	499849	26.5895	.00141443	762	580644	27.6043	.00131234	817	667489	28.5832	.00122399
708	501264	26.6083	.00141243	763	582169	27.6225	.00131062	818	669124	28.6007	.00122249
709	502681	26.6271	.00141044	764	583696	27.6405	.00130890	819	670761	28.6182	.00122100
710	504100	26.6458	.00140845	765	585225	27.6586	.00130719	820	672400	28.6356	.00121951
711	505521	26.6646	.00140647	766	586756	27.6767	.00130548	821	674041	28.6531	.00121803
712	506944	26.6833	.00140449	767	588289	27.6948	.00130378	822	675684	28.6705	.00121655
713	508369	26.7021	.00140252	768	589824	27.7128	.00130208	823	677329	28.6880	.00121507
714	509796	26.7208	.00140056	769	591361	27.7308	.00130039	824	678976	28.7054	.00121359
715	511225	26.7395	.00139860	770	592900	27.7489	.00129870	825	680625	28.7228	.00121212

N	N²	√N	1/N	N	N²	√N	1/N	N	N²	√N	1/N
826	682276	28.7402	.00121065	881	776161	29.6816	.00113507	936	876096	30.5941	.00106838
827	683929	28.7576	.00120919	882	777924	29.6985	.00113379	937	877969	30.6105	.00106724
828	685584	28.7750	.00120773	883	779689	29.7153	.00113250	938	879844	30.6268	.00106610
829	687241	28.7924	.00120627	884	781456	29.7321	.00113122	939	881721	30.6431	.00106496
830	688900	28.8097	.00120482	885	783225	29.7489	.00113994	940	883600	30.6594	.00106383
831	690561	28.8271	.00120337	886	784996	29.7658	.00112867	941	885481	30.6757	.00106270
832	692224	28.8444	.00120192	887	786769	29.7825	.00112740	942	887364	30.6920	.00106157
833	693889	28.8617	.00120048	888	788544	29.7993	.00112613	943	889249	30.7083	.00106045
834	695556	28.8791	.00119904	889	790321	29.8161	.00112486	944	891136	30.7246	.00105932
835	697225	28.8964	.00119760	890	792100	29.8329	.00112360	945	893025	30.7409	.00105820
836	698896	28.9137	.00119617	891	793881	29.8496	.00112233	946	894916	30.7571	.00105708
837	700569	28.9310	.00119474	892	795664	29.8664	.00112108	947	896809	30.7734	.00105597
838	702244	28.9482	.00119332	893	797449	29.8831	.00111982	948	898704	30.7896	.00105485
839	702244	28.9655	.00119190	894	799236	29.8998	.00111857	949	900601	30.8058	.00105374
840	705600	28.9828	.00119048	895	801025	29.9166	.00111732	950	902500	30.8221	.00105263
841	707281	29.0000	.00118906	896	902816	29.9333	.00111607	951	904401	30.8383	.00105152
842	708964	29.0172	.00118765	897	804609	29.9500	.00111483	952	906304	30.8545	.00105042
843	710649	29.0345	.00118624	898	806404	29.9666	.00111359	953	908209	30.8707	.00104932
844	712336	29.0517	.00118483	899	808201	29.9833	.00111235	954	910116	30.8869	.00104822
845	714025	29.0689	.00118343	900	810000	30.0000	.00111111	955	912025	30.9031	.00104712
846	715716	29.0861	.00118203	901	811801	30.0167	.00110988	956	913936	30.9192	.00104603
847	717409	29.1033	.00118064	902	813604	30.0333	.00110865	957	915849	30.9354	.00104493
848	719104	29.1204	.00117925	903	815409	30.0500	.00110742	958	917764	30.9516	.00104384
849	720801	29.1376	.00117786	904	817216	30.0666	.00110619	959	919681	30.9677	.00104275
850	722500	29.1548	.00117647	905	819025	30.0832	.00110497	960	921600	30.9839	.00104167
851	724201	29.1719	.00117509	906	820836	30.0998	.00110375	961	923521	31.0000	.00104058
852	725904	29.1890	.00117371	907	822649	30.1164	.00110254	962	925444	31.0161	.00103950
853	727509	29.2062	.00117233	908	824464	30.1330	.00110132	963	927369	31.0322	.00103842
854	729316	29.2233	.00117096	909	826281	30.1496	.00110011	964	929296	31.0483	.00103734
855	731025	29.2404	.00116959	910	828100	30.1662	.00109890	965	931225	31.0644	.00103627
856	732736	29.2575	.00116822	911	829921	30.1828	.00109769	966	933156	31.0805	.00103520
857	734449	29.2746	.00116686	912	831744	30.1993	.00109649	967	935089	31.0966	.00103413
858	736164	29.2916	.00116550	913	833569	30.2159	.00109529	968	937024	31.1127	.00103306
859	737881	29.3087	.00116414	914	835396	30.2324	.00109409	969	938961	31.1288	.00103199
860	739600	29.3258	.00116279	915	837225	30.2490	.00109290	970	940900	31.1448	.00103093
861	741321	29.3428	.00116144	916	839056	30.2655	.00109170	971	942841	31.1609	.00102987
862	743044	29.3598	.00116009	917	840889	30.2820	.00109051	972	944784	31.1769	.00102881
963	744769	29.3769	.00115875	918	842724	30.2985	.00108932	973	946729	31.1929	.00102775
864	746496	29.3939	.00115741	919	844561	30.3150	.00108814	974	948676	31.2090	.00102669
865	784225	29.4109	.00115607	920	846400	30.3315	.00108696	975	950625	31.2250	.00102564
866	749956	29.4279	.00115473	921	848241	30.3480	.00108578	976	952576	31.2410	.00102459
867	751689	29.4449	.00115340	922	850084	30.3645	.00108460	977	954529	31.2570	.00102354
868	753424	29.4618	.00115207	923	851929	30.3809	.00108342	978	956484	31.2730	.00102249
869	755161	29.4788	.00115075	924	853776	30.3974	.00108225	979	958441	31.2890	.00102145
870	756900	29.4958	.00114943	925	855625	30.4138	.00108108	980	960400	31.3050	.00102041
871	758641	29.5127	.00114811	926	857476	30.4302	.00107991	981	962361	31.3209	.00101937
872	760384	29.5296	.00114679	927	859329	30.4467	.00107875	982	964324	31.3369	.00101833
873	762129	29.5466	.00114548	928	861184	30.4631	.00107759	983	966289	31.3528	.00101729
874	763876	29.5635	.00114416	929	863041	30.4795	.00107643	984	968256	31.3688	.00101626
875	765625	29.5804	.00114286	930	864900	30.4959	.00107527	985	970225	31.3847	.00101523
876	767376	29.5973	.00114155	931	866761	30.5123	.00107411	986	972196	31.4006	.00101420
877	769129	29.6142	.00114025	932	868624	30.5287	.00107296	987	974169	31.4166	.00101317
878	770884	29.6311	.00113895	933	870489	30.5450	.00107181	988	976144	31.4325	.00101215
879	772641	29.6479	.00113766	934	872356	30.5614	.00107066	989	978121	31.4484	.00101112
880	774400	29.6848	.00113636	935	874225	30.5778	.00106952	990	980100	31.4643	.00101010

N	N^2	$\sqrt{N}$	$1/N$	N	N^2	$\sqrt{N}$	$1/N$
991	982081	31.4802	.00100908	996	992016	31.5595	.00100402
992	984064	31.4960	.00100806	997	994009	31.5753	.00103842
993	986049	31.5119	.00100705	998	996004	31.5911	.00100200
994	988036	31.5278	.00100604	999	998001	31.6070	.00100100
995	990025	31.5436	.00100503	1000	1000000	31.6228	.00100000

APPENDIX C

Significance Levels from Normal Curve*

The values in this table represent the proportional area beyond z in the normal curve, with a mean of 0, a standard deviation (s) of 1.00, and a total area of 1.00. Since the normal curve is symmetrical, values are the same for either positive or negative z (one-tail significance level). Two-tail tests of significance would have values twice as large. For example, a $z = 2.33$ would indicate a significant difference (reject the null hypothesis) at the .0099 level for a one-tail test and at .0198 (2 × .0099) for a two-tail test.

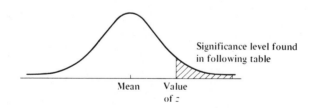

Significance level found in following table

Mean   Value of z

* Taken from "Fundamentals of Behavioral Statistics," 2nd Ed. R. P. Runyon and A. Haber. Addison-Wesley, Reading, Massachusetts (1971).

z	Area beyond z	z	Area beyond z	z	Area beyond z	z	Area beyond z	z	Area beyond z	z	Area beyond z	z	Area beyond z
0.00	.5000	0.55	.2912	1.10	.1357	1.65	.0495	2.20	.0139	2.74	.0031	3.40	.0003
0.01	.4960	0.56	.2877	1.11	.1335	1.66	.0485	2.21	.0136	2.75	.0030	3.45	.0003
0.02	.4920	0.57	.2843	1.12	.1314	1.67	.0475			2.76	.0029	3.50	.0002
0.03	.4880	0.58	.2810	1.13	.1292	1.68	.0465	2.22	.0132	2.77	.0028	3.60	.0002
0.04	.4840	0.59	.2776	1.14	.1271	1.69	.0455	2.23	.0129	2.78	.0027	3.70	.0001
								2.24	.0125			3.80	.0001
0.05	.4801	0.60	.2743	1.15	.1251	1.70	.0446	2.25	.0122				
0.06	.4761	0.61	.2709	1.16	.1230	1.71	.0436	2.26	.0119	2.79	.0026	3.90	.00005
0.07	.4721	0.62	.2676	1.17	.1210	1.72	.0427			2.80	.0026	4.00	.00003
0.08	.4681	0.63	.2643	1.18	.1190	1.73	.0418	2.27	.0116	2.81	.0025		
0.09	.4641	0.64	.2611	1.19	.1170	1.74	.0409	2.28	.0113	2.82	.0024		
								2.29	.0110	2.83	.0023		
0.10	.4602	0.65	.2578	1.20	.1151	1.75	.0401	2.30	.0107				
0.11	.4562	0.66	.2546	1.21	.1131	1.76	.0392	2.31	.0104	2.84	.0023		
0.12	.4522	0.67	.2514	1.22	.1112	1.77	.0384			2.85	.0022		
0.13	.4483	0.68	.2483	1.23	.1093	1.78	.0375	2.32	.0102	2.86	.0021		
0.14	.4443	0.69	.2451	1.24	.1075	1.79	.0367	2.33	.0099	2.87	.0021		
								2.34	.0096	2.88	.0020		
0.15	.4404	0.70	.2420	1.25	.1056	1.80	.0359	2.35	.0094				
0.16	.4364	0.71	.2389	1.26	.1038	1.81	.0351	2.36	.0091	2.89	.0019		
0.17	.4325	0.72	.2358	1.27	.1020	1.82	.0344			2.90	.0019		
0.18	.4286	0.73	.2327	1.28	.1003	1.83	.0336	2.37	.0089	2.91	.0018		
0.19	.4247	0.74	.2296	1.29	.0985	1.84	.0329	2.38	.0087	2.92	.0018		
								2.39	.0084	2.93	.0017		
0.20	.4207	0.75	.2266	1.30	.0968	1.85	.0322	2.40	.0082				
0.21	.4168	0.76	.2236	1.31	.0951	1.86	.0314	2.41	.0080	2.94	.0016		
0.22	.4129	0.77	.2206	1.32	.0934	1.87	.0307			2.95	.0016		
0.23	.4090	0.78	.2177	1.33	.0918	1.88	.0301	2.42	.0078	2.96	.0015		
0.24	.4052	0.79	.2148	1.34	.0901	1.89	.0294	2.43	.0075	2.97	.0015		
								2.44	.0073	2.98	.0014		
0.25	.4013	0.80	.2119	1.35	.0885	1.90	.0287	2.45	.0071				
0.26	.3974	0.81	.2090	1.36	.0869	1.91	.0281	2.46	.0069	2.99	.0014		
0.27	.3936	0.82	.2061	1.37	.0853	1.92	.0274			3.00	.0013		
0.28	.3897	0.83	.2033	1.38	.0838	1.93	.0268	2.47	.0068	3.01	.0013		
0.29	.3859	0.84	.2005	1.39	.0823	1.94	.0262	2.48	.0066	3.02	.0013		
								2.49	.0064	3.03	.0012		
0.30	.3821	0.85	.1977	1.40	.0808	1.95	.0256	2.50	.0062				
0.31	.3783	0.86	.1949	1.41	.0793	1.96	.0250	2.51	.0060	3.04	.0012		
0.32	.3745	0.87	.1922	1.42	.0778	1.97	.0244			3.05	.0011		
0.33	.3707	0.88	.1894	1.43	.0764	1.98	.0239	2.52	.0059	3.06	.0011		
0.34	.3669	0.89	.1867	1.44	.0749	1.99	.0233	2.53	.0057	3.07	.0011		
								2.54	.0055	3.08	.0010		
0.35	.3632	0.90	.1841	1.45	.0735	2.00	.0228	2.55	.0054				
0.36	.3594	0.91	.1814	1.46	.0721	2.01	.0222	2.56	.0052	3.09	.0010		
0.37	.3557	0.92	.1788	1.47	.0708	2.02	.0217			3.10	.0010		
0.38	.3520	0.93	.1762	1.48	.0694	2.03	.0212	2.57	.0051	3.11	.0009		
0.39	.3483	0.94	.1736	1.49	.0681	2.04	.0207	2.58	.0049	3.12	.0009		
								2.59	.0048	3.13	.0009		
0.40	.3446	0.95	.1711	1.50	.0668	2.05	.0202	2.60	.0047				
0.41	.3409	0.96	.1685	1.51	.0655	2.06	.0197	2.61	.0045	3.14	.0008		
0.42	.3372	0.97	.1660	1.52	.0643	2.07	.0192			3.15	.0008		
0.43	.3336	0.98	.1635	1.53	.0630	2.08	.0188	2.62	.0044	3.16	.0008		
0.44	.3300	0.99	.1611	1.54	.0618	2.09	.0183	2.63	.0043	3.17	.0008		
								2.64	.0041	3.18	.0007		
0.45	.3264	1.00	.1587	1.55	.0606	2.10	.0179	2.65	.0040				
0.46	.3228	1.01	.1562	1.56	.0594	2.11	.0174	2.66	.0039	3.19	.0007		
0.47	.3192	1.02	.1539	1.57	.0582	2.12	.0170			3.20	.0007		
0.48	.3156	1.03	.1515	1.58	.0571	2.13	.0166	2.67	.0038	3.21	.0007		
0.49	.3121	1.04	.1492	1.59	.0559	2.14	.0162	2.68	.0037	3.22	.0006		
								2.69	.0036	3.23	.0006		
0.50	.3085	1.05	.1469	1.60	.0548	2.15	.0158	2.70	.0035				
0.51	.3050	1.06	.1446	1.61	.0537	2.16	.0154	2.71	.0034	3.24	.0006		
0.52	.3015	1.07	.1423	1.62	.0526	2.17	.0150			3.25	.0006		
0.53	.2981	1.08	.1401	1.63	.0516	2.18	.0146	2.72	.0033	3.30	.0005		
0.54	.2946	1.09	.1379	1.64	.0505	2.19	.0143	2.73	.0032	3.35	.0004		

APPENDIX D

Table of χ^{2*}

* Taken from "Fundamentals of Behavioral Statistics," 2nd Ed. R. P. Runyon and A. Haber. Addison-Wesley, Reading, Massachusetts (1971).

Degrees of freedom df	P = .99	P = .98	P = .95	P = .90	P = .80	P = .70	P = .50	P = .30	P = .20	P = .10	P = .05	P = .02	P = .01
1	.000157	.000628	.00393	.0158	.0642	.148	.455	1.074	1.642	2.706	3.841	5.412	6.635
2	.0201	.0404	.103	.211	.446	.713	1.386	2.408	3.219	4.605	5.991	7.824	9.210
3	.115	.185	.352	.584	1.005	1.424	2.366	3.665	4.642	6.251	7.815	9.837	11.341
4	.293	.429	.711	1.064	1.649	2.195	3.357	4.878	5.989	7.779	9.488	11.668	13.277
5	.554	.752	1.145	1.610	2.343	3.000	4.351	6.064	7.289	9.236	11.070	13.388	15.086
6	.872	1.134	1.635	2.204	3.070	3.828	5.348	7.231	8.558	10.645	12.592	15.033	16.812
7	1.239	1.564	2.167	2.833	3.822	4.671	6.346	8.383	9.803	12.017	14.067	16.622	18.475
8	1.646	2.032	2.733	3.490	4.594	5.527	7.344	9.524	11.030	13.362	15.507	18.168	20.090
9	2.088	2.532	3.325	4.168	5.380	6.393	8.343	10.656	12.242	14.684	16.919	19.679	21.666
10	2.558	3.059	3.940	4.865	6.179	7.267	9.342	11.781	13.442	15.987	18.307	21.161	23.209
11	3.053	3.609	4.575	5.578	6.989	8.148	10.341	12.899	14.631	17.275	19.675	22.618	24.725
12	3.571	4.178	5.226	6.304	7.807	9.034	11.340	14.011	15.812	18.549	21.026	24.054	26.217
13	4.107	4.765	5.892	7.042	8.634	9.926	12.340	15.119	16.985	19.812	22.362	25.472	27.688
14	4.660	5.368	6.571	7.790	9.467	10.821	13.339	16.222	18.151	21.064	23.685	26.873	29.141
15	5.229	5.985	7.261	8.547	10.307	11.721	14.339	17.322	19.311	22.307	24.996	28.259	30.578
16	5.812	6.614	7.962	9.312	11.152	12.624	15.338	18.418	20.465	23.542	26.296	29.633	32.000
17	6.408	7.255	8.672	10.085	12.002	13.531	16.338	19.511	21.615	24.769	27.587	30.995	33.409
18	7.015	7.906	9.390	10.865	12.857	14.440	17.338	20.601	22.760	25.989	28.869	32.346	34.805
19	7.633	8.567	10.117	11.651	13.716	15.352	18.338	21.689	23.900	27.204	30.144	33.687	36.191
20	8.260	9.237	10.851	12.443	14.578	16.266	19.337	22.775	25.038	28.412	31.410	35.020	37.566
21	8.897	9.915	11.591	13.240	15.445	17.182	20.337	23.858	26.171	29.615	32.671	36.343	38.932
22	9.542	10.600	12.338	14.041	16.314	18.101	21.337	24.939	27.301	30.813	33.924	37.659	40.289
23	10.196	11.293	13.091	14.848	17.187	19.021	22.337	26.018	28.429	32.007	35.172	38.968	41.638
24	10.856	11.992	13.848	15.659	18.062	19.943	23.337	27.096	29.553	33.196	36.415	40.270	42.980
25	11.524	12.697	14.611	16.473	18.940	20.867	24.337	28.172	30.675	34.382	37.652	41.566	44.314
26	12.198	13.409	15.379	17.292	19.820	21.792	25.336	29.246	31.795	35.563	38.885	42.856	45.642
27	12.879	14.125	16.151	18.114	20.703	22.719	26.336	30.319	32.912	36.741	40.113	44.140	46.963
28	13.565	14.847	16.928	18.939	21.588	23.647	27.336	31.391	34.027	37.916	41.337	45.419	48.278
29	14.256	15.574	17.708	19.768	22.475	24.577	28.336	32.461	35.139	39.087	42.557	46.693	49.588
30	14.953	16.306	18.493	20.599	23.364	25.508	29.336	33.530	36.250	40.256	43.773	47.962	50.892

Examples of Tests

This appendix is included with some apprehension. It is clearly not an integral part of the book. Rather it suggests some "next steps" in a few limited areas. The concepts presented in Chapter 8 should be viewed as a prerequisite for this appendix. An understanding of the scope of physical performance and fitness will place this appendix into proper perspective. It would take a series of monographs to deal inclusively with the components of physical performance and fitness. Obviously, one appendix will just begin to scratch the surface and will not necessarily deal with the aspects of performance and fitness most relevant for specific teachers and/or students in particular situations with unique objectives.

With these reservations, this appendix deals with the following questions:

1. What is the recommended sequence of testing for the components of physical performance and fitness?
2. What are some examples of tests of selected aspects of physical performance and fitness?

Sequence of Testing

The specific objectives of participants and/or programs will cause special emphasis to be placed on various levels of particular aspects of performance and fitness. The following testing order is recommended, with appropriate modifications for the specific situations.

1. *Legal and medical waivers.* The person is medically "cleared" to participate in the physical activity program. Unless in a required class, he (or his parent or guardian for minors) has given his "informed consent." Informed consent normally consists of reading a description of the program, then signing a statement that, understanding the program, the person is willing to assume all risks involved.*

* Many of these forms were adapted from those developed under the direction of Drs. T. K. Cureton and B. H. Massey, with assistance of the laboratory staff at the University of Illinois Physical Fitness Research Laboratory. Medical and legal assistance were received from both the University of Illinois and Temple University.

BIOKINETICS RESEARCH LABORATORY
MEDICAL WAIVER

Temple University
Biokinetics Research Laboratory
Department of HPER 787-8707
To the Attending Physician of (Mr., Mrs., Miss)_____:

This person has volunteered to participate in a physical activity program under the supervision of our laboratory. Please advise us concerning his current health status and capability for engaging in such a program.

Sincerely yours,

B. Don Franks, Coordinator

Is there any evidence of:		YES NO
1. Cardiovascular disease	(a) at present	
	(b) past history	
2. Significant disorders of heart rhythm	(a) transient	
	(b) chronic	
3. Defect of cardiac conduction system		
4. Peripheral arterial insufficiency of	(a) central nervous system	
	(b) skeletal muscle	
5. Paroxysmal or chronic disorder of respiratory system especially	(a) asthma	
	(b) emphysema	
6. Central nervous system disorders or residuals thereof		
7. Functional impairment of musculo-skeletal system		
8. Other:		

COMMENTS: (Please comment regarding any of the above and/or indicate any specific limitations to participation.)

The individual named above is capable of engaging in vigorous physical activity.

Date_____   Signed_____
(physician)

BIOKINETICS RESEARCH LABORATORY LEGAL RELEASE

Date_____

I hereby request Temple University to accept me for admission to its Physical Fitness Program as outlined on the attached sheet marked "A" and made a part hereof which is administered by its Department of Health, Physical Education and Recreation. In consideration for such acceptance and admission, I hereby release and discharge the University, its officers, agents, staff members, or employees, and each of them, from any and all claims and demands of whatever nature I may hereafter assert against them on account of any accident, injury, or illness which I may sustain while in attendance in said Physical Fitness Program or as a result of such attendance, and any and all consequences thereof.

I acknowledge that I have read a description of the specific project of the Physical Fitness Program in which I will participate and that I understand the nature of the program and the risk, from overexertion, for example, to me of participation in this program.

In consideration of my acceptance and admission to said Physical Fitness Program, I hereby assume all risks and hazards to me, probable and improbable, associated with participation in said program.

Partial or complete revocation of this RELEASE shall not be effective until notice in writing by me shall have been delivered to _____ at _____.

Witness	Signature	Age

CONSENT OF PARENTS OR GUARDIANS AND RELEASE

Date_____

The undersigned hereby consent to participation in the aforementioned Physical Fitness Program by the above-named person. We acknowledge that we have read a description of the program and recognize the risks inherent in any exertion. We hereby RELEASE Temple University from any and all claim arising therefrom.

Partial or complete revocation of the CONSENT and RELEASE shall not be effective until notice in writing by me shall have been delivered to _____ _____ at _____.

Witness	Parent

Witness	Parent

2. *Background information.* It is useful to determine the type of persons involved in the program. Age, sex, type, and amount of regular physical activity, diet, major health problems, etc., are often included. Personal questions may be appropriate in voluntary programs where people come for help in their physical performance and fitness, but they should be avoided in required classes and in most school situations.

BIOKINETICS RESEARCH LABORATORY
DIETARY RECORD FORM

Please furnish the dietary information requested below as accurately as you can. This form is to be completed for 3 days (2 weekdays and 1 weekend day). Return all the forms when you come for your next test in the Biokinetics Research Laboratory.

Name_____   Date_____

Number of Servings	Food Item Indicate *kind* of food or beverage consumed. (Please indicate components of dishes like casseroles, etc.)
Breakfast	
Lunch	
Supper	
Between-meal snacks	

BIOKINETICS RESEARCH LABORATORY

REMINDER—FITNESS TESTS

Name	Day	Date	Time

Come to Biokinetics Research
Laboratory,

HPER Room_____.

Instructions. Please observe the following (unless given special directions):

1. Bring gym shorts.
2. No meal or food intake for at least three (3) hours prior to test.
3. Minimal physical activity on day of test (no regular work-out prior to test).
4. Drink nothing but water for at least three (3) hours prior to test.
5. No tobacco or medication for at least three (3) hours prior to test.

Cancellation. If you cannot keep this appointment, please call 787-8707 *or* 787-8753.

BIOKINETICS RESEARCH LABORATORY
ADULT PHYSICAL FITNESS QUESTIONNAIRE

Date_____

Name_____ Sex_____ Date of Birth_____

Home Address_____ Phone_____

Work Address_____ Phone_____

Occupation_____ Employer_____

Previous Major Diseases_____

Family History of Major Diseases_____

Regular Medication_____

Weakness from Injuries or Diseases_____

Sleep, hours/night_____ Cigarettes/day_____ Coffee, cups/day_____

    Soft drinks/day_____

Weight at age 20_____ Have you been involved in our Adult Fitness Program?_____ Initial date?_____ Under supervision of_____

Persistent complaints: (Please check those applicable)

Morning fatigue____	Abdominal pain____	Headaches____
Mid-day fatigue____	Low back pain____	Nervousness____
Evening fatigue____	Leg pain____	Constipation____
Frequent colds____	Knee discomfort____	Chest pains____
Sore throat____	Ankle discomfort____	Other (specify)____
Nasal trouble____	Foot discomfort____	
Digestive upsets____	Swollen joints____	

Cont. on p. 202.

Cont. from p. 201.

Indicate those activities participated in regularly (at least weekly during season). Estimate the hours per week and the number of years for each activity.

Type	Hr/wk	Years	Type	Hr/wk	Years
Badminton			Hunting		
Basketball			Ice skating		
Bicycling			Jogging		
Boating			Lawn work		
Bowling			Skiing		
Calisthenics			Softball		
Camping			Squash		
Cross-country skiing			Swimming		
Dancing			Tennis		
Endurance running			Volleyball		
Fishing			Walking		
Gardening			Water skiing		
Golf			Other (specify)		
Handball					
Hiking					
Horseback riding					

BIOKINETICS RESEARCH LABORATORY
SUBJECT CONTROL INFORMATION

Code _____   Name_____   _____   _____
                              Last   First   Middle

Date_____   Time_____

Time Span Covered: _____   _____ *to* _____   _____   Total Hr____
                      Date   Time   Date   Time

Please complete the appropriate items. This information is necessary to properly
evaluate the results of the tests administered.

A. General Health Status
   1. General Feeling: Good_____   Normal_____   Below normal_____
   2. Unusual Conditions:
        Head cold____   Nervous tension____
        Chest cold____   Nasal-head congestion____
        Feverish____   Allergic reactions____
        Headache____   Kind:_____
        Nausea____   _____
        Diziness____   Other: _____
        Cramps____   _____
   3. Menstrual cycle: Date when last period began_____
                       Date when last period terminated_____

B. Rest and Sleep
              Time to bed   Arising time   Duration
              _____   _____   _____
              _____   _____   _____
              _____   _____   _____
                                           Total time_____

C. Physical Activity
                                    Time
          Kind   Time begun   terminated   Duration
          _____   _____   _____   _____
          _____   _____   _____   _____
          _____   _____   _____   _____
                                              Total_____

Cont. on p. 204.

Cont. from p. 203.

D. Food Intake

    1. Amount: Normal_____   Above normal_____   Below normal_____
    2. Last Meal: Time_____   Heavy_____   Average_____   Light_____
    3. Last Food Intake: Same as above_____   Other:_____
       If Other: Kind and amount_____   Time_____
            Hours prior to arrival at lab_____

E. Beverage Intake Other Than with Meals

Kind	Amount	Time of last intake	Hours prior to arrival at lab
Water	_____	_____	_____
Coffee	_____	_____	_____
Tea	_____	_____	_____
Milk	_____	_____	_____
Fruit juice	_____	_____	_____
Soft drinks	_____	_____	_____
Beer or wine	_____	_____	_____
Alcohol	_____	_____	_____
Other: _____	_____	_____	_____
_____	_____	_____	_____
_____	_____	_____	_____
_____	_____	_____	_____

F. Tobacco: None_____   Some_____

Kind	Amount	Time of last intake	Hours prior to arrival at lab
_____	_____	_____	_____
_____	_____	_____	_____

G. Medicine and Drugs: None_____   Some_____

Kind	Amount	Time of last intake	Hours prior to arrival at lab
_____	_____	_____	_____
_____	_____	_____	_____
_____	_____	_____	_____
_____	_____	_____	_____

3. *Sociopsychological variables.* These variables may be appropriate for some situations; however, their use should normally be cleared with participants and appropriate authorities prior to their use.

4. *Body composition.*

5. *Efficiency at rest.* Subject control information can be obtained to determine if the pretest instructions were followed, as well as to find any unusual conditions that might invalidate the test results.

After evaluation of medical information, background information, body composition, and resting efficiency, if further activity is not contraindicated, then proceed with:

6. *Efficiency.* The working efficiency can be determined by testing the response to a standard (submaximal) physical stressor.

7. *Skills.* Both underlying and game skills relevant to the program objectives should be tested.

After evaluation of the working capacity, at submaximal levels, and skills, if further activity is not contraindicated, then proceed with:

8. *Activity program.* The specific activities included will depend on the objectives of the participants and program.

After initial adaptation to the regular, vigorous activity, components of endurance may be evaluated. These might be of little interest in some situations (for example, for senior citizens) and contraindicated in others (some rehabilitation patients).

9. *Muscular endurance*
10. *Cardiovascular endurance*
11. *Continue activity program*
12. *Periodic retests of components of performance and fitness*
13. *Evaluation of participants*
14. *Revision of activity program*

Examples of Tests in Selected Areas

It must be emphasized again that this section will include only a small portion of the possible scope of performance and fitness. These tests will not adequately represent all levels of the components of physical performance and fitness, and they may be irrelevant or im-

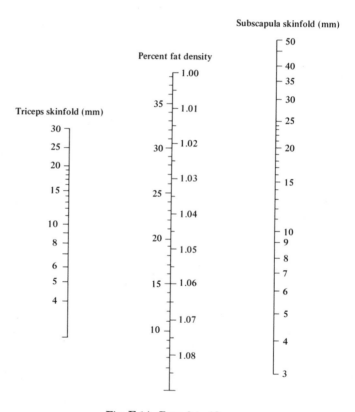

Fig. E.1A. Boys 9 to 12

Fig. E.1. (A–D). Nomograms for estimation of body density/percent fat. Used by permission, J. Parizkova, Total body fat and skinfold thickness in children. *Metabolism*, 1961, **10**, 794–807.

practical for a specific testing situation. Chapter 2 should be reviewed for criteria for test selection. The tests we have selected fall short of optimal criteria. In addition, practical considerations were given high priority in the selection of tests. Examples of practical tests that can be used in mass testing situations are presented. References are included for those who have more research equipment, personnel, and time to test individuals.

BODY COMPOSITION

One of the most useful variables in the area of body composition which can be estimated fairly easily is the percent of the total body weight that is fat. From Parizkova's nomograms (see Fig. E.1) the percent fat can be estimated for boys and girls, 9 to 16 years of age, by

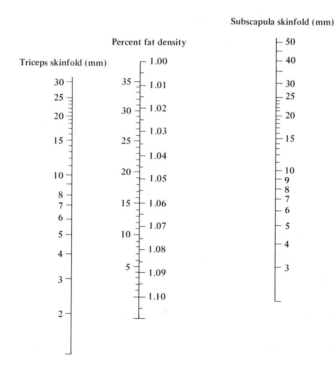

Fig. E.1B. Boys 13 to 16

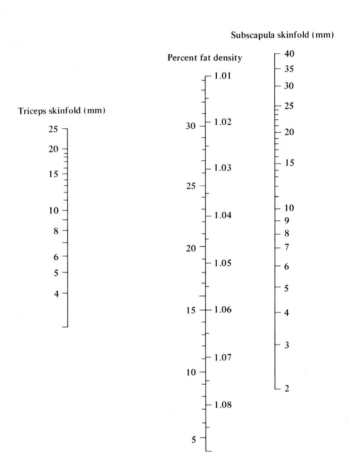

Fig. E.1C. Girls 9 to 12

using skinfold fat measures from the triceps and subscapula. The skin-fold fat measures are taken with skinfold calipers, such as the Lange.*
Take the skinfolds on the right side of the body. Pinch the skin so

* Cambridge Scientific Industries, Cambridge, Maryland.

that the least fold possible is used. Measure the thickness of the fold about 1 cm above the caliper. For the triceps, a vertical fold is taken at the midposterior midpoint between the tip of the acromion and the tip of the olecranon. The fold can be grasped while the elbow is at a 90° angle; then the arm is relaxed (by the side), and the skinfold is measured. For the subscapular, a *diagonal* fold (parallel to the line of the bottom of the scapular) is taken while the subject is standing in a relaxed position. Repeat the measure on each skinfold until three values are within 1 mm of each other. Find the value of the skinfolds on the appropriate nomogram; then find the estimated percent fat by connecting the two values with a piece of string (or straightedge).

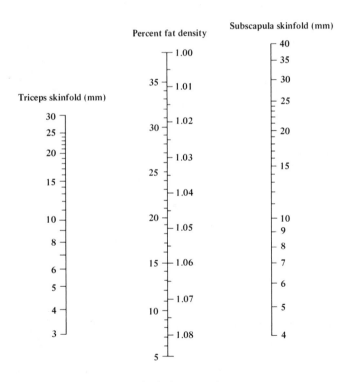

Fig. E.1D. Girls 13 to 16

STRENGTH

Berger has developed the concept of measuring strength by determining a person's one-repetition maximum (1-RM) or the maximum amount of weight that can be lifted (for a particular task) at one time. The advantage of using chinning, or dipping, to determine the I-RM is that it takes the body weight into account. Thus by taking the maximum number of chins and the person's body weight, his estimated 1-RM can be determined from Table E.1.

EFFICIENCY

One simple measure of a person's efficiency is his resting heart rate. The more blood that is ejected per minute (stroke volume), the fewer times the heart needs to beat during the minute to accomplish the same amount of work. It is very easy to teach persons to take their own heart rate. Thus the resting heart rate (before getting out of bed in the morning) can be determined by the students themselves. In addition, a standard amount of exercise can be done by the student, and his heart rate taken immediately after the exercise. Thus the student can see any changes made in his ability to adapt to a standard amount of work.

CARDIOVASCULAR ENDURANCE

There are basically two ways to measure cardiovascular endurance: (1) measure some component of cardiovascular function directly, during work; (2) measure an endurance performance, inferring that persons with better endurance performance have better cardiovascular endurance. The first type of test (direct measure of cardiovascular function) is normally done in research laboratories (for example, maximal $\dot{V}O_2$), and the second type of test (performance test) is normally done in the field. For a performance test, the time for running a certain distance (or distance during a certain time) has been widely used. The longer the run, the more likely it will reflect cardiovascular endurance (rather than skill, explosive power, etc.). The two-mile run is recommended. Whenever possible, students should be given some practice in running this distance and in pacing themselves. In addition, groups of about the same capability should run together.

TABLE E.1

Prediction of Chinning or Dipping Strength from Number of Repetitions Performed at Body Weight[a]

Body weight (pounds)	Number of repetitions																									
	1	2	3	4	5	6	7	8	9	10	11	12	13	14	15	16	17	18	19	20	21	22	23	24	25	26
110	110	113	117	120	124	127	131	134	138	141	145	148	152	155	157	160	164	167	171	174	178	181	185	188	192	195
120	120	124	128	132	136	140	144	148	152	156	160	164	168	172	176	180	184	188	192	196	200	204	208	212	216	220
130	130	135	140	145	150	155	160	165	170	175	180	186	190	195	199	204	209	213	217	222	226	231	236	240	245	250
140	140	145	152	157	163	168	174	179	184	189	193	199	204	209	212	218	223	228	231	236	241	246	251	255	260	266
150	150	156	163	169	176	182	188	193	198	203	207	212	217	222	226	232	237	242	246	251	256	261	266	271	276	281
160	160	166	174	179	186	192	198	203	208	214	219	224	230	235	240	246	251	257	262	266	271	276	282	289	295	301
170	170	177	184	190	196	202	208	213	219	225	231	236	242	248	254	260	266	272	278	284	290	296	302	308	314	320
180	180	187	194	200	206	213	220	225	231	238	244	251	257	263	270	276	283	289	296	302	309	316	322	329	335	341
190	190	197	204	211	217	224	231	238	244	251	258	265	272	279	286	293	300	307	314	321	328	335	343	350	356	363
200	200	207	215	222	228	236	243	250	257	265	271	279	286	294	300	308	315	323	329	337	344	351	359	366	373	380
210	210	218	225	233	240	248	255	263	270	278	285	293	300	308	315	323	330	338	345	353	360	368	375	383	390	398
220	220	228	236	244	252	260	268	276	284	292	300	308	316	324	332	340	348	356	364	372	380	388	396	404	412	420
230	230	238	247	255	264	272	281	289	298	306	314	323	332	340	349	357	366	374	383	391	400	408	417	425	434	442

[a] Used by permission, R. A. Berger, Determination of a method to predict 1-RM chin and dip from repetitive chins and dips. *Research Quarterly*, 1967, *38*; 330–335.

Several can run together, by having the timer stand at the finish line and call out the time as the runners cross the finish line. It is up to the individual to listen for his own time (or appoint a partner to listen for an individual's time).

SPORTS SKILL TESTS

Only a few examples are presented here, with the idea that after carefully reviewing those tests included in this book the student should review tests in an area of his choosing and select two or three which he would administer to his class. By having to defend his selections the student will become more knowledgeable about the available possibilities and will develop an increased understanding of the factors that affect his decisions. The student is referred to AAHPER publications including the *Research Quarterly*, and specific sport test manuals as well as theses and dissertations.

Basketball

The Diagonal Wall Pass Test, originally called the Edgren Ball Handling Test, has been a useful tool to evaluate ball and body handling ability. The test area is marked off by a line 7½ feet (line A) from a wall and parallel to it, which is intercepted by two perpendicular lines beginning at line A and 5½ feet apart (neutral area). The wall is marked with two vertical lines 3 feet apart and equidistant from the neutral area on the floor markings.

The subject stands at either the right or left area with the ball in hand. On the signal "ready go," he throws the ball diagonally across so that the ball rebounds from the far area without landing on a line or within the neutral area. The student then runs to retrieve the ball and again passes the ball diagonally across. The score is the sum total of successful valid passes in three 20-second (for high school) or 30-second (college students) trials.

A foul is incurred if the subject steps on or over any restraining line before releasing the ball or allowing the ball to touch the floor before hitting the wall. Any type of pass may be used.

This test is limited only by the number of areas and basketballs available. To facilitate the testing procedure, one central timer should be used with three helpers per testing station: one watching

for line violations, one counting the number of legal passes, and one
scoring. A rotation system can be easily developed among four to six
students per group.

Golf

The purpose of the West and Thrope eight-iron approach test is
to assess one's "ability to perform on eight-iron approach shot at a
distance of 12 yards from the pin." The equipment includes a 72-
square-foot area with a target which will be described later, 14 regulation golf balls, and one eight-iron per subject as well as one marker.
The target includes six concentric circles with the smallest having a
$1\frac{1}{2}$-yard radius and each circle increasing in size by $1\frac{1}{2}$ yards (radius)
until the outermost circle (sixth circle) has a 9-yard radius. A restraining line is 12 yards from the pin which is located in the center of the
smallest circle. The circles are scored with 7 points for the innermost,
decreasing by 1 point until the outermost circle has a value of 2 and the
remaining area between the restraining line and the target has a value
of 1.

Two to eight students may be tested at one time, with each having
one trial before beginning the second. The test consists in twelve trials.
Approximately 30 students may be tested in a 35-minute period.

Two aspects—angle of projection and final ball position—are considered in scoring this test. The angle of projection is rated by an
experienced evaluator on a three-point basis as follows: 1 point for a
tapped ball; 2 points for an angle of projection of 29 degrees or less;
3 points for an angle of 30 degrees or more. This value is multiplied by
the target point value with a maximum of 21 points per trial. A
student's score is the sum for 12 trials.

Softball

The throw for distance is a measure of coordination, specifically to
see how far someone can throw a softball. The equipment needed is
minimal and includes regulation softballs and a field marked off at
1-foot intervals with a distinctive marking every 10 feet. The distance
should be marked beginning at 30 to 50 feet from a restraining line. A
simple device is to place 2 100-foot tape measures consecutively with
the appropriate markings as listed.

Each student takes three consecutive trials, with the best of the three trials recorded as the score. The student being tested may take only one step and may not step on or beyond the line prior to releasing the ball.

To administer this test most efficiently requires a number of assistants who may also be waiting to be tested. One student should watch for line violations; two students should retrieve the balls and roll them to a collector who stands behind the restraining line; one student should hand the ball to the subject; one student should mark the spot at which the ball first touches the ground; and one student should record the score. A rotating system should be developed. The groups being tested should always have a minimum of two to three students ready to begin immediately after the preceding student completes his turn.

Volleyball

The Liba-Stauff Volleyball Pass Test requires two ropes, one 11 feet and the other 13 feet above the floor, one volleyball per subject, and a 2 × 30-foot target strip marked off in 2 × 2-foot squares with point values from 1 to 8 and back to 1. A restraining line $10\frac{1}{2}$ feet from the ropes and $23\frac{1}{2}$ feet from the center (8 value) of the target area is designated. Therefore, one target box is below the ropes and closer to the subject.

The subject throws the ball into the air and then passes it over the ropes into the target area. The scoring includes distance according to the landing area multiplied by the height attained by the ball. Three points are awarded if the ball goes over the 13-foot rope, 2 points are awarded for a ball going between the ropes, 1 point for a ball going under the 11-foot rope, and 0 point if the ball does not reach the ropes. The score is the sum of ten trials.

Fouls include a pushed or thrown ball and are given a score of 0. If the subject steps on or over the restraining line, he is cautioned but not penalized.

The following modifications should be made for the junior high school level: Rope heights: 12 and 10 feet. Target area: 2 × 28 feet with 2 × 2-foot blocks numbered from 1 to 7 to 1. Restraining line: $6\frac{1}{2}$ feet from ropes and $15\frac{1}{2}$ feet from center of target area (box marked

7). Therefore, boxes 1 and 2 are under the ropes and closer to the subject. Scoring: sum of fifteen trials.

Summary

A sequence for testing components of physical performance and fitness is recommended which progresses from resting to light to moderate to strenuous activities. Examples of tests of selected portions of the components of performance and fitness are described.

Problems

Find better tests for the components of performance and fitness selected in this appendix.

Find tests for other components of performance and fitness.

Modify a current test or construct a new test for a component of performance and fitness.

References

Adams, I. H., Linde, L. M., and Miyake, H. The physical working capacity of normal school children in California. *Pediatrics*, 1961, **28**, 55–64.

Allen, T. H., Peng, M. T., Chen, K. P., Huang, T. F., Chang, C., and Fang, H. S. Prediction of total adiposity from skinfolds and the curvilinear relationship between external and internal adiposity. *Metabolism*, 1956, **5**, 346–352.

Åstrand, I. Aerobic work capacity in men and women with special reference to age. *Acta Physiologica Scandinavica*, 1960, **49**, Suppl. 169, 1.

Åstrand, P. O. *Experimental studies of physical working capacity in relation to sex and age*. Copenhagen: Munksgaard, 1952.

Åstrand, P. O. Human physical fitness with special reference to sex and age. *Physiological Reviews*, 1956, **36**, 307.

Åstrand, P. O. *Work tests with the bicycle ergometer*. Varberg, Sweden: Monark-Cresent AB, 1967.

Åstrand, P. O., and Christensen, E. H. Aerobic work capacity. In F. Dickens, E. Neil, and W. F. Widdas (Eds.), *Proceedings of the Conference on Oxygen in the Animal Organism*. Oxford, England: Pergamon, 1964.

Åstrand, P. O., and Rhyming, I. A nomogram for calculation of aerobic capacity from pulse rate during submaximal work. *Journal of Applied Physiology*, 1954, **7**, 218–221.

Åstrand, P. O., and Rodahl, K. *Textbook of work physiology*. New York: McGraw-Hill, 1970.

Åstrand, P. O., and Saltin, B. Maximal oxygen uptake and heart rate in various types of muscular activity. *Journal of Applied Physiology*, 1961, **16**, 997–981.

Åstrand, P. O., and Saltin, B. Oxygen uptake during the first minutes of heavy muscular exercise. *Journal of Applied Physiology*, 1961, **16**, 971–976.

Balke, B. *Correlation of static and physical endurance*. Report No. 7. Houston Texas: School of Aviation Medicine, 1952.

Balke, B. Circulatory respiratory response to physical work. I. In H. Spector (Ed.), *Symposium on Performance Capacity*. Washington, D.C.: National Research Council, 1961.

Balke, B., and Ware, F. W. An experimental study of physical fitness of air force personnel. *United States Armed Forces Medical Journal*, 1958, **10**, 675–688.

Barry, Alan, Webster, G. W., and Daly, J. W. Validity and reliability of a multi-stage exercise test for older men and women. *Journal of Gerontology*, 1969, **24**, 284–291.

Behnke, A. R. The estimation of lean body weight from "skeletal" measurements. *Human Biology*, 1959, **31**, 295–315.

Behnke, A. R. Anthropometric fractionation of body weight. *Journal of Applied Physiology*, 1961, **16**, 949–954.

Behnke, A. R. Quantitative assessment of body build. *Journal of Applied Physiology*, 1961, **16**, 960–964.

Behnke, A. R., Feen, B. G., and Welham, W. C. The specific gravity of healthy men. *Journal of the American Medical Association*, 1942, **118**, 495–498.

Behnke, A. R., Guttentag, O. E., and Brodsky, C. Quantification of body weight and configuration from anthropometrical measurements. *Human Biology*, 1959, **31**, 213–234.

Berger, R. A. Determination of a method to predict 1-RM chin and dip from repetitive chins and dips. *Research Quarterly*, 1967, **38**, 330–335.

Brook, C. G. D. Determination of body composition of children from skinfold measurements. *Archives of Disease in Childhood*, 1971, **46**, 182–184.

Brouha, L., Graybiel, and Heath, C. W. The step test: a simple method of measuring physical fitness for hard muscular work in adult men. *Revue Canadienne de Biologie*, 1943, **2**, 86–92.

Brouha, L., and Heath, C. W. Resting pulse and blood pressure values in relation to physical fitness in young men. *New England Journal of Medicine*, 1943, **228**, 273.

Brozek, J., and Henschel, A. (Eds.) *Techniques for measuring body composition*. Washington, D.C.: National Academy of Sciences—National Research Council, 1961.

Bruce, R. A., *et al.* Exercise testing in adult normal subjects and cardiac patients. *Pediatrics*, 1963, **32**, 742–756.

Buskirk, E., and Taylor, H. L. Maximal oxygen intake and its relation to body composition, with special reference to chronic physical activity and obesity. *Journal of Applied Physiology*, 1957, **11**, 72–78.

Cardus, D., and Zeigler, R. K. Heart-beat frequency curves, a mathematical model. *Computers and Biomedical Research*, 1968, **1**, 508–526.

Carlson, H. C. Fatigue curve test. *Reserch Quarterly*, 1945, **16**, 169–175.

Check, D. B., Mellits, D., and Elliott, D. Body water, height, and weight during growth in normal children. *American Journal of Diseases of Children*, 1966, **112**, 312–317.

Check, D. B., Schultz, R. B., Parra, A., and Reba, R. C. Overgrowth of lean and adipose tissues in adolescent obesity. *Pediatric Research*, 1970, **4**, 268–279.

Clarke, H. H., and Monroe, R. A. *Test manual. Oregon cable-tension strength test batteries for boys and girls from fourth grade through college.* Eugene, Oregon: Univ. of Oregon, 1970.

Committee on Nutrition. Measurement of skinfold thickness in childhood. *Pediatrics*, 1968, **42**, 538–543.

Consolazio, C. F., Johnson, R. E., and Pecora, L. J. *Physiological measurements of metabolic functions in man.* New York: McGraw-Hill, 1963.

Cooper, K. H. A means of assessing maximal oxygen intake—correlation between field and treadmill testing. *Journal of the American Medical Association*, 1968, **203**, 201–204.

Cooper, K. H. *The new aerobics.* New York: Bantam, 1970.

Corbin, C. B. Standards of subcutaneous fat applied to percentile norms for elementary school children. *American Journal of Clinical Nutrition*, 1969, **22**, 836–841.

Corbin, C. B., and Pletcher, P. Diet and physical activity patterns of obese and nonobese elementary school children. *Research Quarterly*, 1968, **39**, 922–928.

Cotton, F. S. and Dill, D. B. On the relation between the heart rate during exercise and that of immediate post-exercise period. *American Journal of Physiology*, 1935, **3**, 554–556.

Crook, G. H., Bennett, C. A., Norwood, W. D., and Mahaffey, J. A. Evaluation of skin-fold measurements and weight chart to measure body fat. *Journal of the American Medical Association*, 1966, **198**, 157–162.

Cureton, T. K. *Physical fitness and dynamic health.* New York: Dial, 1965.

Cureton, T. K. Comparison of various factor analyses of cardio-respiratory test variables. *Research Quarterly*, 1966, **37**, 317–325.

Cureton, T. K. Improvements in oxygen intake capacity resulting from sports and exercise training programs: A review. *American Corrective Therapy Journal*, 1969, **23**, 143–147.

Davies, C. T. M. Limitations to the prediction of maximal oxygen intake from cardiac frequency measurements. *Journal of Applied Physiology*, 1968, **24**, 700–706.

Day, W., and Ribisl, P. M. *Workshop on bicycle ergometry.* Philadelphia, Pennsylvania: National YMCA Physical Fitness Consultation, 1971.

DeVries, H. A. *Physiology of exercise for physical education and athletics.* Dubuque, Iowa: W. C. Brown, 1969.

DeVries, H. A. and Klafs, C. E. Prediction of maximal oxygen intake from submaximal tests. *Journal of Sports Medicine and Physical Fitness*, 1965, **4**, 207–214.

Doolittle, T. L., and Bigbee, R. The twelve-minute run-walk: A test of cardiorespiratory fitness of adolescent boys. *Research Quarterly*, 1968, **39**, 491–495.

Edgren, H. D. An experiment in the testing of ability and progress in basketball. *Research Quarterly*, 1932, **3**, 159–171.

Edholm, O. G. Fitness for what? *Proceedings of the Royal Society of Medicine*, 1969, **62**, 617–620.

Ekblom, B., Astrand, P. O., Saltin, B., Stenberg, J., and Wallstrom, B. Effect of training on circulatory response to exercise. *Journal of Applied Physiology*, 1968, **24**, 518–528.

Falls, H. B., Ismail, A. H., and MacLeod, D. F. Estimation of maximum oxygen uptake in adults from AAHPER youth fitness test items. *Research Quarterly*, 1966, **37**, 192–201.

Glassford, R. G., Baycroft, H. Y., Sedgwick, A. W., and Macnab, R. B. J. Comparison of maximal oxygen uptake values determined by predicted and actual methods. *Journal of Applied Physiology*, 1965, **20**, 509.

Hall, D. M. *Keeping fit handbook for teachers*. Urbana, Illinois: Extension Service, Univ. of Illinois, 1963. Pp. 9–13.

Harvey, V. P., and Scott, G. D. The validity and reliability of a one minute step test for women. *Journal of Sports Medicine and Physical Fitness*, 1970, **10**, 185–192.

Hebbalinck, M. Ergometry in physical training research. *Journal of Sports Medicine and Physical Fitness*, 1969, **9**, 69–79.

Hermansen, L., and Andersen, K. L. Aerobic work capacity in young Norwegian men and women. *Journal of Applied Physiology*, 1965, **20**, 425–431.

Hettinger, T., Birkhead, N. C., Horvath, S. M., Issekutz, B., and Rodahl, K. Assessment of physical work capacity. *Journal of Applied Physiology*, 1961, **16**, 153–156.

Holmgren, A. Cardiorespiratory determinants of cardiovascular fitness. *Canadian Medical Association Journal*, 1967, **96**, 697–705.

Johnson, B. L., and Nelson, J. K. *Practical measurement for evaluation in physical education*. Minneapolis, Minnesota: Burgess, 1969.

Johnson, W. R. (Ed.) *Science and medicine in sports*. New York: Harper, 1960.

Katch, F. I. Pre and post-test changes in the factors that influence computed body density changes. *Research Quarterly*, 1971, **42**. 280–285.

Katch, F. I., Girandola, R. N., and Katch, V. L. The relationship of body weight on maximum oxygen uptake and heavy-work endurance capacity on the bicycle ergometer. *Medicine and Science in Sports*, 1971, **3**, 101–106.

Katch, F. I., Michael, E. D., and Horvath, S. M. Estimation of body volume by underwater weighing: description of simple method. *Journal of Applied Physiology*, 1967, **23**, 811–813.

Keys, A., Brozek, J., Henschel, A., Mickelson, O., and Taylor, H. L. *The biology of human starvation*. Minneapolis, Minnesota: Univ. of Minnesota Press, 1950. Pp. 689–749.

Klissouras, V. Heritability of adaptive variation. *Journal of Applied Physiology*, 1971, **31**, 338–344.

Knehr, C. A., Dill, D. B., and Neufeld, W. Training and its effects on man at rest and at work. *American Journal of Physiology*, 1942, **136**, 148–156.

Knowlton, R. G., and Weber, H. Effects of progressive endurance training on metabolic and cardiorespiratory adaptations in markedly obese subjects. In B. D. Franks (Ed.), *Exercise and fitness—1969*. Chicago, Illinois: Athletic Institute, 1969.

Kuruez, R., Fox, E., and Mathews, D. Construction of a submaximal cardiovascular step test. *Research Quarterly*, 1969, **40**, 115–124.

Laurent, D., *et al.* Effects of heart rate on corollary flow and cardiac oxygen consumption. *American Journal of Physiology*, 1956, **185**, 355.

Liba, M. R., and Stauff, M. R. A test for the volleyball pass. *Research Quarterly*, 1963, **34**, 56–63.

Margaria, R., Aghemo, P., and Rovelli, E. Indirect determination of maximal O_2 consumption in man. *Journal of Applied Physiology*, 1966, **21**, 1662.

Margaria, R., Ceretelli, P., Aghemo, P., and Sassi, G. Energy cost of running. *Journal of Applied Physiology*, 1963, **18**, 367.

Maritz, J. S., *et al.* A practical method of estimating an individuals maximal oxygen uptake. *Ergonomics*, 1961, **4**, 97.

Mastropaolo, J. A. Prediction of maximal O_2 consumption in middle aged man by multiple regression. *Medicine and Science in Sports*, 1970, **2**, 124–127.

McArdle, W. D., and Magel, J. Physical work capacity and maximum oxygen uptake in treadmill and bicycle exercise. *Medicine and Science in Sports*, 1970, **2**, 118–123.

McArdle, W. D., Glaser, R. M., and Magel, J. R. Metabolic and cardiorespiratory response during free swimming and treadmill walking. *Journal of Applied Physiology*, 1971, **30**, 733–738.

Michael, E. D., Jr., Hutton, K. E., and Horvath, S. M. Cardiorespiratory response during prolonged exercise. *Journal of Applied Physiology*, 1961, **16**, 977–1000.

Mitchell, J., Sproule, B., and Chapman, C. The physiological meaning of the maximal oxygen intake test. *Journal of Clinical Investigation*, 1958, **37**, 538–547.

Montoye, H. J. Physical activity and risk factors associated with coronary heart disease. In B. D. Franks (Ed.), *Exercise in fitness—1969*. Chicago, Illinois: Athletic Institute, 1969.

Montoye, H. J., Willis, P. W., Cunningham, D. A., and Keller, J. B. Heart rate response to a modified Harvard step test: males and females, age 10–69. *Research Quarterly*, 1969, **40**, 153–162.

Montoye, H. J., Epstein, F. H., and Kjelsberg, M. O. The measurement of body fatness. *American Journal of Clinical Nutrition*, 1965. **16**, 417–527.

Morgan, W. P. Psychological effect of weight reduction in the college wrestler. *Medicine and Science in Sports*, 1970, **2**, 24–27.

Murphy, H. F. A comparison of techniques for estimating the amount of fat in the human body; and regression equations for predicting the amount of potassium in the human body. Unpublished doctoral thesis, University of Illinois, 1967.

Murphy, H. F., Lohman, T., Oscai, L., and Pollock, M. The potassium scintillator as a measurer of fat in physical education research. In B. D. Franks (Ed.), *Exercise and fitness—1969*. Chicago, Illinois: Athletic Institute, 1969.

Nagle, F., Balke, G., Baptista, J. A., and Howley, E. Compatibility of progressive treadmill, bicycle and step tests based on oxygen uptake responses. *Medicine and Science in Sports*, 1971, **3**, 149–154.

Nagle, F., Balke, B., and Naughton, J. P. Gradational step tests for assessing work capacity. *Journal of Applied Physiology*, 1965, **20**, 745–748.

Newton, J. L. The assessment of maximal oxygen intake. *Journal of Sports Medicine*, 1963, **2**, 164–169.

Olson, A. L., and Edelstein, E. Spot reduction of subcutaneous adipose tissue. *Research Quarterly*, 1968, **39**, 647–552.

Oscai, L. B., and Hooloszy, J. O. Effects of weight changes produced by exercise, food restriction, or overeating on body composition. *Journal of Clinical Investigation*, 1969, **48**, 2124–2128.

Parizkova, J. Total body fat and skinfold thickness in children. *Metabolism*, 1961, **10**, 794–807.

Pascale, L., Grossman, M., Sloane, H., and Frankel, T. Correlations between thickness of skinfolds and body density in 88 soldiers. *Human Biology*, 1956, **28**, 165–176.

Pollock, M. L., Janeway, R., and Lofland, H. B. Effects of frequency of training on serum lipids, cardiovascular function and body composition. In B. D. Franks (Ed.), *Exercise and fitness—1969*. Chicago, Illinois: Athletic Institute, 1969.

Rauh, J. L., and Schumsky, D. A. Lean and non-lean body mass estimates in urban school children. In D. B. Cheek (Ed.), *Human growth*. Philadelphia, Pennsylvania: Lea and Febiger, 1968.

Reba, R. C., Cheek, D. B., and Leitnaker, F. C. Body potassium and lean body mass. In D. B. Cheek (Ed.), *Human growth*. Philadelphia, Pennsylvania: Lea and Febiger, 1968.

Robinson, S. Experimental studies of physical fitness in relation to age. *Arbeitsphysiologie*, 1938, **10**, 251–323.

Roby, F. B. Effect of exercise on regional fat accumulation. *Research Quarterly*, 1962, **33**, 273–277.

Rowell, L. B. Factors affecting the prediction of maximal oxygen intake from measurements made during submaximal work with observations related to factors which may limit maximal oxygen intake. Unpublished doctoral dissertation, University of Minnesota, 1962.

Rowell, L. B., Taylor, H. L., and Wang, Y. Limitations to prediction of maximal oxygen intake. *Journal of Applied Physiology*, 1964, **19**, 919–927.

Ryhming, I. A modified Harvard step test for the evaluation of physical fitness. *Arbeitsphysiologie*, 1953, **15**, 235.

Saltin, B. Aerobic work capacity and circulation at exercise in man. *Acta Physiologica Scandinavica*, 1964, **62**, Suppl. 230.

Saltin, B., and Astrand, P. O. Maximal oxygen uptake in athletes. *Journal of Applied Physiology*, 1967, **23**, 353–358.

Schade, M., Hellebrandt, F. A., Waterland, J. C., and Carns, M. L. Spot reduction in overweight college women: Its influence on fat distribution as determined by photography. *Research Quarterly*, 1962, **33**, 461–471.

Sharkey, B., and Blake, C. *Fitness for firefighting*. Report to the U.S. Forest Service, Equipment Development Center. Missoula, Montana, 1966.

Shepard, R. J. The relative merits of the step test, bicycle ergometer and treadmill in the assessment of cardio-respiratory fitness. *Internationale Zeitschrift fuer Angewandte Physiologie*, 1966, **23**, 219.

Shepard, R. J., Allen, C., Benade, A. J. S., Davies, C. T. M., Standardization of submaximal exercise tests. *Bulletin of the World Health Organization*, 1968, **38**, 765–775.

Shepard, R. S. The prediction of maximal oxygen consumption using a new progressive step test. *Ergonomics*, 1967, **10**, 1–15.

Sjostrand, T. Changes in the respiratory organs of workmen at an oresmelting works. *Acta Medica Scandinavica*, Suppl. 1947, **196**, 687.

Skinner, J., Buskirk, E. R., and Borg, G. Physiological and perceptual characteristics of young men differing in activity and body composition. In B. D. Franks (Ed.), *Exercise in fitness—1969*. Chicago, Illinois: Athletic Institute, 1969.

Skubic, V., and Hodgkins, J. A cardiovascular efficiency test for girls and women. *Research Quarterly*, 1963, **34**, 191–198.

Sloan, A. W. Estimation of body fat in young men. *Journal of Applied Physiology*, 1967, **23**, 311–315.

Suggs, C. W. An analysis of heart rate response to exericse. *Research Quarterly*, 1968, **39**, 195–205.

Taylor, H. L. Some properties of maximal and submaximal exercise with reference to physiological variation and the measurement of exercise tolerance. *American Journal of Physiology*, 1944, **142**, 200–212.

Taylor, H. L., Buskirk, E., and Henschel, A. Maximal oxygen intake as an objective measure of cardio-respiratory performance. *Journal of Applied Physiology*, 1955, **8**, 73–80.

Teraslinna, P., Ismail, A. H., and MacLeod, D. F. Nomogram by Astrand and Ryhming as a predictor of maximum oxygen intake. *Journal of Applied Physiology*, 1966, **21**, 513.

Van Huss, Wayne D., Heusner, W. W., and Michelson, O. Effects of pre-pubertal exercise on body composition. In B. D. Franks (Ed.), *Exercise and fitness— 1969*. Chicago, Illinois: Athletic Institute, 1969.

Von Dobeln, W. A simple bicycle ergometer. *Journal of Applied Physiology*, 1954, **7**, 222.

Wahlund, H. Determination of the physical working capacity. *Acta Medica Scandinavica*, 1948, **132**, Suppl. 215, 1.

West, C., and Thorpe, J. Construction and validation of an eight-iron approach test. *Research Quarterly*, 1968, **39**, 1115–1120.

Whipple, H. E. (Ed.) Body Composition. Annals of the New York Academy of Science, 1963, **110**, 1.

Wilmore, J. H. The use of actual, predicted and constant residual volumes in the assessment of body composition by underwater weighing. *Medicine and Science in Sports*, 1969, **1**, 87–90.

Wilmore, J. H., and Behnke, A. R. An anthropometric estimation of body density and lean body weight in young women. *American Journal of Clinical Nutrition*, 1970, **23**, 267–274.

Wilmore, J. H., and Behnke, A. R. Predictability of lean body weight through anthropometric assessment in college men. *Journal of Applied Physiology*, 1968, **25**, 4.

Wilson, N. L. (Ed.) *Obesity*. Philadelphia, Pennsylvania: Davis, 1969.

Wyndaham, C. H. Submaximal tests for estimating maximum oxygen intake. *Canadian Medical Association Journal*, 1967, **96**, 736–745.

Wyndham, C. H., and Ward, J. S. An assessment of the exercise capacity of cardiac patients. *Circulation*, 1957, **16**, 384–393.

Young, C. M., Sipin, S. S., and Roe, D. A. Body composition of pre-adolescent and adolescent girls. *Journal of the American Dietetic Association*, 1968, **53**, 357–362.

Index